Top 11 Adobe Programs Keyboard Shortcuts

By

U. C-Abel Books.

Published by U. C-Abel Books

First Edition: 2017

ISBN-13: 978-9785457476
ISBN-10: 9785457478

Published by U. C-Abel Books.

A Summarized List of Contents.

Table of Contents

Acknowledgement.

All thanks to God Almighty for enabling us to bring this work to this point. He is a wonder indeed.

We want to specially appreciate the great company, Adobe Systems for the hard work of her staff and their style of reasoning when it comes to providing the public with helpful programs software and resources and for helping us with some of the tips and keyboard shortcuts included in this book.

Adobe is really changing the world through digital experiences. Their creative, marketing and document solutions empower everyone — from emerging artists to global brands — to bring digital creations to life and deliver them to the right person at the right moment for the best results. And that is what this book has come to do in its own way.

Dedication

The dedication of this title goes to high, medium, and low users of the 11 Adobe programs whose keyboard shortcuts are listed in this book, in any part of the world they are.

Introduction.

After thinking of how to help computer users become more productive in their operation of computers and various fields, it came to our knowledge that there is a smart option many computer users ignore easily and that part has a high yielding capacity that is known to just few people.

We went into a deep research to broaden our knowledge of key combination and found it very helpful, then we started this series "Shortcut Matters" including tips, techniques, keyboard shortcuts, and packaging the title in a way it will attract readers and get a high rating class.

As people who love keyboard shortcuts we treat each topic plainly in an easy-to-read way even to the understanding of a lay man.

Relax and make your mind ready for learning as we go.

How We Began.

We enjoy using shortcuts because they set us on a high plane that astonishes people around us when we work with them. As wonderful shortcuts users, the worst eyesore we witness in computer operation is to see somebody sluggishly struggling to execute a task through mouse usage when in actual sense shortcuts will help to save that person time. Most people have asked us to help them with a list of keyboard shortcuts that can make them work as smartly as we do and that drove us into research to broaden our knowledge and truly help them as they demanded, that is the reason for the existence of this book. It is a great tool for lovers of shortcuts, and those who want to join the group.

Most times the things we love don't come by easily. It is our love for keyboard shortcuts that made us to bear long sleepless nights like owls just to make sure we get the best out of it, and it is the best we got that we are sharing with you in this book. You cannot be the same at computing after reading this book. The time you entrusted to our care is an expensive possession and we promise not to mess it up.

Thank you.

What to Know Before You Begin.

General Notes.

1. Most of the keyboard shortcuts you will see in this book refer to the U.S. keyboard layout. Keys for other layouts might not correspond exactly to the keys on a U.S. keyboard. Keyboard shortcuts for laptop computers might also differ.

2. It is important to note that when using shortcuts to perform any command, you should make sure the target area is active, if not, you may get a wrong result. Example, if you want to highlight all texts you must make sure the text field is active and if an object, make sure the object area is active. The active area is always known by the location where the cursor of your computer blinks.

3. On a Mac keyboard, the Command key is denoted with the ⌘symbol.

4. If a function key doesn't work on your Mac as you expect it to, press the Fn key in addition to the function key. If you don't want to press the Fn key every time, you can change your Apple system preferences.

5. The plus (+) sign that comes in the middle of keyboard shortcuts simply means the keys are meant to be combined or held down together not to be added as one

of the shortcut keys. In a case where plus sign is needed; it will be duplicated (++).

6. Many keyboards assign special functions to function keys, by default. To use the function key for other purposes, you have to press Fn+the function key.

7. For keyboard shortcuts in which you press one key immediately followed by another key, the keys are separated by a comma (,).

8. For chapters that have more than one topic, search for "A fresh topic" to see the beginning of a topic, and "End of Topic" to see the end of a topic.

9. It is also important to note that the keyboard shortcuts, tips, and techniques listed in this book are for users of Adobe programs/applications.

10. To get more information on this title visit ucabelbooks.wordpress.com and search the site using keywords related to it.

11. Our chief website is under construction.

Some Short Forms You Will Find in This Book and Their Full Meaning.

Here are short forms used in this Top 11 Adobe Programs Keyboard Shortcuts book and their full meaning.

1. Win - Windows logo key
2. Tab - Tabulate Key
3. Shft - Shift Key
4. Prt sc - Print Screen
5. Num Lock - Number Lock Key
6. F - Function Key
7. Esc - Escape Key
8. Ctrl - Control Key
9. Caps Lock - Caps Lock Key
10. Alt - Alternate Key

CHAPTER 1.

Fundamental Knowledge of Keyboard Shortcuts.

Without the existence of the keyboard, there wouldn't have been anything like keyboard shortcuts so in this chapter we will learn a little about the computer keyboard before moving to keyboard shortcuts.

1. Definition of Computer Keyboard.

This is an input device that is used to send data to computer memory.

Sketch of a Keyboard

1.1 Types of Keyboard.

i. Standard (Basic) Keyboard.
ii. Enhanced (Extended) Keyboard.

i. **Standard Keyboard:** This is a keyboard designed during the 1800s for mechanical typewriters with just 10 function keys (F keys) placed at the left side of it.
ii. **Enhanced Keyboard:** This is the current 101 to 102-key keyboard that is included in almost all the personal computers (PCs) of nowadays, which has 12 function keys, usually at the top side of it.

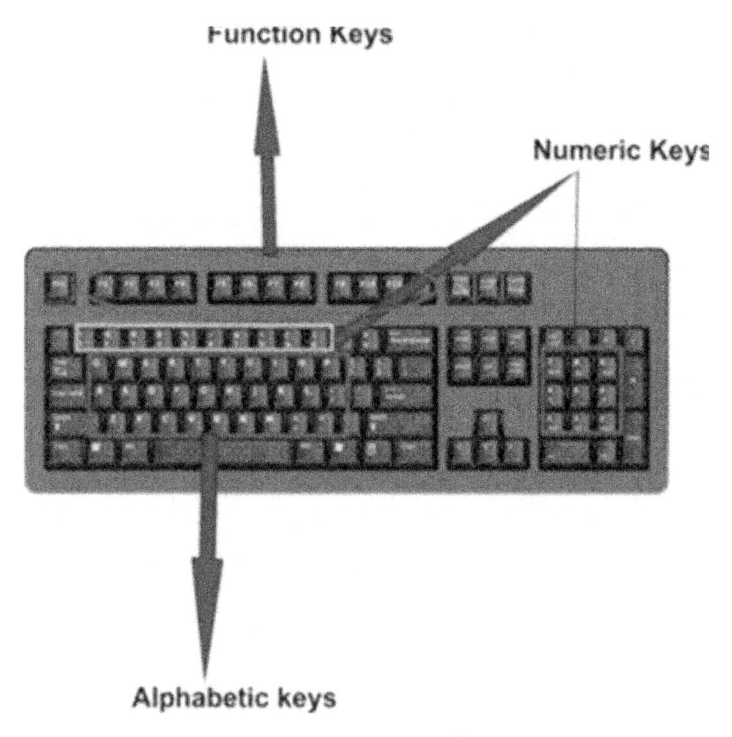

1.2 Segments of the keyboard

- Numeric keys.
- Alphabetic keys.
- Punctuation keys.
- Windows Logo key.
- Function keys.
- Special keys.

Numeric Keys: Numeric keys are keys with numbers from **0 - 9**.

Alphabetic Keys: These are keys that have alphabets on them, ranging from **A** to **Z**.

Punctuation Keys: These are keys of the keyboard used for punctuation, examples include comma, full stop, colon, question marks, hyphen, etc.

Windows Logo Key: A key on Microsoft Computer keyboard with its logo displayed on it. Search for this on your keyboard.

Apple Key: This also known as Command key is a modifier key that you can find on an Apple keyboard. It usually has the image of an apple or command logo on it. Search for this on your Apple keyboard

Function Keys: These are keys that have **F** on them which are usually combined with other keys. They are F1 - F12, and are also in the class called *Special Keys*.

Special Keys: These are keys that perform special functions. They include: Tab, Ctrl, Caps lock, Insert, Prt sc, alt gr, Shift, Home, Num lock, Esc, and many others. Special keys differ according to the type of computer involved. In some keyboard layout, especially laptops, the keys that turn the speaker on/off, the one that increases/decreases volume, the key that turns the computer Wifi on/off are also special keys.

Other Special Keys Worthy of Note.

Enter Key: This is located at the right-hand corner of most keyboards. It is used to send messages to the computer to execute commands, in most cases it is used to mean "Ok" or "Go".

Escape Key (ESC): This is the first key on the upper left of most keyboards. It is used to cancel routines, close menus and select options such as **Save** according to circumstances.

Control Key (CTRL): It is located on the bottom row of the left and right hand side of the keyboard. They also work with the function keys to execute commands using Keyboard shortcuts (key combinations).

Alternate Key (ALT): It is located on the bottom row also of some keyboard, very close to the CTRL key on both side of the keyboard. It enables many editing functions to be accomplished by using some keystroke combinations on the keyboard.

Shift Key: This adds to the roles of function keys. In addition, it enables the use of alternative function of a particular button (key), especially, those with more than one function on a key. E.g. use of capital letters, symbols, and numbers.

1.3. Selecting/Highlighting With Keyboard.

This is a highlighting method or style where data is selected using the computer keyboard instead of a computer mouse.

To do this:

- Move your cursor to the text or object you want to highlight, make sure that area is active,
- Hold down the shift key with one finger,
- Then use another finger to move the arrow key that points to the direction you want to highlight.

1.4 The Operating Modes Of The Keyboard.

Just like the computer mouse, keyboard has two operating modes. The two modes are Text Entering Mode and Command Mode.

a. **Text Entering Mode:** this mode gives the operator/user the opportunity to type text.
b. **Command Mode:** this is used to command the operating system/software/application to execute commands in certain ways.

2. Ways To Improve In Your Typing Skill.

1. Put Your Eyes Off The Keyboard.

This is the aspect of keyboard usage that many don't find funny because they always ask. "How can I put my eyes off the keyboard when I am running away from the occurrence of errors on my file?" My aim is to be fast, is this not going to slow me down?

Of course, there will be errors and at the same time your speed will slow down but the motive behind the introduction to this method is to make you faster than you are. Looking at your keyboard while you type can make you get a sore neck, it is better you learn to touch type because the more you type with your eyes fixed on the screen instead of the keyboard, the faster you become.
An alternative to keeping your eyes off your keyboard is to use the "*Das Keyboard Ultimate*".

2. Errors Challenge You

It is better to fail than to not try at all. Not trying at all is an attribute of the weak and lazybones. When you make mistakes, try again because errors are opportunities for improvement.

3. Good Posture (Position Yourself Well).

Do not adopt an awkward position while typing. You should get everything on your desk organized or arranged before sitting to type. Your posture while typing contributes to your speed and productivity.

4. Practice

Here is the conclusion of everything said above. You have to practice your shortcuts constantly. The practice alone is a way of improvement. "Practice brings improvement". Practice always.

2.1 Software That Will Help You Improve Your Typing Skill.

There are several Software programs for typing that both kids and adults can use for their typing skill. Here is a list of software that can help you improve in your typing: Mavis Beacon, Typing Instructor, Mucky Typing Adventure, Rapid Tying Tutor, Letter Chase Tying Tutor, Alice Touch Typing Tutor and many more. Personally, I love Mavis Beacon.

To learn typing using MAVIS BEACON, install Mavis Beacon software to your computer, start with keyboard lesson, then move to games. Games like ***Penguin Crossing, Creature Lab***, or ***Space Junk*** will help you become a professional in typing. Typing and keyboard shortcuts work hand-in-hand.

Sketch of a computer mouse

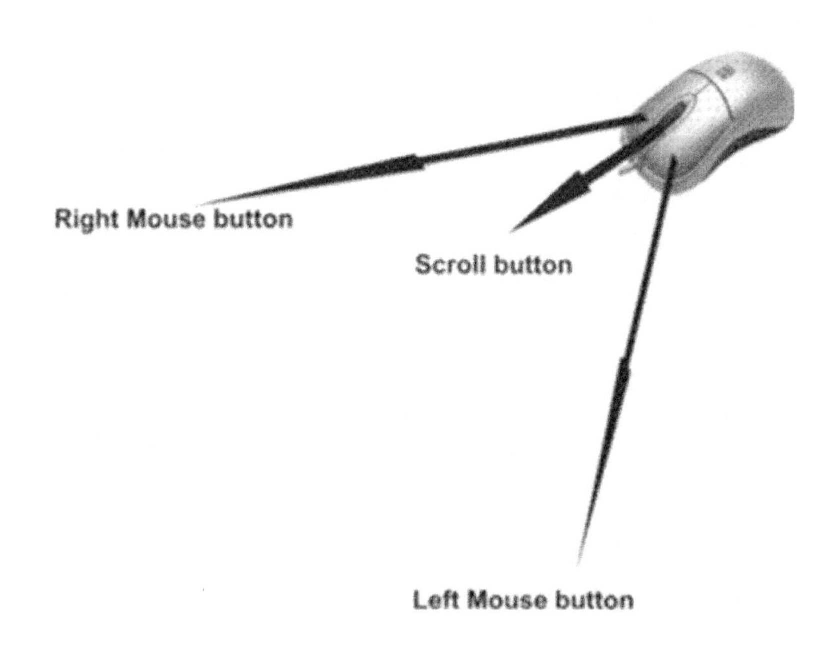

3. Mouse:

This is an oval-shaped portable input device with three buttons for scrolling, left clicking, and right clicking that enables work to be done effectively on a computer. The plural form of mouse is mice.

3.1 Types of Computer Mouse

- Mechanical Mouse.
- Optical Mechanical Mouse (Optomechanical).
- Laser Mouse.
- Optical Mouse.
- BlueTrack Mouse.

3.2 Forms of Clicking:

Left Clicking: This is the process of clicking the left side button of the mouse. It can also be called *clicking* without the addition of *left*.

Right Clicking: It is the process of clicking the right side button of a computer mouse.

Double Clicking: It is the process of clicking the left side button two times (twice) and immediately.

Triple Clicking: It is the process of clicking the left side button three times (thrice) and immediately.

Double clicking is used to select a word while triple clicking is used to select a sentence or paragraph.

Scroll Button: It is the little key attached to the mouse that looks like a tiny wheel. It takes you up and down a page when moved.

3.3 Mouse Pad: This is a small soft mat that is placed under the mouse to make it have a free movement.

3.4 Laptop Mouse Touchpad

This unlike the mouse we explained above is not external, rather it is inbuilt (comes with the laptop computer). With the presence of a laptop mouse touchpad, an external mouse is not needed to use a laptop, except in a case where it is malfunctioning or the operator prefers to use external one for some reasons.

The laptop mouse touchpad is usually positioned at the end of the keyboard section of a laptop computer. It is rectangular in shape with two buttons positioned below it. The two buttons/keys are used for left and right clicking just like the external mouse. Some laptops come with four mouse keys. Two placed above the mouse for left and right clicking and two other keys placed below it for the same function.

4. Definition Of Keyboard Shortcuts.

Keyboard shortcuts are defined as a series of keys, most times with combination that execute tasks which typically involve the use of mouse or other input devices.

5. Why You Should Use Shortcuts.

1. One may not be able to use a computer mouse easily because of disability or pain.

2. One may not be able to see the mouse pointer as a result of vision impairment, in such case what will the person do? The answer is SHORTCUT.

3. Research has made it known that Extensive mouse usage is related to Repetitive Syndrome Injury (RSI) greatly than the use of keyboard.

4. Keyboard shortcuts speed up computer users, making learning them a worthwhile effort.

5. When performing a job that requires precision, it is wise that you use the keyboard instead of mouse, for instance, if you are dealing with Text Editing, it is better you handle it using keyboard shortcuts than spending more time doing it with your computer mouse alone.

6. Studies calculate that using keyboard shortcuts allows working 10 times faster than working with the mouse. The time you spend looking for the mouse and then getting the cursor to the position you want is lost! Reducing your work duration by 10 times gives you greater results.

5.1 Ways To Become A Lover Of Shortcuts.

1. Always have the urge to learn new shortcut keys associated with the programs you use.
2. Be happy whenever you learn a new shortcut.
3. Try as much as you can to apply the new shortcuts you learnt.
4. Always bear it in mind that learning new shortcuts is worth it.
5. Always remember that the use of keyboard shortcuts keeps people healthy while performing computer activities.

5.2 How To Learn New Shortcut Keys

1. Do a research on them: quick references (a cheat sheet comprehensively compiled like ours) can go a long way to help you improve.
2. Buy applications that show you keyboard shortcuts every time you execute an action with mouse.
3. Disconnect your mouse if you must learn this fast.
4. Read user manuals and help topics (Whether offline or online).

5.3 Your Reward For Knowing Shortcut Keys.

1. You will get faster unimaginably.
2. Your level of efficiency will increase.
3. You will find it easy to use.
4. Opportunities are high that you will become an expert in what you do.

5. You won't have to go for **Office button**, click **New,** click **Blank and Recent**, and click **Create** just to insert a fresh/blank page. **Ctrl +N** takes care of that in a second.

A Funny Note: Keyboarding and Mousing are in a marital union with Keyboarding being the head, so it will be unfair for anybody to put asunder between them.

5.4 Why We Emphasize On The Use of Shortcuts.

You may never leave your mouse completely unless you are ready to make your brain a box of keyboard shortcuts which will really be frustrating, just imagine yourself learning all shortcuts that go with the programs you use and their various versions. You shouldn't learn keyboard shortcuts that way.

Why we are emphasizing on the use of shortcuts is because mouse usage is becoming unusually common and unhealthy, too. So we just want to make sure both are combined so you can get fast, productive and healthy in your computer activities. All you need to know is just the most important ones associated with the programs you use.

CHAPTER 2.

15 (Fifteen) Special Keyboard Shortcuts.

The fifteen special keyboard shortcuts are fifteen (15) shortcuts every computer user should know.

The following is a list of keyboard shortcuts every computer user should know:

1. **Ctrl + A:** Control A, highlights or selects everything you have in the environment where you are working.

   If you are like ***"Wow, the content of this document is large and there is no time to select all of it, besides, it's going to mount pressure on my computer?"*** *Using the mouse for this is an outdated method of handling a task like selecting all, Ctrl+A will take care of that in a second.*

2. **Ctrl + C:** Control C copies any highlighted or selected element within the work environment.

   Saves the time and stress which would have been used to right click and click again just to copy. Use ctrl+c.

3. **Ctrl + N:** Control N opens a new window or file.

   Instead of clicking **File, New, blank/ template** and another **click,** *just press **Ctrl + N*** and a fresh page or window will appear instantly.

4. **Ctrl + O:** Control O opens a new program.

   Use ctrl +O when you want to locate / open a file or program.

5. **Ctrl + P:** Control P prints the active document.

   Always use this to locate the printer dialog box, and thereafter print.

6. **Ctrl + S:** Control S saves a new document or file and changes made by the user.

   Please stop! Don't use the mouse. Just press Ctrl+S and everything will be saved.

7. **Ctrl +V:** Control V pastes copied elements into the active area of the program in use.

   Using ctrl+V in a case like this Saves the time and stress of right clicking and clicking again just to paste.

8. **Ctrl + W:** Control W is used to close the page you are working on when you want to leave the work environment.

"There is a way Debby does this without using the mouse. Oh my God, why didn't I learn it then?" Don't worry, I have the answer. Debby presses Ctrl+W to close active windows.

9. **Ctrl + X:** Control X cuts elements (making the elements to disappear from their original place). The difference between cutting and deleting elements is that in Cutting, what was cut doesn't get lost permanently but prepares itself so that it can be pasted on another location defined by the user.

   Use ctrl+x when you think ***"this shouldn't be here and I can't stand the stress of retyping or redesigning it on the rightful place it belongs".***

10. **Ctrl + Y:** Control Y undoes already done actions.

    Ctrl+Z brought back what you didn't need? Press Ctrl+ Y to remove it again.

11. **Ctrl + Z:** Control Z redoes actions.
    Can't find what you typed now or a picture you inserted, it suddenly disappeared or you mistakenly removed it? Press Ctrl+Z to bring it back.

12. **Alt + F4:** Alternative F4 closes active windows or items.

*You don't need to move the mouse in order to close an active window, just press **Alt** + **F4**. Also use it when you are done or you don't want somebody who is coming to see what you are doing.*

13. **Ctrl + F6:** Control F6 Navigates between open windows, making it possible for a user to see what is happening in windows that are active.

    Are you working in Microsoft Word and want to find out if the other active window where your browser is loading a page is still progressing? Use Ctrl + F6.

14. **F1:** This displays the help window.

    *Is your computer malfunctioning? Use **F1** to find help when you don't know what next to do.*

15. **F12:** This enables user to make changes to an already saved document.

    F12 is the shortcut to use when you want to change the format in which you saved your existing document, password it, change its name, change the file location or destination, or make other changes to it. It will save you time.

CHAPTER 3.

Tips, and Keyboard Shortcuts for use in Adobe Photoshop.

About the program: Adobe Photoshop is a raster graphics editor developed, published, and sold by Adobe Systems Incorporated for MacOS and Windows operating systems.

A fresh topic ↳

Download Photoshop CC.

Welcome to Photoshop CC! Whether you purchased a Complete, a Photography, or a Single-App plan, the process is the same. Simply download Photoshop from the adobe.com website and install it on your desktop.

1. Go to the Creative Cloud apps catalog. Locate Photoshop, and click **Download**.

   If you are not signed in, you will be asked to sign in with your Adobe ID and password. Follow the onscreen instructions.

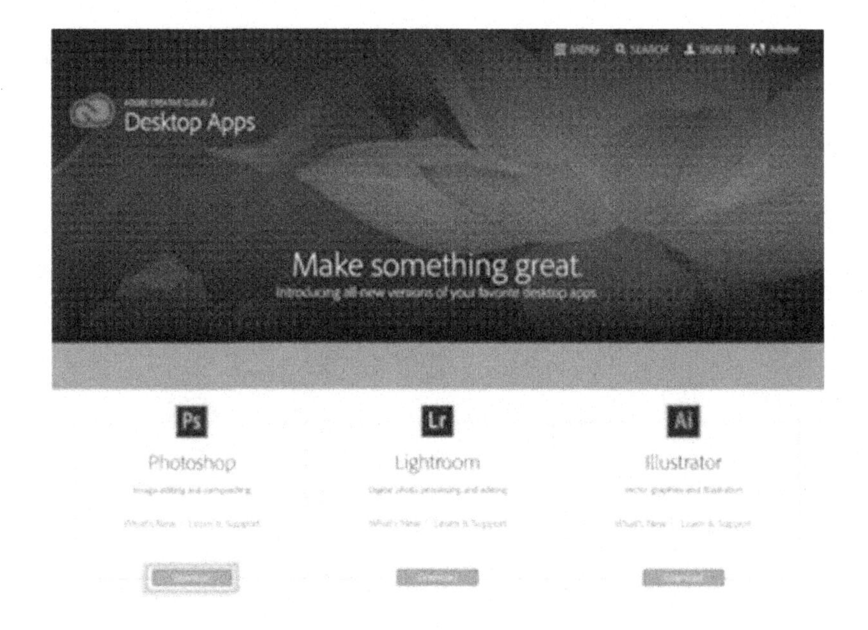

Note:

If you have a free trial membership to Creative Cloud, please refer to Download and install a Creative Cloud trial.

2. Your app begins to download.

   At the same time, the Adobe Creative Cloud desktop app appears, and it will manage the rest of the installation process. Check your download progress in the status bar next to the app's name.

   Note:

   Depending on your network's speed, it could take some time to download your app.

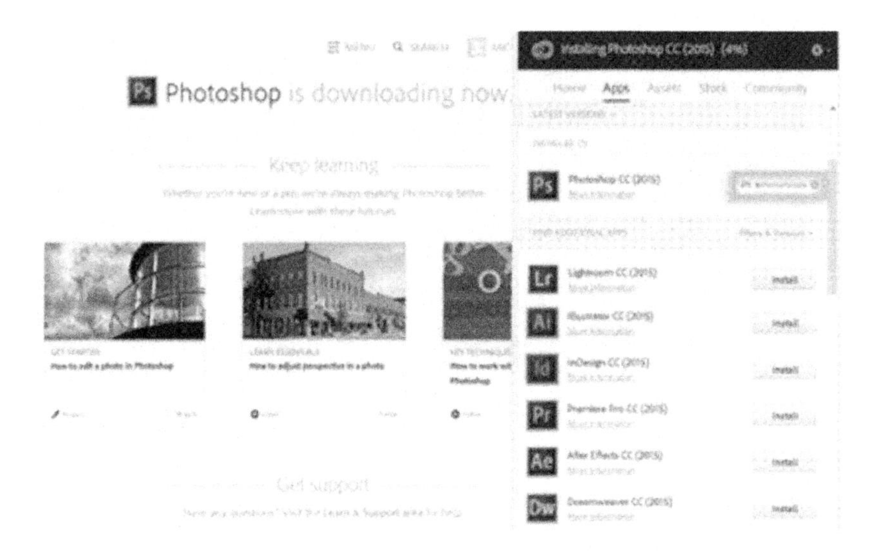

3. To launch your new app, find the Photoshop icon in the Apps panel and click Open.

   You can also launch Photoshop as you normally launch any app on your computer. Photoshop is installed in the same location where your applications are normally installed, such as the Program Files folder (Windows) or the Applications folder (Mac OS).

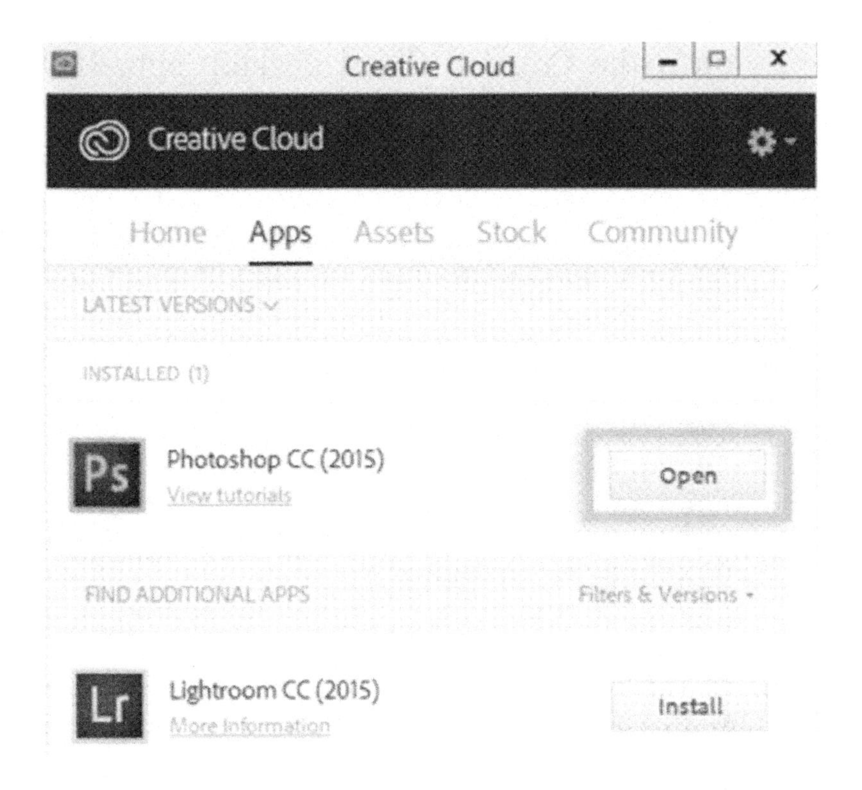

Note:

Having trouble with your first download? See Troubleshoot Creative Cloud download and installation issues.

Install Photoshop CS6.

You can download previous versions of Photoshop, such as CS6, directly from the Creative Cloud desktop app. You can have multiple versions of Photoshop installed on your computer at the same time, if you choose.

1. Click the **Creative Cloud icon**, located in the taskbar (Windows) or Apple menu bar (Mac OS), to

open the Creative Cloud desktop app. If it's not already selected, click the **Apps** tab at the top of the window.

2. In the Find Additional Apps section, click **Filters & Versions** and choose **Previous Version**.

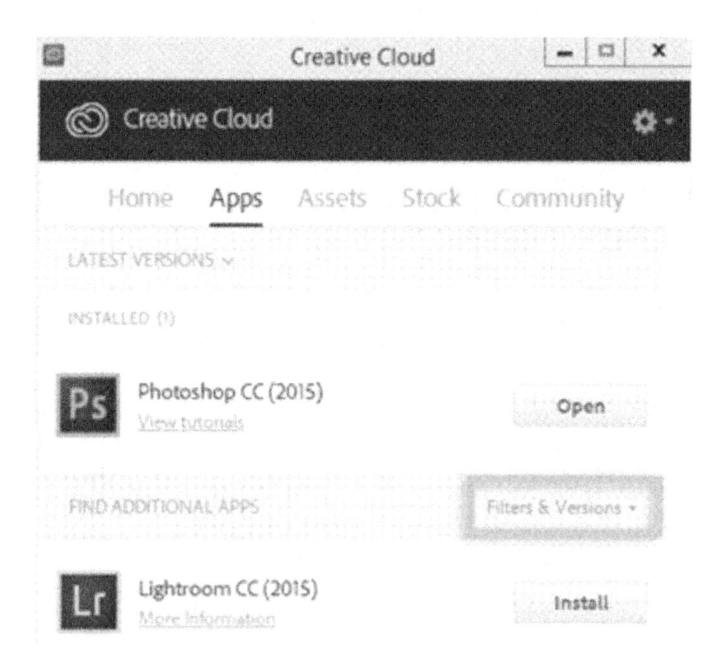

3. Find Photoshop in the list, and click the Install menu. Choose **CS6**.

   Photoshop CS6 downloads and is installed on your computer.

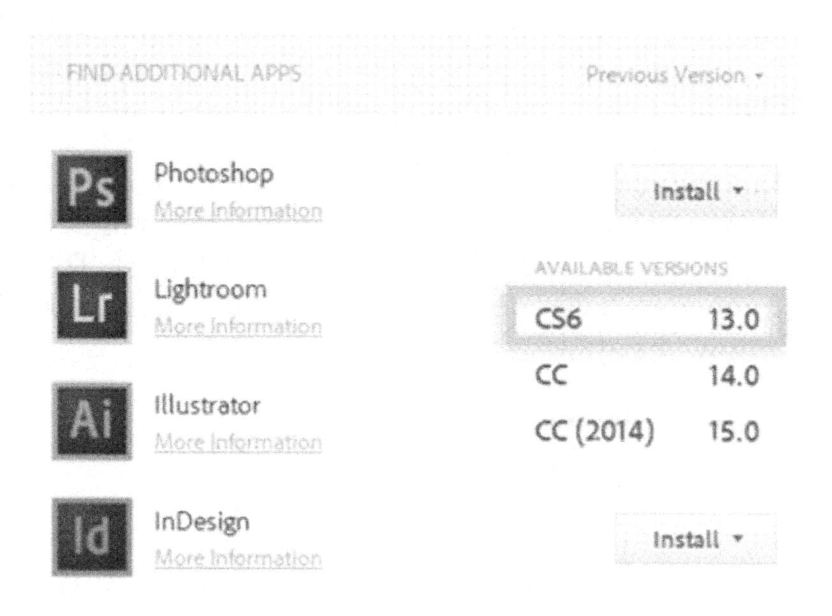

Note:

Previous product versions do not overwrite existing versions. You can have two versions of the same app running simultaneously on your computer, except for Acrobat XI (Windows) and Acrobat DC. Installation of these Acrobat versions will uninstall other versions of Acrobat.

A fresh topic

Customize Keyboard Shortcuts.

Note:

In addition to using keyboard shortcuts, you can access many commands using context-sensitive menus that are relevant to the active tool, selection, or panel. To display a context-sensitive menu, right-click in the document window or panel.

Define New Keyboard Shortcuts

1. Do one of the following:
    - Choose Edit > Keyboard Shortcuts.
    - Choose Window > Workspace > Keyboard Shortcuts & Menus and click the Keyboard Shortcuts tab.
2. Choose a set of shortcuts from the Set menu at the top of the Keyboard Shortcuts & Menus dialog box.
3. Choose a shortcut type from the Shortcuts For menu:

    Application Menus

    Lets you customize keyboard shortcuts for items in the menu bar.

    Panel Menus

Lets you customize keyboard shortcuts for items in panel menus.

Tools

Lets you customize keyboard shortcuts for tools in the toolbox.

4. In the Shortcut column of the scroll list, select the shortcut you want to modify.
5. Type a new shortcut.

   If the keyboard shortcut is already assigned to another command or tool in the set, an alert appears. Click Accept to assign the shortcut to the new command or tool and erase the previously assigned shortcut. After you reassign a shortcut, you can click Undo Changes to undo the change, or click Accept and Go To Conflict to assign a new shortcut to the other command or tool.

6. When you're finished changing shortcuts, do one of the following:
   - To save all changes to the current set of keyboard shortcuts, click the Save Set button. Changes to a custom set are saved. If you're saving changes to the Photoshop Defaults set, the Save dialog box opens. Enter a name for the new set and click Save.
   - To create a new set based on the current set of shortcuts, click the Save Set As button. In the Save dialog box, enter a name for the new set in the Name text box, and click Save.

The new keyboard shortcut set will appear in the pop-up menu under the new name.

- To discard the last saved change without closing the dialog box, click Undo.
- To return a new shortcut to the default, click Use Default.
- To discard all changes and exit the dialog box, click Cancel.

Note:

If you haven't saved the current set of changes, you can click Cancel to discard all changes and exit the dialog box.

Clear shortcuts from a command or tool

1. Choose Edit > Keyboard Shortcuts.
2. In the Keyboard Shortcuts dialog box, select the command or tool name whose shortcut you want to delete.
3. Click Delete Shortcut.

Delete a set of shortcuts

1. Choose Edit > Keyboard Shortcuts.
2. In the Set pop-up menu, choose the shortcut set that you want to delete.
3. Click the Delete icon and then click OK to exit the dialog box.

View a list of current shortcuts

To view a list of current shortcuts, export them to an HTML file, which you can display or print with a web browser.

1. Choose Edit > Keyboard Shortcuts.
2. From the Shortcuts For menu, choose a shortcut type: Application Menus, Panel Menus, or Tools.
3. Click Summarize.

A fresh topic

Default Keyboard Shortcuts in Adobe Photoshop.

Use the following list of keyboard shortcuts to enhance your productivity in Adobe Photoshop.

Keys for Invoking Search Experience.

Result	Windows Shortcut	Mac OS Shortcut
Search across Photoshop UI, Help & Learn content, and Adobe Stock assets.	Control + F	Command + F

Function Keys

Result	Windows	Mac OS
Start Help	F1	Help key
Undo/Redo		F1
Cut	F2	F2
Copy	F3	F3
Paste	F4	F4
Show/Hide Brush panel	F5	F5
Show/Hide Color panel	F6	F6
Show/Hide Layers panel	F7	F7
Show/Hide Info panel	F8	F8
Show/Hide Actions panel	F9	Option + F9
Revert	F12	F12
Fill	Shift + F5	Shift + F5
Feather Selection	Shift + F6	Shift + F6
Inverse Selection	Shift + F7	Shift + F7

Keys for Selecting Tools.

Holding down a key temporarily activates a tool. Letting go of the key returns to the previous tool.

Note:

In rows with multiple tools, repeatedly press the same shortcut to toggle through the group.

Result	Windows Shortcut	Mac OS Shortcut
Cycle through tools with the	Shift-press shortcut key (if Use Shift Key for	Shift-press shortcut key (if Use Shift Key for

same shortcut key	Tool Switch preference is selected)	Tool Switch preference is selected)
Cycle through hidden tools	Alt-click + tool (except Add Anchor Point, Delete Anchor Point, and Convert Point tools)	Option-click + tool (except Add Anchor Point, Delete Anchor Point, and Convert Point tools)
Move tool	V	V
Rectangular Marquee tool† Elliptical Marquee tool	M	M
Lasso tool Polygonal Lasso tool Magnetic Lasso tool	L	L
Magic Wand tool Quick Selection tool	W	W
Crop tool Slice tool Slice Select tool	C	C

Eyedropper tool[†] Color Sampler tool Ruler tool Note tool Count tool[*]	I	I
Spot Healing Brush tool Healing Brush tool Patch tool Red Eye tool	J	J
Brush tool Pencil tool Color Replacement tool Mixer Brush tool	B	B
Clone Stamp tool	S	S

Pattern Stamp tool		
History Brush tool Art History Brush tool	Y	Y
Eraser tool[†] Background Eraser tool Magic Eraser tool	E	E
Gradient tool Paint Bucket tool	G	G
Dodge tool Burn tool Sponge tool	O	O
Pen tool Freeform Pen tool	P	P
Horizontal Type tool Vertical Type tool	T	T

Horizontal Type mask tool Vertical Type mask tool		
Path Selection tool Direct Selection tool	A	A
Rectangle tool Rounded Rectangle tool Ellipse tool Polygon tool Line tool Custom Shape tool	U	U
3D Object Rotate tool* 3D Object Roll tool* 3D Object Pan tool*	K	K

3D Object Slide tool* 3D Object Scale tool*		
3D Camera Rotate tool* 3D Camera Roll tool* 3D Camera Pan tool* 3D Camera Walk tool* 3D Camera Zoom*	N	N
Hand tool†	H	H
Rotate View tool	R	R
Zoom tool†	Z	Z
†Use same shortcut key for Liquify *Photoshop Extended only		

Keys For Viewing Images.

This partial list provides shortcuts that don't appear in menu commands or tool tips.

Result	**Windows Shortcut**	**Mac OS Shortcut**

Cycle through open documents	Control + Tab	Control + Tab
Switch to previous document	Shift + Control + Tab	Shift + Command + `(grave accent)
Close a file in Photoshop and open Bridge	Shift-Control-W	Shift-Command-W
Toggle between Standard mode and Quick Mask mode	Q	Q
Toggle (forward) between Standard screen mode, Full screen mode with menu bar, and Full screen mode	F	F
Toggle (backward) between Standard screen mode, Full screen mode with menu bar, and Full screen mode	Shift + F	Shift + F
Toggle (forward) canvas color	Spacebar + F (or right-click canvas background and select color)	Spacebar + F (or Control-click canvas background and select color)
Toggle (backward) canvas color	Spacebar + Shift + F	Spacebar + Shift + F
Fit image in window	Double-click Hand tool	Double-click Hand tool

Magnify 100%	Double-click Zoom tool or Ctrl + 1	Double-click Zoom tool or Command + 1
Switch to Hand tool (when not in text-edit mode)	Spacebar	Spacebar
Simultaneously pan multiple documents with Hand tool	Shift-drag	Shift-drag
Switch to Zoom In tool	Control + spacebar	Command + spacebar
Switch to Zoom Out tool	Alt + spacebar	Option + spacebar
Move Zoom marquee while dragging with the Zoom tool	Spacebar-drag	Spacebar-drag
Apply zoom percentage, and keep zoom percentage box active	Shift + Enter in Navigator panel zoom percentage box	Shift + Return in Navigator panel zoom percentage box
Zoom in on specified area of an image	Control-drag over preview in Navigator panel	Command-drag over preview in Navigator panel
Temporarily zoom into an image	Hold down H and then click in the image and hold down	Hold down H and then click in the image and hold down

	the mouse button	the mouse button
Scroll image with Hand tool	Spacebar-drag, or drag view area box in Navigator panel	Spacebar-drag, or drag view area box in Navigator panel
Scroll up or down 1 screen	Page Up or Page Down†	Page Up or Page Down†
Scroll up or down 10 units	Shift + Page Up or Page Down†	Shift + Page Up or Page Down†
Move view to upper-left corner or lower-right corner	Home or End	Home or End
Toggle layer mask on/off as rubylith (layer mask must be selected)	\ (backslash)	\ (backslash)
†Hold down Ctrl (Windows) or Command (Mac OS) to scroll left (Page Up) or right (Page Down)		

Keys for Puppet Warp.

This partial list provides shortcuts that don't appear in menu commands or tool tips.

Result	**Windows Shortcut**	**Mac OS Shortcut**
Cancel completely	Esc	Esc
Undo last pin adjustment	Ctrl + Z	Command + Z
Select all pins	Ctrl + A	Command + A

Deselect all pins	Ctrl + D	Command + D
Select multiple pins	Shift-click	Shift-click
Move multiple selected pins	Shift-drag	Shift-drag
Temporarily hide pins	H	H

Keys for Refine Edge.

Result	**Windows Shortcut**	**Mac OS Shortcut**
Open the Refine Edge dialog box	Control + Alt + R	Command + Option + R
Cycle (forward) through preview modes	F	F
Cycle (backward) through preview modes	Shift + F	Shift + F
Toggle between original image and selection preview	X	X
Toggle between original selection and refined version	P	P
Toggle radius preview on and off	J	J
Toggle between Refine Radius and Erase Refinements tools	Shift + E	Shift + E

Keys for the Filter Gallery.

Result	Windows Shortcut	Mac OS Shortcut
Apply a new filter on top of selected	Alt-click a filter	Option-click a filter
Reapply last-used filter	Control + Alt + F	Command + Alt + F
Open/close all disclosure triangles	Alt-click a disclosure triangle	Option-click a disclosure triangle
Change Cancel button to Default	Control	Command
Change Cancel button to Reset	Alt	Option
Undo/Redo	Control + Z	Command + Z
Step forward	Control + Shift + Z	Command + Shift + Z
Step backward	Control + Alt + Z	Command + Option + Z

Keys for Liquify.

Result	Windows Shortcut	Mac OS Shortcut
Forward Warp tool	W	W
Reconstruct tool	R	R
Twirl Clockwise tool	C	C
Pucker tool	S	S
Bloat tool	B	B
Push Left tool	O	O

Mirror tool	M	M
Turbulence tool	T	T
Freeze Mask tool	F	F
Thaw Mask tool	D	D
Reverse direction for Bloat, Pucker, Push Left, and Mirror tools	Alt + tool	Option + tool
Continually sample the distortion	Alt-drag in preview with Reconstruct tool, Displace, Amplitwist, or Affine mode selected	Option-drag in preview with Reconstruct tool, Displace, Amplitwist, or Affine mode selected
Decrease/increase brush size by 2, or density, pressure, rate, or turbulent jitter by 1	Down Arrow/Up Arrow in Brush Size, Density, Pressure, Rate, or Turbulent Jitter text box[†]	Down Arrow/Up Arrow in Brush Size, Density, Pressure, Rate, or Turbulent Jitter text box[†]
Decrease/increase brush size by 2, or density, pressure, rate, or turbulent jitter by 1	Left Arrow/Right Arrow with Brush Size, Density, Pressure, Rate, or Turbulent Jitter slider showing[†]	Left Arrow/Right Arrow with Brush Size, Density, Pressure, Rate, or Turbulent Jitter slider showing[†]

Cycle through controls on right from top	Tab	Tab
Cycle through controls on right from bottom	Shift + Tab	Shift + Tab
Change Cancel to Reset	Alt	Option
†Hold down Shift to decrease/increase by 10		

Keys for Vanishing Point.

Result	**Windows Shortcut**	**Mac OS Shortcut**
Zoom 2x (temporary)	X	X
Zoom in	Control + + (plus)	Command + + (plus)
Zoom out	Control + - (hyphen)	Command + - (hyphen)
Fit in view	Control + 0 (zero), Double-click Hand tool	Command + 0 (zero), Double-click Hand tool
Zoom to center at 100%	Double-click Zoom tool	Double-click Zoom tool
Increase brush size (Brush, Stamp tools)	]	]
Decrease brush size (Brush, Stamp tools)	[	[

Increase brush hardness (Brush, Stamp tools)	Shift +]	Shift +]
Decrease brush hardness (Brush, Stamp tools)	Shift + [	Shift + [
Undo last action	Control + Z	Command + Z
Redo last action	Control + Shift + Z	Command + Shift + Z
Deselect all	Control + D	Command + D
Hide selection and planes	Control + H	Command + H
Move selection 1 pixel	Arrow keys	Arrow keys
Move selection 10 pixels	Shift + arrow keys	Shift + arrow keys
Copy	Control + C	Command + C
Paste	Control + V	Command + V
Repeat last duplicate and move	Control + Shift + T	Command + Shift + T
Create a floating selection from the current selection	Control + Alt + T	
Fill a selection with image under the pointer	Control-drag	Command-drag
Create a duplicate of the selection as a floating selection	Control + Alt-drag	Command + Option-drag
Constrain selection to a 15° rotation	Alt + Shift to rotate	Option + Shift to rotate

Select a plane under another selected plane	Control-click the plane	Command-click the plane
Create 90 degree plane off parent plane	Control-drag	Command-drag
Delete last node while creating plane	Backspace	Delete
Make a full canvas plane, square to the camera	Double-click the Create Plane tool	Double-click the Create Plane tool
Show/hide measurements (Photoshop Extended only)	Control + Shift + H	Command + Shift + H
Export to a DFX file (Photoshop Extended only)	Control + E	Command + E
Export to a 3DS file (Photoshop Extended only)	Control + Shift + E	Command + Shift + E

Keys for the Camera Raw Dialog Box.

Note:

Holding down a key temporarily activates a tool. Letting go of the key returns to the previous tool.

Result	Windows Shortcut	Mac OS Shortcut
Zoom tool	Z	Z

Hand tool	H	H
White Balance tool	I	I
Color Sampler tool	S	S
Crop tool	C	C
Straighten tool	A	A
Spot Removal tool	B	B
Red Eye Removal tool	E	E
Basic panel	Ctrl + Alt + 1	Command + Option + 1
Tone Curve panel	Ctrl + Alt + 2	Command + Option + 2
Detail panel	Ctrl + Alt + 3	Command + Option + 3
HSL/Grayscale panel	Ctrl + Alt + 4	Command + Option + 4
Split Toning panel	Ctrl + Alt + 5	Command + Option + 5
Lens Corrections panel	Ctrl + Alt + 6	Command + Option + 6
Camera Calibration panel	Ctrl + Alt + 7	Command + Option + 7
Presets panel	Ctrl + Alt + 9	Command + Option + 9 (Mac OS Universal Access zoom shortcut must be disabled in System Preferences)
Open Snapshots panel	Ctrl + Alt + 9	Command + Option + 9

Parametric Curve Targeted Adjustment tool	Ctrl + Alt + Shift + T	Command + Option + Shift + T
Hue Targeted Adjustment tool	Ctrl + Alt + Shift + H	Command + Option + Shift + H
Saturation Targeted Adjustment tool	Ctrl + Alt + Shift + S	Command + Option + Shift + S
Luminance Targeted Adjustment tool	Ctrl + Alt + Shift + L	Command + Option + Shift + L
Grayscale Mix Targeted Adjustment tool	Ctrl + Alt + Shift + G	Command + Option + Shift + G
Last-used Targeted Adjustment tool	T	T
Adjustment Brush tool	K	K
Graduated Filter tool	G	G
Increase/decrease brush size	] / [	] / [
Increase/decrease brush feather	Shift +] / Shift + [	Shift +] / Shift + [
Increase/decrease Adjustment Brush tool flow in increments of 10	= (equal sign) / - (hyphen)	= (equal sign) / - (hyphen)
Temporarily switch from Add to Erase mode for the Adjustment Brush tool, or from Erase to Add mode	Alt	Option

Increase/decrease temporary Adjustment Brush tool size	Alt +] / Alt + [	Option +] / Option + [
Increase/decrease temporary Adjustment Brushtool feather	Alt + Shift +] / Alt + Shift + [	Option + Shift +] / Option + Shift + [
Increase/decrease temporary Adjustment Brush tool flow in increments of 10	Alt + = (equal sign) / Alt + - (hyphen)	Option = (equal sign) / Option + - (hyphen)
Switch to New mode from Add or Erase mode of the Adjustment Brush tool or the Graduated Filter	N	N
Toggle Auto Mask for Adjustment Brush tool	M	M
Toggle Show Mask for Adjustment Brush tool	Y	Y
Toggle pins for Adjustment Brush tool	V	V
Toggle overlay for Graduated Filter, Spot Removal tool, or Red Eye Removal tool.	V	V
Rotate image left	L or Ctrl +]	L or Command +]
Rotate image right	R or Ctrl + [	R or Command + [

Zoom in	Ctrl + + (plus)	Command + + (plus)
Zoom out	Ctrl + - (hyphen)	Command + - (hyphen)
Temporarily switch to Zoom In tool (Doesn't work when Straighten tool is selected. If Crop tool is active, temporarily switches to Straighten tool.)	Ctrl	Command
Temporarily switch to Zoom Out tool and change the Open Image button to Open Copy and the Cancel button to Reset.	Alt	Option
Toggle preview	P	P
Full screen mode	F	F
Temporarily activate the White Balance tool and change the Open Image button to Open Object. (Does not work if Crop tool is active)	Shift	Shift
Select multiple points in Curves panel	Click the first point; Shift-click additional points	Click the first point; Shift-click additional points

Add point to curve in Curves panel	Control-click in preview	Command-click in preview
Move selected point in Curves panel (1 unit)	Arrow keys	Arrow keys
Move selected point in Curves panel (10 units)	Shift-arrow	Shift-arrow
Open selected images in Camera Raw dialog box from Bridge	Ctrl + R	Command + R
Open selected images from Bridge bypassing Camera Raw dialog box	Shift + double-click image	Shift + double-click image
Display highlights that will be clipped in Preview	Alt-drag Exposure, Recovery, or Black sliders	Option-drag Exposure, Recovery, or Black sliders
Highlight clipping warning	O	O
Shadows clipping warning	U	U
(Filmstrip mode) Add 1 - 5 star rating	Ctrl +1 - 5	Command + 1 – 5
(Filmstrip mode) Increase/decrease rating	Ctrl +. (period) / Ctrl+, (comma)	Command + . (period) / Command+, (comma)
(Filmstrip mode) Add red label	Ctrl + 6	Command + 6
(Filmstrip mode) Add yellow label	Ctrl + 7	Command + 7

(Filmstrip mode) Add green label	Ctrl + 8	Command + 8
(Filmstrip mode) Add blue label	Ctrl + 9	Command + 9
(Filmstrip mode) Add purple label	Ctrl + Shift + 0	Command + Shift + 0
Camera Raw preferences	Ctrl + K	Command + K
Deletes Adobe Camera Raw preferences	Ctrl + Alt (on open)	Option + Shift (on open)

Keys for the Black-and-White Dialog Box.

Result	**Windows Shortcut**	**Mac OS Shortcut**
Open the Black-and-White dialog box	Shift + Control + Alt + B	Shift + Command + Option+ B
Increase/decrease selected value by 1%	Up Arrow/Down Arrow	Up Arrow/Down Arrow
Increase/decrease selected value by 10%	Shift + Up Arrow/Down Arrow	Shift + Up Arrow/Down Arrow
Change the values of the closest color slider	Click-drag on the image	Click-drag on the image

Keys for Curves.

Result	**Windows Shortcut**	**Mac OS Shortcut**

Open the Curves dialog box	Control + M	Command + M
Select next point on the curve	+ (plus)	+ (plus)
Select the previous point on the curve	– (minus)	– (minus)
Select multiple points on the curve	Shift-click the points	Shift-click the points
Deselect a point	Control + D	Command + D
To delete a point on the curve	Select a point and press Delete	Select a point and press Delete
Move the selected point 1 unit	Arrow keys	Arrow keys
Move the selected point 10 units	Shift + Arrow keys	Shift + Arrow keys
Display highlights and shadows that will be clipped	Alt-drag black/white point sliders	Option-drag black/white point sliders
Set a point to the composite curve	Control-click the image	Command-click the image
Set a point to the channel curves	Shift + Control-click the image	Shift + Command-click the image
Toggle grid size	Alt-click the field	Option-click the field

Keys for Selecting and Moving Objects.

This partial list provides shortcuts that don't appear in menu commands or tool tips.

Result	Windows Shortcut	Mac OS Shortcut
Reposition marquee while selecting[‡]	Any marquee tool (except single column and single row) + spacebar-drag	Any marquee tool (except single column and single row) + spacebar-drag
Add to a selection	Any selection tool + Shift-drag	Any selection tool + Shift-drag
Subtract from a selection	Any selection tool + Alt-drag	Any selection tool + Option-drag
Intersect a selection	Any selection tool (except Quick Selection tool) + Shift-Alt-drag	Any selection tool (except Quick Selection tool) + Shift-Option-drag
Constrain marquee to square or circle (if no other selections are active)[‡]	Shift-drag	Shift-drag
Draw marquee from center (if no other selections are active)[‡]	Alt-drag	Option-drag
Constrain shape and draw marquee from center[‡]	Shift + Alt-drag	Shift + Option-drag
Switch to Move tool	Control (except when Hand, Slice, Path,	Command (except when Hand, Slice,

	Shape, or any Pen tool is selected)	Path, Shape, or any Pen tool is selected)
Switch from Magnetic Lasso tool to Lasso tool	Alt-drag	Option-drag
Switch from Magnetic Lasso tool to polygonal Lasso tool	Alt-click	Option-click
Apply/cancel an operation of the Magnetic Lasso	Enter/Esc or Control + . (period)	Return/Esc or Command + . (period)
Move copy of selection	Move tool + Alt-drag selection‡	Move tool + Option-drag selection‡
Move selection area 1 pixel	Any selection + Right Arrow, Left Arrow, Up Arrow, or Down Arrow†	Any selection + Right Arrow, Left Arrow, Up Arrow, or Down Arrow†
Move selection 1 pixel	Move tool + Right Arrow, Left Arrow, Up Arrow, or Down Arrow†‡	Move tool + Right Arrow, Left Arrow, Up Arrow, or Down Arrow†‡
Move layer 1 pixel when nothing selected on layer	Control + Right Arrow, Left Arrow, Up Arrow, or Down Arrow†	Command + Right Arrow, Left Arrow, Up Arrow, or Down Arrow†
Increase/decrease detection width	Magnetic Lasso tool + [or]	Magnetic Lasso tool + [or]
Accept cropping or exit cropping	Crop tool + Enter or Esc	Crop tool + Return or Esc

Toggle crop shield off and on	/ (forward slash)	/ (forward slash)
Make protractor	Ruler tool + Alt-drag end point	Ruler tool + Option-drag end point
Snap guide to ruler ticks (except when View > Snap is unchecked)	Shift-drag guide	Shift-drag guide
Convert between horizontal and vertical guide	Alt-drag guide	Option-drag guide
†Hold down Shift to move 10 pixels ‡Applies to shape tools		

Keys for Transforming Selections, Selection Borders, and Paths.

This partial list provides shortcuts that don't appear in menu commands or tool tips.

Result	**Windows Shortcut**	**Mac OS Shortcut**
Transform from center or reflect	Alt	Option
Constrain	Shift	Shift
Distort	Control	Command
Apply	Enter	Return
Cancel	Control + . (period) or Esc	Command + . (period) or Esc

Free transform with duplicate data	Control + Alt + T	Command + Option + T
Transform again with duplicate data	Control + Shift + Alt + T	Command + Shift + Option + T

Keys for Editing Paths.

This partial list provides shortcuts that don't appear in menu commands or tool tips.

Result	**Windows Shortcut**	**Mac OS Shortcut**
Select multiple anchor points	Direct selection tool + Shift-click	Direct selection tool + Shift-click
Select entire path	Direct selection tool + Alt-click	Direct selection tool + Option-click
Duplicate a path	Pen (any Pen tool), Path Selection or Direct Selection tool + Control + Alt-drag	Pen (any Pen tool), Path Selection or Direct Selection tool + Command + Option-drag
Switch from Path Selection, Pen, Add Anchor Point, Delete Anchor Point, or Convert Point tools to	Control	Command

Direct Selection tool		
Switch from Pen tool or Freeform Pen tool to Convert Point tool when pointer is over anchor or direction point	Alt	Option
Close path	Magnetic Pen tool-double-click	Magnetic Pen tool-double-click
Close path with straight-line segment	Magnetic Pen tool + Alt-double-click	Magnetic Pen tool + Option-double-click

Keys For Painting.

This partial list provides shortcuts that don't appear in menu commands or tool tips.

Result	**Windows Shortcut**	**Mac OS Shortcut**
Select foreground color from color picker	Any painting tool + Shift + Alt + right-click and drag	Any painting tool + Control + Option + Command and drag
Select foreground color from image with	Any painting tool + Alt or any shape tool + Alt (except	Any painting tool + Option or any shape tool + Option (except

Eyedropper tool	when Paths option is selected)	when Paths option is selected)
Select background color	Eyedropper tool + Alt-click	Eyedropper tool + Option-click
Color sampler tool	Eyedropper tool + Shift	Eyedropper tool + Shift
Deletes color sampler	Color sampler tool + Alt-click	Color sampler tool + Option-click
Sets opacity, tolerance, strength, or exposure for painting mode	Any painting or editing tool + number keys (e.g., 0 = 100%, 1 = 10%, 4 then 5 in quick succession = 45%) (when airbrush option is enabled, use Shift + number keys)	Any painting or editing tool + number keys (e.g., 0 = 100%, 1 = 10%, 4 then 5 in quick succession = 45%) (when airbrush option is enabled, use Shift + number keys)
Sets flow for painting mode	Any painting or editing tool + Shift + number keys (e.g., 0 = 100%, 1 = 10%, 4 then 5 in quick succession = 45%) (when airbrush option is enabled, omit Shift)	Any painting or editing tool + Shift + number keys (e.g., 0 = 100%, 1 = 10%, 4 then 5 in quick succession = 45%) (when airbrush option is enabled, omit Shift)
Mixer Brush changes Mix setting	Alt + Shift + number	Option + Shift + number

Mixer Brush changes Wet setting	Number keys	Number keys
Mixer Brush changes Wet and Mix to zero	00	00
Cycle through blending modes	Shift + + (plus) or – (minus)	Shift + + (plus) or – (minus)
Open Fill dialog box on background or standard layer	Backspace or Shift + Backspace	Delete or Shift + Delete
Fill with foreground or background color	Alt + Backspace or Control + Backspace†	Option + Delete or Command + Delete†
Fill from history	Control + Alt + Backspace†	Command + Option + Delete†
Displays Fill dialog box	Shift + Backspace	Shift + Delete
Lock transparent pixels on/off	/ (forward slash)	/ (forward slash)
Connects points with a straight line	Any painting tool + Shift-click	Any painting tool + Shift-click
†Hold down Shift to preserve transparency		

Keys For Blending Modes.

Result	Windows Shortcut	Mac OS Shortcut
Cycle through blending modes	Shift + + (plus) or – (minus)	Shift + + (plus) or – (minus)
Normal	Shift + Alt + N	Shift + Option + N
Dissolve	Shift + Alt + I	Shift + Option + I
Behind (Brush tool only)	Shift + Alt + Q	Shift + Option + Q
Clear (Brush tool only)	Shift + Alt + R	Shift + Option + R
Darken	Shift + Alt + K	Shift + Option + K
Multiply	Shift + Alt + M	Shift + Option + M
Color Burn	Shift + Alt + B	Shift + Option + B
Linear Burn	Shift + Alt + A	Shift + Option + A
Lighten	Shift + Alt + G	Shift + Option + G
Screen	Shift + Alt + S	Shift + Option + S
Color Dodge	Shift + Alt + D	Shift + Option + D
Linear Dodge	Shift + Alt + W	Shift + Option + W
Overlay	Shift + Alt + O	Shift + Option + O

Soft Light	Shift + Alt + F	Shift + Option + F
Hard Light	Shift + Alt + H	Shift + Option + H
Vivid Light	Shift + Alt + V	Shift + Option + V
Linear Light	Shift + Alt + J	Shift + Option + J
Pin Light	Shift + Alt + Z	Shift + Option + Z
Hard Mix	Shift + Alt + L	Shift + Option + L
Difference	Shift + Alt + E	Shift + Option + E
Exclusion	Shift + Alt + X	Shift + Option + X
Hue	Shift + Alt + U	Shift + Option + U
Saturation	Shift + Alt + T	Shift + Option + T
Color	Shift + Alt + C	Shift + Option + C
Luminosity	Shift + Alt + Y	Shift + Option + Y
Desaturate	Sponge tool + Shift + Alt + D	Sponge tool + Shift + Option + D
Saturate	Sponge tool + Shift + Alt + S	Sponge tool + Shift + Option + S
Dodge/burn shadows	Dodge tool/Burn tool	Dodge tool/Burn tool

	+ Shift + Alt + S	+ Shift + Option + S
Dodge/burn midtones	Dodge tool/Burn tool + Shift + Alt + M	Dodge tool/Burn tool + Shift + Option + M
Dodge/burn highlights	Dodge tool/Burn tool + Shift + Alt + H	Dodge tool/Burn tool + Shift + Option + H
Set blending mode to Threshold for bitmap images, Normal for all other images	Shift + Alt + N	Shift + Option + N

Keys for Selecting and Editing Text.

This partial list provides shortcuts that don't appear in menu commands or tool tips.

Result	**Windows Shortcut**	**Mac OS Shortcut**
Move type in image	Control-drag type when Type layer is selected	Command-drag type when Type layer is selected
Select 1 character left/right or 1 line down/up, or 1 word left/right	Shift + Left Arrow/Right Arrow or Down Arrow/Up Arrow, or Control + Shift + Left	Shift + Left Arrow/Right Arrow or Down Arrow/Up Arrow, or Command + Shift + Left

	Arrow/Right Arrow	Arrow/Right Arrow
Select characters from insertion point to mouse click point	Shift-click	Shift-click
Move 1 character left/right, 1 line down/up, or 1 word left/right	Left Arrow/Right Arrow, Down Arrow/Up Arrow, or Control + Left Arrow/Right Arrow	Left Arrow/Right Arrow, Down Arrow/Up Arrow, or Command + Left Arrow/Right Arrow
Create a new text layer, when a text layer is selected in the Layers panel	Shift-click	Shift-click
Select a word, line, paragraph, or story	Double-click, triple-click, quadruple-click, or quintuple-click	Double-click, triple-click, quadruple-click, or quintuple-click
Show/Hide selection on selected type	Control + H	Command + H
Display the bounding box for transforming text when editing text, or activate Move tool if cursor is	Control	Command

inside the bounding box		
Scale text within a bounding box when resizing the bounding box	Control-drag a bounding box handle	Command-drag a bounding box handle
Move text box while creating text box	Spacebar-drag	Spacebar-drag

Keys for Formatting Type.

This partial list provides shortcuts that don't appear in menu commands or tool tips.

Result	**Windows Shortcut**	**Mac OS Shortcut**
Align left, center, or right	Horizontal Type tool + Control + Shift + L, C, or R	Horizontal Type tool + Command + Shift + L, C, or R
Align top, center, or bottom	Vertical Type tool + Control + Shift + L, C, or R	Vertical Type tool + Command + Shift + L, C, or R
Choose 100% horizontal scale	Control + Shift + X	Command + Shift + X
Choose 100% vertical scale	Control + Shift + Alt + X	Command + Shift + Option + X

Choose Auto leading	Control + Shift + Alt + A	Command + Shift + Option + A
Choose 0 for tracking	Control + Shift + Q	Command + Control + Shift + Q
Justify paragraph, left aligns last line	Control + Shift + J	Command + Shift + J
Justify paragraph, justifies all	Control + Shift + F	Command + Shift + F
Toggle paragraph hyphenation on/off	Control + Shift + Alt + H	Command + Control + Shift + Option + H
Toggle single/every-line composer on/off	Control + Shift + Alt + T	Command + Shift + Option + T
Decrease or increase type size of selected text 2 points or pixels	Control + Shift + < or >[†]	Command + Shift + < or >[†]
Decrease or increase leading 2 points or pixels	Alt + Down Arrow or Up Arrow[††]	Option + Down Arrow or Up Arrow[††]
Decrease or increase baseline shift 2 points or pixels	Shift + Alt + Down Arrow or Up Arrow[††]	Shift + Option + Down Arrow or Up Arrow[††]
Decrease or increase kerning/tracking 20/1000 ems	Alt + Left Arrow or Right Arrow[††]	Option + Left Arrow or Right Arrow[††]
[†]Hold down Alt (Win) or Option (macOS) to decrease/increase by 10 [††]Hold down Ctrl (Windows) or Command (macOS) to decrease/increase by 10		

Keys for Slicing and Optimizing.

Result	Windows Shortcut	Mac OS Shortcut
Toggle between Slice tool and Slice Selection tool	Control	Command
Draw square slice	Shift-drag	Shift-drag
Draw from center outward	Alt-drag	Option-drag
Draw square slice from center outward	Shift + Alt-drag	Shift + Option-drag
Reposition slice while creating slice	Spacebar-drag	Spacebar-drag
Open context-sensitive menu	Right-click slice	Control-click slice

Keys for using Panels.

This partial list provides shortcuts that don't appear in menu commands or tool tips.

Result	Windows Shortcut	Mac OS Shortcut
Set options for new items (except for Actions, Animation, Styles, Brushes, Tool Presets, and Layer Comps panels)	Alt-click New button	Option-click New button

Delete without confirmation (except for the Brush panel)	Alt-click Delete button	Option-click Delete button
Apply value and keep text box active	Shift + Enter	Shift + Return
Show/Hide all panels	Tab	Tab
Show/Hide all panels except the toolbox and options bar	Shift + Tab	Shift + Tab
Highlight options bar	Select tool and press Enter	Select tool and press Return
Increase/decrease selected values by 10	Shift + Up Arrow/Down Arrow	Shift + Up Arrow/Down Arrow

Keys for the Actions Panel.

Result	**Windows Shortcut**	**Mac OS Shortcut**
Turn command on and all others off, or turn all commands on	Alt-click the check mark next to a command	Option-click the check mark next to a command
Turn current modal control on and toggle all other modal controls	Alt-click	Option-click
Change action or action set options	Alt + double-click action or action set	Option + double-click action or action set

Display Options dialog box for recorded command	Double-click recorded command	Double-click recorded command
Play entire action	Control + double-click an action	Command + double-click an action
Collapse/expand all components of an action	Alt-click the triangle	Option-click the triangle
Play a command	Control-click the Play button	Command-click the Play button
Create new action and begin recording without confirmation	Alt-click the New Action button	Option-click the New Action button
Select contiguous items of the same kind	Shift-click the action/command	Shift-click the action/command
Select discontiguous items of the same kind	Control-click the action/command	Command-click the action/command

Keys for Adjustment Layers

Note:

If you prefer channel shortcuts starting with Alt/Option + 1 for red, choose Edit > Keyboard Shortcuts, and select Use Legacy Channel Shortcuts. Then restart Photoshop.

Result	Windows Shortcut	Mac OS Shortcut
Choose specific channel for adjustment	Alt + 3 (red), 4 (green), 5 (blue)	Option + 3 (red), 4 (green), 5 (blue)
Choose composite channel for adjustment	Alt + 2	Option + 2
Delete adjustment layer	Delete or Backspace	Delete
Define Auto options for Levels or Curves	Alt-click Auto button	Option-click Auto button

Keys for the Animation panel in Frames Mode.

Result	Windows Shortcut	Mac OS Shortcut
Select/deselect multiple contiguous frames	Shift-click second frame	Shift-click second frame
Select/deselect multiple discontiguous frames	Control-click multiple frames	Command-click multiple frames
Paste using previous settings	Alt + Paste Frames	Option + Paste Frames

without displaying the dialog box	command from the Panel pop-up menu	command from the Panel pop-up menu

Keys for the Animation Panel in Timeline Mode (Photoshop Extended).

Note:

To enable all shortcuts, choose Enable Timeline Shortcut Keys from the Animation (Timeline) panel menu.

Result	**Windows Shortcut**	**Mac OS Shortcut**
Start playing the timeline or Animation panel	Spacebar	Spacebar
Switch between timecode and frame numbers (current time view)	Alt + click the current-time display in the upper-left corner of the timeline.	Option + click the current-time display in the upper-left corner of the timeline.
Expand and collapse list of layers	Alt + click	Option + click on list triangles
Jump to the next/previous whole second in timeline	Hold down the Shift key when clicking the Next/Previous Frame buttons (on either side of the Play button).	Hold down the Shift key when clicking the Next/Previous Frame buttons (on either side of the Play button)

Increase playback speed	Hold down the Shift key while dragging the current time.	Hold down the Shift key while dragging the current time.
Decrease playback speed	Hold down the Control key while dragging the current time.	Hold down the Command key while dragging the current time.
Snap an object (keyframe, the current time, layer in point, and so on) to the nearest object in timeline	Shift-drag	Shift-drag
Scale (evenly distribute to condensed or extended length) a selected group of multiple keyframes	Alt-drag (first or last keyframe in the selection)	Option-drag (first or last keyframe in the group)
Back one frame	Left Arrow or Page Up	Left Arrow or Page Up
Forward one frame	Right Arrow or Page Down	Right Arrow or Page Down
Back ten frames	Shift + Left Arrow or Shift + Page Up	Shift + Left Arrow or Shift Page Up
Forward ten frames	Shift + Right Arrow or Shift + Page Down	Shift + Right Arrow or Shift + Page Down

Move to the beginning of the timeline	Home	Home
Move to the end of the timeline	End	End
Move to the beginning of the work area	Shift + Home	Shift + Home
Move to the end of the work area	Shift + End	Shift + End
Move to In point of the current layer	Up Arrow	Up Arrow
Move to the Out point of the current layer	Down Arrow	Down Arrow
Back 1 second	Shift + Up Arrow	Shift + Up Arrow
Foward 1 second	Shift + Down Arrow	Shift + Down Arrow
Return a rotated document to its original orientation	Esc	Esc

Keys for the Brush Panel.

Result	**Windows Shortcut**	**Mac OS Shortcut**
Delete brush	Alt-click brush	Option-click brush
Rename brush	Double-click brush	Double-click brush

Change brush size	Alt + right-click + drag left or right	Ctrl + Option + drag left or right
Decrease/increase brush softness/hardness	Alt + right-click + drag up or down	Ctrl + Option + drag up or down
Select previous/next brush size	, (comma) or . (period)	, (comma) or . (period)
Select first/last brush	Shift + , (comma) or . (period)	Shift + , (comma) or . (period)
Display precise cross hair for brushes	Caps Lock or Shift + Caps Lock	Caps Lock
Toggle airbrush option	Shift + Alt + P	Shift + Option + P

Keys for the Channels Panel.

Note:

If you prefer channel shortcuts starting with Ctrl/Command + 1 for red, choose Edit > Keyboard Shortcuts, and select Use Legacy Channel Shortcuts.

Result	**Windows Shortcut**	**Mac OS Shortcut**
Select individual channels	Ctrl + 3 (red), 4 (green), 5 (blue)	Command + 3 (red), 4 (green), 5 (blue)
Select composite channel	Ctrl + 2	Command + 2

Load channel as selection	Control-click channel thumbnail, or Alt + Ctrl + 3 (red), 4 (green), 5 (blue)	Command-click channel thumbnail, or Option + Command + 3 (red), 4 (green), 5 (blue)
Add to current selection	Control + Shift-click channel thumbnail	Command + Shift-click channel thumbnail
Subtract from current selection	Control + Alt-click channel thumbnail	Command + Option-click channel thumbnail
Intersect with current selection	Control + Shift + Alt-click channel thumbnail	Command + Shift + Option-click channel thumbnail
Set options for Save Selection As Channel button	Alt-click Save Selection As Channel button	Option-click Save Selection As Channel button
Create a new spot channel	Control-click Create New Channel button	Command-click Create New Channel button
Select/deselect multiple color-channel selection	Shift-click color channel	Shift-click color channel
Select/deselect alpha channel and show/hide as a rubylith overlay	Shift-click alpha channel	Shift-click alpha channel

Display channel options	Double-click alpha or spot channel thumbnail	Double-click alpha or spot channel thumbnail
Toggle composite and grayscale mask in Quick Mask mode	~ (tilde)	~ (tilde)

Keys for the Clone Source Panel.

Result	**Windows Shortcut**	**Mac OS Shortcut**
Show Clone Source (overlays image)	Alt + Shift	Option + Shift
Nudge Clone Source	Alt + Shift + arrow keys	Option + Shift + arrow keys
Rotate Clone Source	Alt + Shift + < or >	Option + Shift + < or >
Scale (increase or reduce size) Clone Source	Alt + Shift + [or]	Option + Shift + [or]

Keys for the Color Panel.

Result	**Windows Shortcut**	**Mac OS Shortcut**
Select background color	Alt-click color in color bar	Option-click color in color bar
Display Color Bar menu	Right-click color bar	Control-click color bar

Cycle through color choices	Shift-click color bar	Shift-click color bar

Keys for the History Panel.

Result	**Windows Shortcut**	**Mac OS Shortcut**
Create a new snapshot	Alt + New Snapshot	Option + New Snapshot
Rename snapshot	Double-click snapshot name	Double-click snapshot name
Step forward through image states	Control + Shift + Z	Command + Shift + Z
Step backward through image states	Control + Alt + Z	Command + Option + Z
Duplicate any image state, except the current state	Alt-click the image state	Option-click the image state
Permanently clear history (no Undo)	Alt + Clear History (in History panel pop-up menu)	Option + Clear History (in History panel pop-up menu)

Keys for the Info Panel

Result	**Windows Shortcut**	**Mac OS Shortcut**

Change color readout modes	Click eyedropper icon	Click eyedropper icon
Change measurement units	Click crosshair icon	Click crosshair icon

Keys for the Layers Panel.

Result	**Windows Shortcut**	**Mac OS Shortcut**
Load layer transparency as a selection	Control-click layer thumbnail	Command-click layer thumbnail
Add to current selection	Control + Shift-click layer thumbnail	Command + Shift-click layer thumbnail
Subtract from current selection	Control + Alt-click layer thumbnail	Command + Option-click layer thumbnail
Intersect with current selection	Control + Shift + Alt-click layer thumbnail	Command + Shift + Option-click layer thumbnail
Load filter mask as a selection	Control-click filter mask thumbnail	Command-click filter mask thumbnail
Group layers	Control + G	Command + G
Ungroup layers	Control + Shift + G	Command + Shift + G
Create/release clipping mask	Control + Alt + G	Command + Option + G
Select all layers	Control + Alt + A	Command + Option + A

Merge visible layers	Control + Shift + E	Command + Shift + E
Create new empty layer with dialog box	Alt-click New Layer button	Option-click New Layer button
Create new layer below target layer	Control-click New Layer button	Command-click New Layer button
Select top layer	Alt + . (period)	Option + . (period)
Select bottom layer	Alt + , (comma)	Option + , (comma)
Add to layer selection in Layers panel	Shift + Alt + [or]	Shift + Option + [or]
Select next layer down/up	Alt + [or]	Option + [or]
Move target layer down/up	Control + [or]	Command + [or]
Merge a copy of all visible layers into target layer	Control + Shift + Alt + E	Command + Shift + Option + E
Merge layers	Highlight layers you want to merge, then Control + E	Highlight the layers you want to merge, then Command + E
Move layer to bottom or top	Control + Shift + [or]	Command + Shift + [or]
Copy current layer to layer below	Alt + Merge Down command from the Panel pop-up menu	Option + Merge Down command from the Panel pop-up menu

Merge all visible layers to a new layer above the currently selected layer	Alt + Merge Visible command from the Panel pop-up menu	Option + Merge Visible command from the Panel pop-up menu
Show/hide this layer/layer group only or all layers/layer groups	Right-click the eye icon	Control-click the eye icon
Show/hide all other currently visible layers	Alt-click the eye icon	Option-click the eye icon
Toggle lock transparency for target layer, or last applied lock	/ (forward slash)	/ (forward slash)
Edit layer effect/style, options	Double-click layer effect/style	Double-click layer effect/style
Hide layer effect/style	Alt-double-click layer effect/style	Option-double-click layer effect/style
Edit layer style	Double-click layer	Double-click layer
Disable/enable vector mask	Shift-click vector mask thumbnail	Shift-click vector mask thumbnail
Open Layer Mask Display Options dialog box	Double-click layer mask thumbnail	Double-click layer mask thumbnail
Toggle layer mask on/off	Shift-click layer mask thumbnail	Shift-click layer mask thumbnail

Toggle filter mask on/off	Shift-click filter mask thumbnail	Shift-click filter mask thumbnail
Toggle between layer mask/composite image	Alt-click layer mask thumbnail	Option-click layer mask thumbnail
Toggle between filter mask/composite image	Alt-click filter mask thumbnail	Option-click filter mask thumbnail
Toggle rubylith mode for layer mask on/off	\ (backslash), or Shift + Alt-click	\ (backslash), or Shift + Option-click
Select all type; temporarily select Type tool	Double-click type layer thumbnail	Double-click type layer thumbnail
Create a clipping mask	Alt-click the line dividing two layers	Option-click the line dividing two layers
Rename layer	Double-click the layer name	Double-click the layer name
Edit filter settings	Double-click the filter effect	Double-click the filter effect
Edit the Filter Blending options	Double-click the Filter Blending icon	Double-click the Filter Blending icon
Create new layer group below current layer/layer set	Control-click New Group button	Command-click New Group button

Create new layer group with dialog box	Alt-click New Group button	Option-click New Group button
Create layer mask that hides all/selection	Alt-click Add Layer Mask button	Option-click Add Layer Mask button
Create vector mask that reveals all/path area	Control-click Add Layer Mask button	Command-click Add Layer Mask button
Create vector mask that hides all or displays path area	Control + Alt-click Add Layer Mask button	Command + Option-click Add Layer Mask button
Display layer group properties	Right-click layer group and choose Group Properties, or double-click group	Control-click the layer group and choose Group Properties, or double-click group
Select/deselect multiple contiguous layers	Shift-click	Shift-click
Select/deselect multiple discontiguous layers	Control-click	Command-click

Note:

If Kotoeri is your Japanese language input method, the "Toggle rubylith mode for layer mask on/off" shortcut starts an action in Kotoeri. Please switch to another mode (for example, "U.S.") to enable this shortcut.

Keys for the Layer Comps Panel.

Result	Windows Shortcut	Mac OS Shortcut
Create new layer comp without the New Layer Comp box	Alt-click Create New Layer Comp button	Option-click Create New Layer Comp button
Open Layer Comp Options dialog box	Double-click layer comp	Double-click layer comp
Rename in-line	Double-click layer comp name	Double-click layer comp name
Select/deselect multiple contiguous layer comps	Shift-click	Shift-click
Select/deselect multiple discontiguous layer comps	Control-click	Command-click

Keys for the Paths Panel

Result	Windows Shortcut	Mac OS Shortcut
Load path as selection	Control-click pathname	Command-click pathname
Add path to selection	Control + Shift-click pathname	Command + Shift-click pathname

Subtract path from selection	Control + Alt-click pathname	Command + Option-click pathname
Retain intersection of path as selection	Control + Shift + Alt-click pathname	Command + Shift + Option-click pathname
Hide path	Control + Shift + H	Command + Shift + H
Set options for Fill Path with Foreground Color button, Stroke Path with Brush button, Load Path as a Selection button, Make Work Path from Selection button, and Create New Path button	Alt-click button	Option-click button

Keys for the Swatches Panel.

Result	**Windows Shortcut**	**Mac OS Shortcut**
Create new swatch from foreground color	Click in empty area of panel	Click in empty area of panel
Set swatch color as background color	Control-click swatch	Command-click swatch
Delete swatch	Alt-click swatch	Option-click swatch

Keys for 3D tools (Photoshop Extended).

Result	Windows Shortcut	Mac OS Shortcut
Enable 3D object tools	K	K
Enable 3D camera tools	N	N
Hide nearest surface	Alt + Ctrl + X	Option + Command + X
Show all surfaces	Alt + Shift + Ctrl + X	Option + Shift + Command + X
3D Object Tool	**Right-click (Windows) / Control-click (Mac OS)**	**Alt (Windows) / Option (Mac OS)**
Rotate	Changes to Drag tool	Changes to Roll tool
Roll	Changes to Slide tool	Changes to Rotate tool
Drag	Changes to Orbit tool	Changes to Slide tool
Slide	Changes to Roll tool	Changes to Drag tool
Scale	Scales on the Z plane	Scales on the Z plane

Note:

To scale on the Y plane, hold down the Shift key.

Camera Tool	Right-click (Windows) / Control-click (Mac OS)	Alt (Windows) / Option (Mac OS)
Orbit	Changes to Drag tool	Changes to Roll tool
Roll	Changes to Slide tool	Changes to Rotate tool
Pan	Changes to Orbit tool	Changes to Slide tool
Walk	Changes to Roll tool	Changes to Drag tool

Keys for Measurement (Photoshop Extended).

Result	Windows Shortcut	Mac OS Shortcut
Record a measurement	Shift + Control + M	Shift + Command + M
Deselects all measurements	Control + D	Command + D
Selects all measurements	Control + A	Command + A
Hide/show all measurements	Shift + Control + H	Shift + Command + H
Removes a measurement	Backspace	Delete
Nudge the measurement	Arrow keys	Arrow keys
Nudge the measurement in increments	Shift + arrow keys	Shift + arrow keys

Extend/shorten selected measurement	Ctrl + Left/Right Arrow key	Command + Left/Right Arrow key
Extend/shorten selected measurement in increments	Shift + Ctrl + Left/Right Arrow key	Shift + Command + Left/Right Arrow key
Rotate selected measurement	Ctrl + Up/Down Arrow key	Command + Up/Down Arrow key
Rotate selected measurement in increments	Shift + Ctrl + Up/Down Arrow key	Shift + Command + Up/Down Arrow key

Keys for DICOM files (Photoshop Extended).

Result	**Windows Shortcut**	**Mac OS Shortcut**
Zoom tool	Z	Z
Hand tool	H	H
Window Level tool	W	W
Select all frames	Control + A	Command + A
Deselect all frames except the current frame	Control + D	Command + D
Navigate through frames	Arrow keys	Arrow keys

Keys for Extract and Pattern Maker (optional plug-ins).

Result (Extract and Pattern Maker)	Windows Shortcut	Mac OS Shortcut
Fit in window	Control + 0	Command + 0
Zoom in	Control + + (plus)	Command + + (plus)
Zoom out	Control + - (hyphen)	Command + - (hyphen)
Cycle through controls on right from top	Tab	Tab
Cycle through controls on right from bottom	Shift + Tab	Shift + Tab
Temporarily activate Hand tool	Spacebar	Spacebar
Change Cancel to Reset	Alt	Option
Result (Extract only)	**Windows Shortcut**	**Mac OS Shortcut**
Edge Highlighter tool	B	B
Fill tool	G	G
Eyedropper tool	I	I
Cleanup tool	C	C
Edge Touchup tool	T	T

Toggle between Edge Highlighter tool and Eraser tool	Alt + Edge Highlighter/Eraser tool	Option + Edge Highlighter/Eraser tool
Toggle Smart Highlighting	Control with Edge Highlighter tool selected	Command with Edge Highlighter tool selected
Remove current highlight	Alt + Delete	Option + Delete
Highlight entire image	Control + Delete	Command + Delete
Fill foreground area and preview extraction	Shift-click with Fill tool selected	Shift-click with Fill tool selected
Move mask when Edge Touchup tool is selected	Control-drag	Command-drag
Add opacity when Cleanup tool is selected	Alt-drag	Option-drag
Toggle Show menu options in preview between Original and Extracted	X	X
Enable Cleanup and Edge Touchup tools before preview	Shift + X	Shift + X
Cycle through Display menu in	F	F

preview from top to bottom		
Cycle through Display menu in preview from bottom to top	Shift + F	Shift + F
Decrease/increase brush size by 1	Down Arrow/Up Arrow in Brush Size text box†	Down Arrow or Up Arrow in Brush Size text box†
Decrease/increase brush size by 1	Left Arrow/Right Arrow with Brush Size Slider showing†	Left Arrow/Right Arrow with Brush Size Slider showing†
Set strength of Cleanup or Edge Touch-up tool	0–9	0–9

†Hold down Shift to decrease/increase by 10

Result (Pattern Maker only)	**Windows Shortcut**	**Mac OS Shortcut**
Delete current selection	Control + D	Command + D
Undo a selection move	Control + Z	Command + Z
Generate or generate again	Control + G	Command + G
Intersect with current selection	Shift + Alt + select	Shift + Option + select
Toggle view: original/generated pattern	X	X

Go to first tile in Tile History	Home	Home
Go to last tile in Tile History	End	End
Go to previous tile in Tile History	Left Arrow, Page Up	Left Arrow, Page Up
Go to next tile in Tile History	Right Arrow, Page Down	Right Arrow, Page Down
Delete current tile from Tile History	Delete	Delete
Nudge selection when viewing the original	Right Arrow, Left Arrow, Up Arrow, or Down Arrow	Right Arrow, Left Arrow, Up Arrow, or Down Arrow
Increase selection nudging when viewing the original	Shift + Right Arrow, Left Arrow, Up Arrow, or Down Arrow	Shift + Right Arrow, Left Arrow, Up Arrow, or Down Arrow

CHAPTER 4.

Tips, Tricks, and Keyboard Shortcuts for Use in After Effect.

About the program: This is an industry-standard tool for video composition, motion graphics design, and animation developed by adobe Systems.

A fresh topic

How to Improve Performance in After Effect.

You can improve performance by optimizing your computer system, After Effects, your project, and your workflow. Some of the suggestions here improve performance not by increasing rendering speed but by decreasing time that other operations require, such as opening a project.

By far, the best way to improve performance overall is to plan ahead, run early tests of your workflow and output pipeline, and confirm that what you are delivering is what your client actually wants and expects. (Check Planning your work.)

Improve performance before starting After Effects.

- Make sure that you've installed the current version of After Effects, including any available updates. To check for and install updates, choose Help > Updates.
- Make sure that you've installed the latest versions of drivers and plug-ins, especially video card drivers. To download updates for drivers and plug-ins, go to the provider's website.
- Make sure that your system has enough RAM. Optimum performance is achieved with computer systems with at least 2 GB of installed RAM per processor core. See the documentation for your operating system and computer for details on how to check the amount of installed RAM and how to install RAM.
- Quit applications that are not necessary for your work. If you run applications other than those with which After Effects shares a memory pool, and you don't allocate adequate memory to other applications, performance can be greatly reduced when the operating system swaps RAM to the hard disk.
- Stop or pause resource-intensive operations in other applications, such as video previews in Adobe Bridge.
- Make sure that your system includes a display card that supports OpenGL 2.0 or later. Though After Effects can function without it, OpenGL accelerates various types of rendering, including rendering to the screen for previews.

- When possible, keep the source footage files for your project on a fast local disk drive. If your source footage files are on a slow disk drive (or across a slow network connection), then performance will be poor. Ideally, use separate fast local disk drives for source footage files and rendered output.
- A separate fast disk (or disk array) to assign the disk cache folder to, is ideal. Because of their speed, SSDs work well for this function.

Improve performance by optimizing memory, cache, and multiprocessing settings.

- Allocate adequate memory for other applications.
- Enable caching frames to disk for previews by selecting the Enable Disk Cache preference. In After Effects, assign as much space as possible to the Disk Cache folder (on a separate fast drive) for best performance. See Disk cache.

Improve performance using Global Performance Cache | CC, CS6.

Import projects from After Effects CS5.5 and earlier into After Effects to take advantage of the Global Performance Cache.

Persistent disk cache improves performance by retaining frames stored in the disk cache between sessions, saving rendering time as you work on a project or other projects that might use the same cached frames.

Improve performance by simplifying your project.

By simplifying and dividing your project, you can prevent After Effects from using memory and other resources to process elements that you are not currently working with. Also, by controlling when After Effects performs certain processing, you can greatly improve overall performance. For example, you can avoid repeating an action that needs to happen only once, or you can postpone an action until it is more convenient for you.

- Delete unused elements from your project.
- Divide complex projects into simpler projects, and then recombine them before you render the finished movie. To recombine projects, import all of the projects into a single project.
- Before rendering, put all of your source footage files on a fast, local disk—not the one that you're rendering and exporting to. A good way to do this is with the Collect Files command. See Collect files in one location.
- Pre-render nested compositions. Render a completed composition as a movie so that After Effects doesn't rerender the composition every time it is displayed.
- Substitute a low-resolution or still-image proxy for a source item when not working directly with that item.
- Lower the resolution for the composition.
- Isolate the layer you're working on by using the Solo switch.

Improve performance by modifying screen output.

You can improve performance in many ways that don't affect how After Effects treats your project data, only how output is drawn to the screen as you work. Although it is often useful to see certain items and information as you work, After Effects uses memory and processor resources to update this information, so be selective in what you choose to display as you work. You will likely need to see different aspects of your project at different points in your workflow, so you may apply the following suggestions in various combinations at various stages.

- Turn off display color management and output simulation when not needed. See Simulate how colors will appear on a different output device. The speed and quality of color management for previews are controlled by the Viewer Quality preferences.
- Enable hardware acceleration of previews, which uses the GPU to assist in drawing previews to the screen. Choose Edit > Preferences > Display (Windows) or After Effects > Preferences > Display (Mac OS), and select Hardware Accelerate Composition, Layer, And Footage Panels.
- Close unneeded panels. After Effects must use memory and processor resources to update open panels, which may slow the work that you are doing in another panel.
- Create a region of interest. If you are working on a small part of your composition, limit which portion

of the composition is rendered to the screen during previews.

- Deselect Show Cache Indicators in the Timeline panel menu to prevent After Effects from displaying green and blue bars in the time ruler to indicate cached frames. See Caches: RAM cache, disk cache, and media cache.
- Deselect the Show Rendering Progress In Info Panel And Flowchart preference to prevent the details of each render operation for each frame from being written to the screen.
- Hide Current Render Details in the Render Queue panel by clicking the triangle beside Current Render Details in the Render Queue panel.
- Press Caps Lock to prevent After Effects from updating Footage, Layer, or Composition panels. When you make a change that would otherwise appear in a panel, After Effects adds a red bar with a text reminder at the bottom of the panel. After Effects continues to update panel controls such as motion paths, anchor points, and mask outlines as you move them. To resume panel updates and display all changes, press Caps Lock again.

Note:

Pressing Caps Lock suspends updates (disables refresh) of previews in viewers during rendering for final output, too, although no red reminder bar appears.

- Lower the display quality of a layer to Draft.
- Select Draft 3D in the Timeline panel menu, which disables all lights and shadows that fall on 3D

layers. It also disables the depth-of-field blur for a camera.

- Use fast draft mode while laying out and previewing a ray-traced 3D composition by selecting an option other than "Off" from the Fast Previews button.
- Deselect Live Update in the Timeline panel menu to prevent After Effects from updating compositions dynamically.
- Display audio waveforms in the Timeline panel only when necessary.
- Disable pixel aspect ratio correction by clicking the Toggle Pixel Aspect Ratio Correction button at the bottom of a Composition, Layer, or Footage panel. The speed and quality of pixel aspect ratio correction and other scaling for previews are controlled by the Viewer Quality preferences.
- Deselect Mirror On Computer Monitor when previewing video on an external video monitor.
- Hide layer controls, such as masks, 3D reference axes, and layer handles. See Show or hide layer controls in the Composition panel.
- Lower the magnification for a composition. When After Effects displays the Composition, Layer, and Footage panels at magnifications greater than 100%, screen redraw speed decreases.
- Set the Resolution/Down Sample Factor value of the composition to Auto in the Composition panel, which prevents the unnecessary rendering of rows or columns of pixels that aren't drawn to the screen at low zoom levels.

Improve performance when using effects

Some effects, such as blurs and distortions, require large amounts of memory and processor resources. By being selective about when and how you apply these effects, you can greatly improve overall performance.

- Apply memory-intensive and processor-intensive effects later. Animate your layers and do other work that requires real-time previews before you apply memory-intensive or processor-intensive effects (such as glows and blurs), which may make previews slower than real time.
- Temporarily turn off effects to increase the speed of previews.
- Limit the number of particles generated by particle effects.
- Rather than apply the same effect with the same settings to multiple layers, apply the effect to an adjustment layer. When an effect is applied to an adjustment layer, it is processed once, on the composite of all of the layers beneath it.

A fresh topic

Keyboard Shortcuts in Adobe After Effect.

Use the following list of keyboard shortcuts to enhance your productivity in Adobe After Effect.

General.

Result	Windows Shortcut	Mac OS Shortcut
Select all	Ctrl+A	Command+A
Deselect all	F2 or Ctrl+Shift+A	F2 or Command+Shift+A
Rename selected layer, composition, folder, effect, group, or mask	Enter on main keyboard	Return
Open selected layer, composition, or footage item	Enter on numeric keypad	Enter on numeric keypad
Move selected layers, masks, effects, or render items down (back) or up (forward)	Ctrl+Alt+Down Arrow or Ctrl+Alt+Up Arrow	Command+Option+Down Arrow or Command+Option+Up Arrow

in stacking order		
Move selected layers, masks, effects, or render items to bottom (back) or top (front) of stacking order	Ctrl+Alt+Shift+ Down Arrow or Ctrl+Alt+Shift+ Up Arrow	Command+Option+Shift+Down Arrow or Command+Option+Shift+Up Arrow
Extend selection to next item in Project panel, Render Queue panel, or Effect Controls panel	Shift+Down Arrow	Shift+Down Arrow
Extend selection to previous item in Project panel, Render	Shift+Up Arrow	Shift+Up Arrow

Queue panel, or Effect Controls panel		
Duplicate selected layers, masks, effects, text selectors, animators, puppet meshes, shapes, render items, output modules, or compositi ons	Ctrl+D	Command+D
Quit	Ctrl+Q	Command+Q
Undo	Ctrl+Z	Command+Z
Redo	Ctrl+Shift+Z	Command+Shift+Z
Purge All Memory	Ctrl+Alt+/ (on numeric keypad)	Command+Option+/ (on numeric keypad)
Interrupt running a script	Esc	Esc

Display filename correspon ding to the frame at the current time in the Info panel	Ctrl+Alt+E	Command+Option+E

Projects.

Result	Windows Shortcut	Mac OS Shortcut
New project	Ctrl+Alt+N	Command+Option+N
Open project	Ctrl+O	Command+O
Open most recent project	Ctrl+Alt+Shift+ P	Command+Option+Shift+ P
New folder in Project panel	Ctrl+Alt+Shift+ N	Command+Option+Shift+ N
Open Project Setting s dialog box	Ctrl+Alt+Shift+ K	Command+Option+Shift+ K

Find in Project panel	Ctrl+F	Command+F
Cycle through color bit depths for project	Alt-click bit-depth button at bottom of Project panel	Option-click bit-depth button at bottom of Project panel
Open Project Settings dialog box	Click bit-depth button at bottom of Project panel	Click bit-depth button at bottom of Project panel

Preferences.

Result	**Windows Shortcut**	**Mac OS Shortcut**
Open Preferences dialog box	Ctrl+Alt+; (semicolon)	Command+Option+; (semicolon)
Restore default preferences settings	Hold down Ctrl+Alt+Shift while starting After Effects	Hold down Command+Option+Shift while starting After Effects

Panels, Viewers, Workspaces, and Windows.

Note:

(Mac OS) Shortcuts involving function keys F9-F12 may conflict with shortcuts used by the operating system. See Mac OS Help for instructions to reassign Dashboard & Expose shortcuts.

Result	Windows Shortcut	Mac OS Shortcut
Open or close Project panel	Ctrl+0	Command+0
Open or close Render Queue panel	Ctrl+Alt+0	Command+Option+0
Open or close Tools panel	Ctrl+1	Command+1
Open or close Info panel	Ctrl+2	Command+2
Open or close Preview panel	Ctrl+3	Command+3
Open or close Audio panel	Ctrl+4	Command+4
Open or close Effects & Presets panel	Ctrl+5	Command+5
Open or close Character panel	Ctrl+6	Command+6

Open or close Paragraph panel	Ctrl+7	Command+7
Open or close Paint panel	Ctrl+8	Command+8
Open or close Brushes panel	Ctrl+9	Command+9
Open or close Effect Controls panel for selected layer	F3 or Ctrl+Shift+T	F3 or Command+Shift+T
Open Flowchart panel for project flowchart	Ctrl+F11	Command+F11
Switch to workspace	Shift+F10, Shift+F11, or Shift+F12	Shift+F10, Shift+F11, or Shift+F12
Close active viewer or panel (closes content first)	Ctrl+W	Command+W
Close active panel or all viewers of type of active viewer (closes content first). For example,	Ctrl+Shift+W	Command+Shift+W

if a Timeline panel is active, this command closes all Timeline panels.		
Split the frame containing the active viewer and create a new viewer with opposite locked/unlocked state	Ctrl+Alt+Shift+N	Command+Option+Shift+N
Maximize or restore panel under pointer	` (accent grave)	` (accent grave)
Resize application window or floating window to fit screen. (Press again to resize window so that contents fill the screen.)	Ctrl+\ (backslash)	Command+\ (backslash)

Move application window or floating window to main monitor; resize window to fit screen. (Press again to resize window so that contents fill the screen.)	Ctrl+Alt+\ (backslash)	Command+Option+\ (backslash)
Toggle activation between Composition panel and Timeline panel for current composition	\ (backslash)	\ (backslash)
Cycle to previous or next item in active viewer (for example, cycle through open compositions)	Shift+, (comma) or Shift+. (period)	Shift+, (comma) or Shift+. (period)

Cycle to previous or next panel in active frame (for example, cycle through open Timeline panels)	Alt+Shift+, (comma) or Alt+Shift+. (period)	Option+Shift+, (comma) or Option+Shift+. (period)
Activate a view in a multi-view layout in the Composition panel without affecting layer selection	Click with middle mouse button	Click with middle mouse button

Activate Tools.

Note:

You can activate some tools only under certain circumstances. For example, you can activate a camera tool only when the active composition contains a camera layer.

Note:

To momentarily activate a tool with a single-letter keyboard shortcut, hold down the key; release the key to return to the previously active tool. To activate a tool and keep it active, press the key and immediately release it.

Result	**Windows Shortcut**	**Mac OS Shortcut**
Cycle through tools	Alt-click tool button in Tools panel	Option-click tool button in Tools panel
Activate Selection tool	V	V
Activate Hand tool	H	H
Temporarily activate Hand tool	Hold down spacebar or the middle mouse button	Hold down spacebar or the middle mouse button
Activate Zoom In tool	Z	Z
Activate Zoom Out tool	Alt (when Zoom In tool is active)	Option (when Zoom In tool is active)
Activate Rotation tool	W	W
Activate Roto Brush tool	Alt+W	Option+W
Activate Refine Edge tool	Alt+W	Option+W
Activate and cycle through Camera tools (Unified Camera, Orbit	C	C

Camera, Track XY Camera, and Track Z Camera)		
Activate Pan Behind tool	Y	Y
Activate and cycle through mask and shape tools (Rectangle, Rounded Rectangle, Ellipse, Polygon, Star)	Q	Q
Activate and cycle through Type tools (Horizontal and Vertical)	Ctrl+T	Command+T
Activate and cycle between the Pen and Mask Feather tools. (Note: You can turn off this setting in the Preferences dialog box.)	G	G
Temporarily activate Selection tool when a pen tool is selected	Ctrl	Command
Temporarily activate Pen tool when the Selection tool is selected and pointer is over a	Ctrl+Alt	Command+Option

path (Add Vertex tool when pointer is over a segment; Convert Vertex tool when pointer is over a vertex)		
Activate and cycle through Brush, Clone Stamp, and Eraser tools	Ctrl+B	Command+B
Activate and cycle through Puppet tools	Ctrl+P	Command+P
Temporarily convert Selection tool to Shape Duplication tool	Alt (in shape layer)	Option (in shape layer)
Temporarily convert Selection tool to Direct Selection tool	Ctrl (in shape layer)	Command (in shape layer)

Compositions and the Work Area.

Result	Windows Shortcut	Mac OS Shortcut
New composition	Ctrl+N	Command+N
Open Composition Settings dialog	Ctrl+K	Command+K

box for selected composition		
Set beginning or end of work area to current time	B or N	B or N
Set work area to duration of selected layers or, if no layers are selected, set work area to composition duration	Ctrl+Alt+B	Command+Option+B
Open Composition Mini-Flowchart for active composition	Tab	Tab
Activate the most recently active composition that is in the same composition hierarchy (network of nested compositions) as the currently active composition	Shift+Esc	Shift+Esc

Trim Composition to work area	Ctrl+Shift+X	Command+Shift+X
New Composition from selection	Alt+\	Option+\

Time Navigation.

Result	Windows Shortcut	Mac OS Shortcut
Go to specific time	Alt+Shift+J	Option+Shift+J
Go to beginning or end of work area	Shift+Home or Shift+End	Shift+Home or Shift+End
Go to previous or next visible item in time ruler (keyframe, layer marker, work area beginning or end)	J or K	J or K

(Note: Also goes to beginning, end, or base frame of Roto Brush span if viewing Roto Brush in Layer panel.)		
Go to beginning of composition, layer, or footage item	Home or Ctrl+Alt+Left Arrow	Home or Command+Option+Left Arrow
Go to end of composition, layer, or footage item	End or Ctrl+Alt+Right Arrow	End or Command+Option+Right Arrow
Go forward 1 frame	Page Down or Ctrl+Right Arrow	Page Down or Command+Right Arrow

Go forward 10 frames	Shift+Page Down or Ctrl+Shift+Right Arrow	Shift+Page Down or Command+Shift+Right Arrow
Go backward 1 frame	Page Up or Ctrl+Left Arrow	Page Up or Command+Left Arrow
Go backward 10 frames	Shift+Page Up or Ctrl+Shift+Left Arrow	Shift+Page Up or Command+Shift+Left Arrow
Go to layer In point	I	I
Go to layer Out point	O	O
Go to previous In point or Out point	Ctrl+Alt+Shift+ Left Arrow	Command+Option+Shift+Left Arrow
Go to next In point or Out point	Ctrl+Alt+Shift+ Right Arrow	Command+Option+Shift+Right Arrow
Scroll to current time in Timeline panel	D	D

Previews.

Result	Windows Shortcut	Mac OS Shortcut
Start or stop preview	Spacebar, 0 on numeric keypad, Shift+0 on numeric keypad	Spacebar, 0 on numeric keypad, Shift+0 on numeric keypad
Reset preview settings to replicate RAM Preview and Standard Preview behaviors	Alt-click Reset in Preview panel	Option-click Reset in Preview panel
Preview only audio, from current time	. (decimal point) on numeric keypad*	. (decimal point) on numeric keypad* or Control+. (period) on main keyboard
Preview only audio, in work area	Alt+. (decimal point) on numeric keypad*	Option+. (decimal point) on numeric keypad* or Control+Option+. (period) on main keyboard
Manually preview	Drag or Alt-drag current-time indicator,	Drag or Option-drag current-time

(scrub) video	depending on Live Update setting	indicator, depending on Live Update setting
Manually preview (scrub) audio	Ctrl-drag current-time indicator	Command-drag current-time indicator
Preview number of frames specified by Alternate Preview preference (defaults to 5)	Alt+0 on numeric keypad*	Option+0 on numeric keypad* or Control+Option+0 (zero) on main keyboard
Toggle Mercury Transmit video preview	/ (on numeric keypad)	/ (on numeric keypad), Control+/ on main keyboard
Take snapshot	Shift+F5, Shift+F6, Shift+F7, or Shift+F8	Shift+F5, Shift+F6, Shift+F7, or Shift+F8
Display snapshot in active viewer	F5, F6, F7, or F8	F5, F6, F7, or F8
Purge snapshot	Ctrl+Shift+F5, Ctrl+Shift+F6, Ctrl+Shift+F7, or Ctrl+Shift+F8	Command+Shift+F5, Command+Shift+F6, Command+Shift+F7,

		or Command+Shift+F8
Fast Previews > Off	Ctrl+Alt+1	Command+Option+1
Fast Previews > Adaptive Resolution	Ctrl+Alt+2	Command+Option+2
Fast Previews > Draft	Ctrl+Alt+3	Command+Option+3
Fast Previews > Fast Draft	Ctrl+Alt+4	Command+Option+4
Fast Previews > Wireframe	Ctrl+Alt+5	Command+Option+5

Note:

Some shortcuts are marked with an asterisk (*) to remind you to make sure that Num Lock is on when you use the numeric keypad.

Views

Result	**Windows Shortcut**	**Mac OS Shortcut**
Turn display color	Shift+/ (on numeric keypad)	Shift+/ (on numeric keypad)

management on or off for active view		
Show red, green, blue, or alpha channel as grayscale	Alt+1, Alt+2, Alt+3, Alt+4	Option+1, Option+2, Option+3, Option+4
Show colorized red, green, or blue channel	Alt+Shift+1, Alt+Shift+2, Alt+Shift+3	Option+Shift+1, Option+Shift+2, Option+Shift+3
Toggle showing straight RGB color	Alt+Shift+4	Option+Shift+4
Show alpha boundary (outline between transparent and opaque regions) in Layer panel	Alt+5	Option+5
Show alpha overlay (colored overlay on transparent regions) in Layer panel	Alt+6	Option+6

Show Refine Edge X-ray	Alt+X	Option+X
Center composition in the panel	Double-click Hand tool	Double-click Hand tool
Zoom-in in Compositio n, Layer, or Footage panel	. (period) on main keyboard	. (period) on main keyboard
Zoom-out in Compositio n, Layer, or Footage panel	, (comma)	, (comma)
Zoom to 100% in Compositio n, Layer, or Footage panel	/ (on main keyboard)	/ (on main keyboard)
Zoom to fit in Compositio n, Layer, or Footage panel	Shift+/ (on main keyboard)	Shift+/ (on main keyboard)
Zoom up to 100% to fit in Compositio n, Layer, or	Alt+/ (on main keyboard)	Option+/ (on main keyboard)

Footage panel		
Set resolution to Full, Half, or Custom in Composition panel	Ctrl+J, Ctrl+Shift+J, Ctrl+Alt+J	Command+J, Command+Shift+J, Command+Option+J
Open View Options dialog box for active Composition panel	Ctrl+Alt+U	Command+Option+U
Zoom in time	= (equal sign) on main keyboard	= (equal sign) on main keyboard
Zoom out time	- (hyphen) on main keyboard	- (hyphen) on main keyboard
Zoom in Timeline panel to single-frame units (Press again to zoom out to show entire composition duration.)	; (semicolon)	; (semicolon)

Zoom out in Timeline panel to show the entire composition duration (Press again to zoom back in to the duration specified by the Time Navigator.)	Shift+; (semicolon)	Shift+; (semicolon)
Prevent images from being rendered for previews in viewer panels	Caps Lock	Caps Lock
Show or hide safe zones	' (apostrophe)	' (apostrophe)
Show or hide grid	Ctrl+' (apostrophe)	Command+' (apostrophe)
Show or hide proportiona l grid	Alt+' (apostrophe)	Option+' (apostrophe)
Show or hide rulers	Ctrl+R	Command+R

Show or hide guides	Ctrl+; (semicolon)	Command+; (semicolon)
Turn snapping to grid on or off	Ctrl+Shift+' (apostrophe)	Command+Shift+' (apostrophe)
Turn snapping to guides on or off	Ctrl+Shift+; (semicolon)	Command+Shift+; (semicolon)
Lock or unlock guides	Ctrl+Alt+Shift +; (semicolon)	Command+Option+Shift +; (semicolon)
Show or hide layer controls (masks, motion paths, light and camera wireframes, effect control points, and layer handles)	Ctrl+Shift+H	Command+Shift+H

Footage.

Result	Windows Shortcut	Mac OS Shortcut
Import one file or image sequence	Ctrl+I	Command+I

Import multiple files or image sequences	Ctrl+Alt+I	Command+Option+I
Open movie in an After Effects Footage panel	Double-click the footage item in the Project panel	Double-click the footage item in the Project panel
Add selected items to most recently activated composition	Ctrl+/ (on main keyboard)	Command+/ (on main keyboard)
Replace selected source footage for selected layers with footage item selected in Project panel	Ctrl+Alt+/ (on main keyboard)	Command+Option+/ (on main keyboard)
Replace source for a selected layer	Alt-drag footage item from Project panel onto selected layer	Option-drag footage item from Project panel onto selected layer
Delete a footage item without a warning	Ctrl+Backspace	Command+Delete
Open Interpret	Ctrl+Alt+G	Command+Option+G

Footage dialog box for selected footage item		
Remember footage interpretatio n	Ctrl+Alt+C	Command+Option+C
Edit selected footage item in application with which it's associated (Edit Original)	Ctrl+E	Command+E
Replace selected footage item	Ctrl+H	Command+H
Reload selected footage items	Ctrl+Alt+L	Command+Option+L
Set proxy for selected footage item	Ctrl+Alt+P	Command+Option+P

Effects and Animation Presets.

Result	**Windows Shortcut**	**Mac OS Shortcut**
Delete all effects from	Ctrl+Shift+E	Command+Shift+E

selected layers		
Apply most recently applied effect to selected layers	Ctrl+Alt+Shift+E	Command+Option+Shift+E
Apply most recently applied animation preset to selected layers	Ctrl+Alt+Shift+F	Command+Option+Shift+F

Layers.

Note:

Some operations do not affect shy layers.

Result	**Windows Shortcut**	**Mac OS Shortcut**
New solid layer	Ctrl+Y	Command+Y
New null layer	Ctrl+Alt+Shift+Y	Command+Option+Shift+Y

New adjustment layer	Ctrl+Alt+Y	Command+Option+Y
Select layer (1-999) by its number (enter digits rapidly for two-digit and three-digit numbers)	0-9 on numeric keypad*	0-9 on numeric keypad*
Toggle selection of layer (1-999) by its number (enter digits rapidly for two-digit and three-digit numbers)	Shift+0-9 on numeric keypad*	Shift+0-9 on numeric keypad*
Select next layer in stacking order	Ctrl+Down Arrow	Command+Down Arrow
Select previous layer in stacking order	Ctrl+Up Arrow	Command+Up Arrow

Extend selection to next layer in stacking order	Ctrl+Shift+Down Arrow	Command+Shift+Down Arrow
Extend selection to previous layer in stacking order	Ctrl+Shift+Up Arrow	Command+Shift+Up Arrow
Deselect all layers	Ctrl+Shift+A	Command+Shift+A
Scroll topmost selected layer to top of Timeline panel	X	X
Show or hide Parent column	Shift+F4	Shift+F4
Show or hide Layer Switches and Modes columns	F4	F4
Setting the sampling method for selected layers	Alt+B	Option+B

(Best/Bilinear)		
Setting the sampling method for selected layers (Best/Bicubic)	Alt+Shift+B	Option+Shift+B
Turn off all other solo switches	Alt-click solo switch	Option-click solo switch
Turn Video (eyeball) switch on or off for selected layers	Ctrl+Alt+Shift+V	Command+Option+Shift+V
Turn off Video switch for all video layers other than selected layers	Ctrl+Shift+V	Command+Shift+V
Open settings dialog box for selected solid, light, camera, null, or adjustment layer	Ctrl+Shift+Y	Command+Shift+Y

Paste layers at current time	Ctrl+Alt+V	Command+Option+V
Split selected layers. (If no layers are selected, split all layers.)	Ctrl+Shift+D	Command+Shift+D
Precompose selected layers	Ctrl+Shift+C	Command+Shift+C
Open Effect Controls panel for selected layers	Ctrl+Shift+T	Command+Shift+T
Open layer in Layer panel (opens source composition for precomposition layer in Composition panel)	Double-click a layer	Double-click a layer
Open source of a layer in Footage panel (opens precomposit	Alt-double-click a layer	Option-double-click a layer

ion layer in Layer panel)		
Reverse selected layers in time	Ctrl+Alt+R	Command+Option+R
Enable time remapping for selected layers	Ctrl+Alt+T	Command+Option+T
Move selected layers so that their In point or Out point is at the current time	[(left bracket) or] (right bracket)	[(left bracket) or] (right bracket)
Trim In point or Out point of selected layers to current time	Alt+[(left bracket) or Alt+] (right bracket)	Option+[(left bracket) or Option+] (right bracket)
Add or remove expression for a property	Alt-click stopwatch	Option-click stopwatch
Add an effect (or multiple selected effects) to	Double-click effect selection in Effects & Presets panel	Double-click effect selection in Effects & Presets panel

selected layers		
Set In point or Out point by time-stretching	Ctrl+Shift+, (comma) or Ctrl+Alt+, (comma)	Command+Shift+, (comma) or Command+Option+, (comma)
Move selected layers so that their In point is at beginning of composition	Alt+Home	Option+Home
Move selected layers so that their Out point is at end of composition	Alt+End	Option+End
Lock selected layers	Ctrl+L	Command+L
Unlock all layers	Ctrl+Shift+L	Command+Shift+L
Set Quality to Best, Draft, or Wireframe for selected layers	Ctrl+U, Ctrl+Shift+U, or Ctrl+Alt+Shift+U	Command+U, Command+Shift+U, Command+Option+Shift+U

Cycle forward or backward through blending modes for selected layers	Shift+- (hyphen) or Shift+= (equal sign) on the main keyboard	Shift+- (hyphen) or Shift+= (equal sign) on the main keyboard
Find in Timeline panel	Ctrl+F	Command+F

Note:

Some shortcuts are marked with an asterisk (*) to remind you to make sure that Num Lock is on when you use the numeric keypad.

Showing Properties and Groups in the Timeline Panel.

Note:

This table contains double-letter shortcuts (for example, LL). To use these shortcuts, press the letters in quick succession.

Result	Windows Shortcut	Mac OS Shortcut
Find in Timeline panel	Ctrl+F	Command+F

Toggle expansion of selected layers to show all properties	Ctrl+` (accent grave)	Command+` (accent grave)
Toggle expansion of property group and all child property groups to show all properties	Ctrl-click triangle to the left of the property group name	Command-click triangle to the left of the property group name
Show only Anchor Point property (for lights and cameras, Point Of Interest)	A	A
Show only Audio Levels property	L	L
Show only Mask Feather property	F	F
Show only Mask Path property	M	M
Show only Mask Opacity property	TT	TT

Show only Opacity property (for lights, Intensity)	T	T
Show only Position property	P	P
Show only Rotation and Orientation properties	R	R
Show only Scale property	S	S
Show only Time Remap property	RR	RR
Show only instances of missing effects	FF	FF
Show only Effects property group	E	E
Show only mask property groups	MM	MM
Show only Material Options	AA	AA

property group		
Show only expressions	EE	EE
Show properties with keyframes	U	U
Show only modified properties	UU	UU
Show only paint strokes, Roto Brush strokes, and Puppet pins	PP	PP
Show only audio waveform	LL	LL
Show only selected properties and groups	SS	SS
Hide property or group	Alt+Shift-click property or group name	Option+Shift-click property or group name
Add or remove property or group from set that is shown	Shift+property or group shortcut	Shift+property or group shortcut
Add or remove	Alt+Shift+property shortcut	Option+property shortcut

keyframe at current time		

Showing Properties in the Effect Controls Panel.

Result	Windows Shortcut	Mac OS Shortcut
Toggle expansion of selected effects to show all properties	Ctrl+` (accent grave)	Command+` (accent grave)
Toggle expansion of property group and all child property groups to show all properties	Ctrl-click triangle to the left of the property group name	Command-click triangle to the left of the property group name

Modifying Layer Properties.

Result	Windows Shortcut	Mac OS Shortcut
Modify property value by default increments	Drag property value	Drag property value
Modify property value by	Shift-drag property value	Shift-drag property value

10x default increments		
Modify property value by 1/10 default increments	Ctrl-drag property value	Command-drag property value
Open Auto-Orientation dialog box for selected layers	Ctrl+Alt+O	Command+Alt+O
Open Opacity dialog box for selected layers	Ctrl+Shift+O	Command+Shift+O
Open Rotation dialog box for selected layers	Ctrl+Shift+R	Command+Shift+R
Open Position dialog box for selected layers	Ctrl+Shift+P	Command+Shift+P
Center selected layers in view (modifies Position	Ctrl+Home	Command+Home

property to place anchor points of selected layers in center of current view)		
Center anchor point in the visible content	Ctrl+Alt+Home	Command+Option+Home
Move selected layers 1 pixel at current magnification (Position)	Arrow key	Arrow key
Move selected layers 10 pixels at current magnification (Position)	Shift+arrow key	Shift+arrow key
Move selected layers 1	Alt+Page Up or Alt+Page Down	Option+Page Up or Option+Page Down

frame earlier or later		
Move selected layers 10 frames earlier or later	Alt+Shift+Page Up or Alt+Shift+Page Down	Option+Shift+Page Up or Option+Shift+Page Down
Increase or decrease Rotation (Z Rotation) of selected layers by 1°	+ (plus) or - (minus) on numeric keypad	+ (plus) or - (minus) on numeric keypad
Increase or decrease Rotation (Z Rotation) of selected layers by 10°	Shift++ (plus) or Shift+- (minus) on numeric keypad	Shift++ (plus) or Shift+- (minus) on numeric keypad
Increase or decrease Opacity (or Intensity for light layers) of selected layers by 1%	Ctrl+Alt++ (plus) or Ctrl+Alt+- (minus) on numeric keypad	Control+Option++ (plus) or Control+Option+- (minus) on numeric keypad
Increase or decrease	Ctrl+Alt+Shift ++ (plus) or	Control+Option+Shift+ + (plus) or

Opacity (or Intensity for light layers) of selected layers by 10%	Ctrl+Alt+Shift +- (minus) on numeric keypad	Control+Option+Shift+ - (minus) on numeric keypad
Increase Scale of selected layers by 1%	Ctrl++ (plus) or Alt++ (plus) on numeric keypad	Command++ (plus) or Option++ (plus) on numeric keypad
Decrease Scale of selected layers by 1%	Ctrl+- (minus) or Alt+- (minus) on numeric keypad	Command+- (minus) or Option+- (minus) on numeric keypad
Increase Scale of selected layers by 10%	Ctrl+Shift++ (plus) or Alt+Shift++ (plus) on numeric keypad	Command+Shift++ (plus) or Option+Shift++ (plus) on numeric keypad
Decrease Scale of selected layers by 10%	Ctrl+Shift+- (minus) or Alt+Shift+- (minus) on numeric keypad	Command+Shift+- (minus) or Option+Shift+- (minus) on numeric keypad
Modify Rotation or Orientation	Shift-drag with Rotation tool	Shift-drag with Rotation tool

in 45° increments		
Modify Scale, constrained to footage frame aspect ratio	Shift-drag layer handle with Selection tool	Shift-drag layer handle with Selection tool
Reset Rotation to 0°	Double-click Rotation tool	Double-click Rotation tool
Reset Scale to 100%	Double-click Selection tool	Double-click Selection tool
Scale and reposition selected layers to fit compositio n	Ctrl+Alt+F	Command+Option+F
Scale and reposition selected layers to fit compositio n width, preserving image aspect ratio for each layer	Ctrl+Alt+Shift +H	Command+Option+Shif t+H
Scale and reposition selected	Ctrl+Alt+Shift +G	Command+Option+Shif t+G

layers to fit composition height, preserving image aspect ratio for each layer		

3D Layers.

Note:

(Mac OS) Shortcuts involving function keys F9-F12 may conflict with shortcuts used by the operating system. See Mac OS Help for instructions to reassign Dashboard & Expose shortcuts.

Result	Windows Shortcut	Mac OS Shortcut
Switch to 3D view 1 (defaults to Front)	F10	F10
Switch to 3D view 2 (defaults to	F11	F11

Custom View 1)		
Switch to 3D view 3 (defaults to Active Camera)	F12	F12
Return to previous view	Esc	Esc
New light	Ctrl+Alt+Shift+L	Command+Option+Shift+L
New camera	Ctrl+Alt+Shift+C	Command+Option+Shift+C
Move the camera and its point of interest to look at selected 3D layers	Ctrl+Alt+Shift+\	Command+Option+Shift+\
With a camera tool selected	F	F

, move the camera and its point of interest to look at selected 3D layers		
With a camera tool selected, move the camera and its point of interest to look at all 3D layers	Ctrl+Shift+F	Command+Shift+F
Turn Casts Shadows property on or off for selected 3D layers	Alt+Shift+C	Option+Shift+C

Keyframes and the Graph Editor

Note:

(Mac OS) Shortcuts involving function keys F9-F12 may conflict with shortcuts used by the operating system. See Mac OS Help for instructions to reassign Dashboard & Expose shortcuts.

Result	Windows Shortcut	Mac OS Shortcut
Toggle between Graph Editor and layer bar modes	Shift+F3	Shift+F3
Select all keyframes for a property	Click property name	Click property name
Select all visible keyframes and properties	Ctrl+Alt+A	Command+Option+A
Deselect all keyframes, properties, and	Shift+F2 or Ctrl+Alt+Shift+A	Shift+F2 or Command+Option+Shift+A

property groups		
Move keyframe 1 frame later or earlier	Alt+Right Arrow or Alt+Left Arrow	Option+Right Arrow or Option+Left Arrow
Move keyframe 10 frames later or earlier	Alt+Shift+Right Arrow or Alt+Shift+Left Arrow	Option+Shift+Right Arrow or Option+Shift+Left Arrow
Set interpolati on for selected keyframes (layer bar mode)	Ctrl+Alt+K	Command+Option+K
Set keyframe interpolati on method to hold or Auto Bezier	Ctrl+Alt+H	Command+Option+H
Set keyframe interpolati on method to linear or Auto Bezier	Ctrl-click in layer bar mode	Command-click in layer bar mode

Set keyframe interpolation method to linear or hold	Ctrl+Alt-click in layer bar mode	Command+Option-click in layer bar mode
Easy ease selected keyframes	F9	F9
Easy ease selected keyframes in	Shift+F9	Shift+F9
Easy ease selected keyframes out	Ctrl+Shift+F9	Command+Shift+F9
Set velocity for selected keyframes	Ctrl+Shift+K	Command+Shift+K
Add or remove keyframe at current time. For property shortcuts	Alt+Shift+property shortcut	Option+property shortcut

Result	Windows Shortcut	Mac OS Shortcut
New text layer	Ctrl+Alt+Shift+T	Command+Option+Shift+T
Align selected horizontal text left, center, or right	Ctrl+Shift+L, Ctrl+Shift+C, or Ctrl+Shift+R	Command+Shift+L, Command+Shift+C, or Command+Shift+R
Align selected vertical text top, center, or bottom	Ctrl+Shift+L, Ctrl+Shift+C, or Ctrl+Shift+R	Command+Shift+L, Command+Shift+C, or Command+Shift+R
Extend or reduce selection by one character to right or left in horizontal text	Shift+Right Arrow or Shift+Left Arrow	Shift+Right Arrow or Shift+Left Arrow
Extend or reduce selection by one	Ctrl+Shift+Right Arrow or Ctrl+Shift+Left Arrow	Command+Shift+Right Arrow or Command+Shift+Left Arrow

word to right or left in horizontal text		
Extend or reduce selection by one line up or down in horizontal text	Shift+Up Arrow or Shift+Down Arrow	Shift+Up Arrow or Shift+Down Arrow
Extend or reduce selection by one line to right or left in vertical text	Shift+Right Arrow or Shift+Left Arrow	Shift+Right Arrow or Shift+Left Arrow
Extend or reduce selection one word up or down in	Ctrl+Shift+Up Arrow or Ctrl+Shift+Down Arrow	Command+Shift+Up Arrow or Command+Shift+Down Arrow

vertical text		
Extend or reduce selection by one character up or down in vertical text	Shift+Up Arrow or Shift+Down Arrow	Shift+Up Arrow or Shift+Down Arrow
Select text from insertion point to beginning or end of line	Shift+Home or Shift+End	Shift+Home or Shift+End
Move insertion point to beginning or end of line	Home or End	Home or End
Select all text on a layer	Double-click text layer	Double-click text layer
Select text from insertion	Ctrl+Shift+Home or Ctrl+Shift+End	Command+Shift+Home or Command+Shift+End

point to beginning or end of text frame		
Select text from insertion point to mouse-click point	Shift-click	Shift-click
In horizontal text, move insertion point one character left or right; one line up or down; one word left or right; or one paragraph up or down	Left Arrow or Right Arrow; Up Arrow or Down Arrow; Ctrl+Left Arrow or Ctrl+Right Arrow; or Ctrl+Up Arrow or Ctrl+Down Arrow	Left Arrow or Right Arrow; Up Arrow or Down Arrow; Command+Left Arrow or Command+Right Arrow; or Command+Up Arrow or Command+Down Arrow

In vertical text, move insertion point one character up or down; one left or right; one word up or down; or one paragraph left or right	Up Arrow or Down Arrow; Left Arrow or Right Arrow; Ctrl+Up Arrow or Ctrl+Down Arrow; or Ctrl+Left Arrow or Ctrl+Right Arrow	Up Arrow or Down Arrow; Left Arrow or Right Arrow; Command+Up Arrow or Command+Down Arrow; or Command+Left Arrow or Command+Right Arrow
Select word, line, paragraph, or entire text frame	Double-click, triple-click, quadruple-click, or quintuple-click with Type tool	Double-click, triple-click, quadruple-click, or quintuple-click with Type tool
Turn All Caps on or off for selected text	Ctrl+Shift+K	Command+Shift+K
Turn Small	Ctrl+Alt+Shift+K	Command+Option+Shift+K

Caps on or off for selected text		
Turn Superscript on or off for selected text	Ctrl+Shift+= (equal sign)	Command+Shift+= (equal sign)
Turn Subscript on or off for selected text	Ctrl+Alt+Shift+= (equal sign)	Command+Option+Shift += (equal sign)
Set horizontal scale to 100% for selected text	Ctrl+Shift+X	Command+Shift+X
Set vertical scale to 100% for selected text	Ctrl+Alt+Shift+X	Command+Option+Shift +X
Auto leading for	Ctrl+Alt+Shift+A	Command+Option+Shift +A

selected text		
Reset tracking to 0 for selected text	Ctrl+Shift+Q	Command+Shift+Control+Q
Justify paragraph; left align last line	Ctrl+Shift+J	Command+Shift+J
Justify paragraph; right align last line	Ctrl+Alt+Shift+J	Command+Option+Shift+J
Justify paragraph; force last line	Ctrl+Shift+F	Command+Shift+F
Decrease or increase font size of selected text by 2 units	Ctrl+Shift+, (comma) or Ctrl+Shift+. (period)	Command+Shift+, (comma) or Command+Shift+. (period)
Decrease or increase font size	Ctrl+Alt+Shift+, (comma) or Ctrl+Alt+Shift+. (period)	Command+Option+Shift+, (comma) or Command+Option+Shift+. (period)

of selected text by 10 units		
Increase or decrease leading by 2 units	Alt+Down Arrow or Alt+Up Arrow	Option+Down Arrow or Option+Up Arrow
Increase or decrease leading by 10 units	Ctrl+Alt+Down Arrow or Ctrl+Alt+Up Arrow	Command+Option+Down Arrow or Command+Option+Up Arrow
Decrease or increase baseline shift by 2 units	Alt+Shift+Down Arrow or Alt+Shift+Up Arrow	Option+Shift+Down Arrow or Option+Shift+Up Arrow
Decrease or increase baseline shift by 10 units	Ctrl+Alt+Shift+ Down Arrow or Ctrl+Alt+Shift+ Up Arrow	Command+Option+Shift +Down Arrow or Command+Option+Shift +Up Arrow
Decrease or increase kerning or	Alt+Left Arrow or Alt+Right Arrow	Option+Left Arrow or Option+Right Arrow

tracking 20 units (20/1000 ems)		
Decrease or increase kerning or tracking 100 units (100/1000 ems)	Ctrl+Alt+Left Arrow or Ctrl+Alt+Right Arrow	Command+Option+Left Arrow or Command+Option+Right Arrow
Toggle paragraph composer	Ctrl+Alt+Shift+T	Command+Option+Shift+T

Masks.

Result	Windows Shortcut	Mac OS Shortcut
New mask	Ctrl+Shift+N	Command+Shift+N
Select all points in a mask	Alt-click mask	Option-click mask
Select next or previous mask	Alt+` (accent grave) or Alt+Shift+` (accent grave)	Option+` (accent grave) or Option+Shift+` (accent grave)

Enter free-transform mask editing mode	Double-click mask with Selection tool or select mask in Timeline panel and press Ctrl+T	Double-click mask with Selection tool or select mask in Timeline panel and press Command+T
Exit free-transform mask editing mode	Esc	Esc
Scale around center point in Free Transform mode	Ctrl-drag	Command-drag
Move selected path points 1 pixel at current magnification	Arrow key	Arrow key
Move selected path points 10 pixels at current magnification	Shift+arrow key	Shift+arrow key
Toggle between smooth and corner points	Ctrl+Alt-click vertex	Command+Option-click vertex
Redraw Bezier handles	Ctrl+Alt-drag vertex	Command+Option-drag vertex

Invert selected mask	Ctrl+Shift+I	Command+Shift+I
Open Mask Feather dialog box for selected mask	Ctrl+Shift+F	Command+Shift+F
Open Mask Shape dialog box for selected mask	Ctrl+Shift+M	Command+Shift+M

Paint Tools.

Result	**Windows Shortcut**	**Mac OS Shortcut**
Swap paint background color and foreground colors	X	X
Set paint foreground color to black and background color to white	D	D
Set foreground color to the color currently under any paint tool pointer	Alt-click	Option-click
Set foreground color to the	Ctrl+Alt-click	Command+Option-click

average color of a 4-pixel x 4-pixel area under any paint tool pointer		
Set brush size for a paint tool	Ctrl-drag	Command-drag
Set brush hardness for a paint tool	Ctrl-drag, then release Ctrl while dragging	Command-drag, then release Command while dragging
Join current paint stroke to the previous stroke	Hold Shift while beginning stroke	Hold Shift while beginning stroke
Set starting sample point to point currently under Clone Stamp tool pointer	Alt-click	Option-click
Momentarily activate Eraser tool with Last Stroke Only option	Ctrl+Shift	Command+Shift
Show and move overlay (change Offset value of *aligned* Clone Stamp tool or change Source Position value of	Alt+Shift-drag with Clone Stamp tool	Option+Shift-drag with Clone Stamp tool

unaligned Clone Stamp tool)		
Activate a specific Clone Stamp tool preset	3, 4, 5, 6, or 7 on the main keyboard	3, 4, 5, 6, or 7 on the main keyboard
Duplicate a Clone Stamp tool preset in Paint panel	Alt-click the button for the preset	Option-click the button for the preset
Set opacity for a paint tool	Digit on numeric keypad (for example, 9=90%, 1=10%)*	Digit on numeric keypad (for example, 9=90%, 1=10%)*
Set opacity for a paint tool to 100%	. (decimal) on numeric keypad*	. (decimal) on numeric keypad*
Set flow for a paint tool	Shift+ a digit on numeric keypad (for example, 9=90%, 1=10%)*	Shift+ a digit on numeric keypad (for example, 9=90%, 1=10%)*
Set flow for a paint tool to 100%	Shift+. (decimal) on numeric keypad*	Shift+. (decimal) on numeric keypad*
Move earlier or later by number of frames	Ctrl+Page Up or Ctrl+Page Down (or 1	Command+Page Up or Command+Page Down (or 1 or 2 on the main keyboard)

specified for stroke Duration	or 2 on the main keyboard)	

Note:

Some shortcuts are marked with an asterisk (*) to remind you to make sure that Num Lock is on when you use the numeric keypad.

Shape Layers.

Result	**Windows Shortcut**	**Mac OS Shortcut**
Group selected shapes	Ctrl+G	Command+G
Ungroup selected shapes	Ctrl+Shift+G	Command+Shift+G
Enter free-transform path editing mode	Select Path property in Timeline panel and press Ctrl+T	Select Path property in Timeline panel and press Command+T
Increase star inner roundness	Page Up when dragging to create shape	Page Up when dragging to create shape
Decrease star inner roundness	Page Down when dragging to create shape	Page Down when dragging to create shape

Increase number of points for star or polygon; increase roundness for rounded rectangle	Up Arrow when dragging to create shape	Up Arrow when dragging to create shape
Decrease number of points for star or polygon; decrease roundness for rounded rectangle	Down Arrow when dragging to create shape	Down Arrow when dragging to create shape
Reposition shape during creation	Hold spacebar when dragging to create shape	Hold spacebar when dragging to create shape
Set rounded rectangle roundness to 0 (sharp corners); decrease polygon and star outer roundness	Left Arrow when dragging to create shape	Left Arrow when dragging to create shape
Set rounded rectangle roundness to maximum; increase	Right Arrow when dragging to create shape	Right Arrow when dragging to create shape

polygon and star outer roundness		
Constrain rectangles to squares; constrain ellipses to circles; constrain polygons and stars to zero rotation	Shift when dragging to create shape	Shift when dragging to create shape
Change outer radius of star	Ctrl when dragging to create shape	Command when dragging to create shape

Markers.

Result	**Windows Shortcut**	**Mac OS Shortcut**
Set marker at current time (works during preview and audio-only preview)	* (multiply) on numeric keypad	* (multiply) on numeric keypad or Control+8 on main keyboard
Set marker at current time and open marker dialog box	Alt+* (multiply) on numeric keypad	Option+* (multiply) on numeric keypad or Control+Option+8 on main keyboard

Set and number a composition marker (0-9) at the current time	Shift+0-9 on main keyboard	Shift+0-9 on main keyboard
Go to a composition marker (0-9)	0-9 on main keyboard	0-9 on main keyboard
Display the duration between two layer markers or keyframes in the Info panel	Alt-click the markers or keyframes	Option-click the markers or keyframes
Remove marker	Ctrl-click marker	Command-click marker

Motion Tracking.

Result	**Windows Shortcut**	**Mac OS Shortcut**
Move feature region, search region, and attach point 1 pixel at current magnification	Arrow key	Arrow key
Move feature region, search region, and attach point 10 pixels at	Shift+arrow key	Shift+arrow key

current magnification		
Move feature region and search region 1 pixel at current magnification	Alt+arrow key	Option+arrow key
Move feature region and search region 10 pixels at current magnification	Alt+Shift+arrow key	Option+Shift+arrow key

Saving, Exporting, and Rendering.

Result	**Windows Shortcut**	**Mac OS Shortcut**
Save project	Ctrl+S	Command+S
Increment and save project	Ctrl+Alt+Shift +S	Command+Option+Shif t+S
Save As	Ctrl+Shift+S	Command+Shift+S
Add active compositio n or selected items to render queue	Ctrl+Shift+/ (on main keyboard)	Command+Shift+/ (on main keyboard)

Add current frame to render queue	Ctrl+Alt+S	Command+Option+S
Duplicate render item with same output filename as original	Ctrl+Shift+D	Command+Shift+D
Add a composition to the Adobe Media Encoder encoding queue	Ctrl+Alt+M	Cmd+Option+M

Note:

On Mac OS, some keyboard commands used to interact with the operating system conflict with keyboard commands for interacting with After Effects. Select Use System Shortcut Keys in the General preferences to override the After Effects keyboard command in some cases in which there's a conflict with the Mac OS keyboard command.

Applies to: Adobe After Effects.

CHAPTER 5.

Keyboard Shortcuts for Use in Adobe Lightroom.

About the program: It is an application developed and marketed by Adobe for processing, editing, sharing and organizing photography.

Keyboard Shortcuts in Lightroom.

Use the following list of keyboard shortcuts to enhance your productivity in Adobe Lightroom.

Keys for Working with Panels.

Result	Windows Shortcut	Mac OS Shortcut
Show/hide side panels	Tab	Tab
Show/hide all panels	Shift + Tab	Shift + Tab
Show/hide toolbar	T	T
Show/hide Module Picker	F5	F5
Show/hide Filmstrip	F6	F6
Show/hide left panels	F7	F7
Show/hide right panels	F8	F8

Toggle solo mode	Alt-click a panel	Option-click a panel
Open a new panel without closing soloed panel	Shift-click a panel	Shift-click a panel
Open/close all panels	Ctrl-click a panel	Command-click a panel
Open/close left panels, top to bottom	Ctrl + Shift + 0 - 5	Command + Control + 0 - 5
Open/close right panels, Library and Develop modules, top to bottom	Ctrl + 0 - 9	Command + 0 - 9
Open/close right panels, Slideshow, Print, and Web modules, top to bottom	Ctrl + 1 - 7	Command + 1 - 7

Keys for Navigating Modules.

Result	**Windows Shortcut**	**Mac OS Shortcut**
Go to Library module	Ctrl + Alt + 1	Command + Option + 1
Go to Develop module	Ctrl + Alt + 2	Command + Option + 2
Go to Slideshow module	Ctrl + Alt + 3	Command + Option + 3
Go to Print module	Ctrl + Alt + 4	Command + Option + 4

Go to Web module	Ctrl + Alt + 5	Command + Option + 5
Go back / go forward	Ctrl + Alt + Left Arrow / Ctrl + Alt + RIght Arrow	Command + Option + Left Arrow / Command + Option + Right Arrow
Go back to previous module	Ctrl + Alt + Up Arrow	Command + Option + Up Arrow

Keys for Changing Views and Screen Modes.

Result	**Windows Shortcut**	**Mac OS Shortcut**
Enter Library Loupe view	E	E
Enter Library Grid view	G	G
Enter Library Compare view	C	C
Enter Library Survey view	N	N
Open selected photo in the Develop module	D	D
Cycle forward / backward through Lights Out modes	L / Shift + L	L / Shift + L
Toggle Lights Dim mode	Ctrl + Shift + L	Command + Shift + L
Cycle screen modes	F	F
Previous screen mode		Shift + F

Switch between Normal and full-screen, hide panels	Ctrl + Shift + F	Command + Shift + F
Go to Normal screen mode	Ctrl + Alt + F	Command + Option + F
Cycle info overlay	I	I
Show/hide info overlay	Ctrl + I	Command + I

Keys for Using a Secondary Window.

Note:

The shortcuts for using the secondary window are the same as the equivalent shortcuts in the Library module, with the Shift key added.

Result	**Windows Shortcut**	**Mac OS Shortcut**
Open secondary window	F11	Command + F11
Enter Grid view	Shift + G	Shift + G
Enter normal Loupe view	Shift + E	Shift + E
Enter locked Loupe view	Ctrl + Shift + Enter	Command + Shift + Return
Enter Compare view	Shift + C	Shift + C
Enter Survey view	Shift + N	Shift + N
Enter Slideshow view	Ctrl + Alt + Shift + Enter	Command + Option + Shift + Return

Enter full-screen mode (requires a second monitor)	Shift + F11	Command + Shift + F11
Show/hide Filter bar	Shift + \	Shift + \
Zoom in / zoom out	Ctrl + Shift + = / Ctrl + Shift -	Command + Shift + = / Command + Shift + -

Keys for Managing Photos and Catalogs.

Result	Windows Shortcut	Mac OS Shortcut
Import photos from disk	Ctrl + Shift + I	Command + Shift + I
Open catalog	Ctrl + O	Command +Shift + O
Open Preferences	Ctrl + , (comma)	Command + , (comma)
Open Catalog Settings	Ctrl + Alt + , (comma)	Command + Option + , (comma)
Create new subfolder (segmented tethered capture)	Ctrl + Shift + T	Command +Shift + T
Hide/show tether capture bar	Ctrl + T	Command + T
Create a new folder in the Library module	Ctrl + Shift + N	Command + Shift + N
Create virtual copy (Library and Develop module only)	Ctrl + ' (apostrophe)	Command + ' (apostrophe)

Show in Explorer/Finder (Library and Develop module only)	Ctrl + R	Command + R
Go to next/previous photo in the Filmstrip	Right Arrow/Left Arrow	Right Arrow/Left Arrow
Select multiple folders or collections (in Library, Slideshow, Print, and Web modules)	Shift-click or Ctrl-click	Shift-click or Command-click
Rename photo (in Library module)	F2	F2
Delete selected photo(s)	Backspace or Delete	Delete
Remove selected photo(s) from catalog	Alt + Backspace	Option + Delete
Delete selected photo(s) and move to Recycling Bin (Windows) or Trash (Mac OS)	Ctrl + Alt + Shift + Backspace	Command + Option + Shift + Delete
Delete rejected photo(s)	Ctrl + Backspace	Command + Delete
Edit in Photoshop	Ctrl + E	Command + E
Open in other editor	Ctrl + Alt + E	Command + Option + E
Export selected photo(s)	Ctrl + Shift + E	Command + Shift + E
Export with previous settings	Ctrl + Alt + Shift + E	Command + Option + Shift + E

Open plug-in manager	Ctrl + Alt + Shift + , (comma)	Command + Option + Shift + , (comma)
Print selected photo	Ctrl + P	Command + P
Open Page Setup dialog box	Ctrl + Shift + P	Command + Shift + P

Keys for Comparing Photos in the Library Module.

Result	**Windows Shortcut**	**Mac OS Shortcut**
Switch to Loupe view	E or Enter	E or Return
Switch to Grid view	G or Esc	G or Esc
Switch to Compare view	C	C
Switch to Survey view	N	N
Switch from Grid to Loupe view	Spacebar or E	Spacebar or E
Swap select and candidate photos in Compare view	Down Arrow	Down Arrow
Make next photos select and candidate in Compare view	Up Arrow	Up Arrow
Toggle Zoom view	Z	Z
Zoom in / zoom out in Loupe view	Ctrl + = / Ctrl + -	Command + = / Command + -
Scroll up/down zoomed photo in Loupe view	Page Up / Page Down	Page Up / Page Down

(also works in Develop and Web modules)	on full-size keyboard	on full-size keyboard
Go to beginning/end of Grid view	Home / End	Home / End
Play impromptu slide show	Ctrl + Enter	Command + Return
Rotate photo right (clockwise)	Ctrl +]	Command +]
Rotate photo left (counterclockwise)	Ctrl + [	Command + [
Increase/decrease Grid thumbnail size	= / -	= / -
Scroll up/down Grid thumbnails	Page Up / Page Down on full-size keyboard	Page Up / Page Down on full-size keyboard
Toggle cell extras	Ctrl + Shift + H	Command + Shift + H
Show/hide badges	Ctrl + Alt + Shift + H	Command + Option + Shift + H
Cycle Grid views	J	J
Open Library view options	Ctrl + J	Command + J
Select multiple discrete photos	Ctrl-click	Command-click
Select multiple contiguous photos	Shift-click	Shift-click
Select all photos	Ctrl + A	Command + A
Deselect all photos	Ctrl + D	Command + D or

		Command + Shift + A
Select only active photo	Ctrl + Shift + D	Command + Shift + D
Deselect active photo	/	/
Add previous/next photo to selection	Shift + Left/Right Arrow	Shift + Left/Right Arrow
Select flagged photos	Ctrl + Alt + A	Command + Option + A
Deselect unflagged photos	Ctrl + Alt + Shift + D	Command + Option + Shift + D
Group into stack	Ctrl + G	Command + G
Unstack	Ctrl + Shift + G	Command + Shift + G
Toggle stack	S	S
Move to top of stack	Shift + S	Shift + S
Move up in stack	Shift + [	Shift + [
Move down in stack	Shift +]	Shift +]

Keys for Rating and Filtering Photos.

Result	**Windows Shortcut**	**Mac OS Shortcut**
Set star rating	1 - 5	1 - 5
Set star rating and go to next photo	Shift + 1 - 5	Shift + 1 - 5
Remove star rating	0	0
Remove star rating and go to next photo	Shift + 0	Shift + 0

Increase/decrease rating by one star	] / [	] / [
Assign a red label	6	6
Assign a yellow label	7	7
Assign a green label	8	8
Assign a blue label	9	9
Assign a color label and go to next photo	Shift + 6 - 9	Shift + 6 - 9
Flag photo as a pick	P	P
Flag photo as a pick and go to next photo	Shift + P	Shift + P
Flag photo as a reject	X	X
Flag photo as a reject and go to next photo	Shift + X	Shift + X
Unflag photo	U	U
Unflag photo and go to next photo	Shift + U	Shift + U
Increase/decrease flag status	Ctrl + Up Arrow / Ctrl + Down Arrow	Command + Up Arrow / Command + Down Arrow
Cycle flag settings	‘ (back quote)	‘ (back quote)
Refine photos	Ctrl + Alt + R	Command + Option + R
Show/hide Library Filter bar	\	\
Open multiple filters in the Filter bar	Shift-click filter labels	Shift-click filter labels
Toggle filters on/off	Ctrl + L	Command + L
Find photo in the Library module	Ctrl + F	Command + F

Keys for Working with Collections.

Result	Windows Shortcut	Mac OS Shortcut
Create a new collection in the Library module	Ctrl + N	Command + N
Add to Quick Collection	B	B
Add to Quick Collection and go to next photo	Shift + B	Shift + B
Show Quick Collection	Ctrl + B	Command + B
Save Quick Collection	Ctrl + Alt + B	Command + Option + B
Clear Quick Collection	Ctrl + Shift + B	Command + Shift + B
Set as target collection	Ctrl + Alt + Shift + B	Command + Option + Shift + B

Keys for Working with Metadata and Keywords in the Library Module.

Result	Windows Shortcut	Mac OS Shortcut
Add keywords	Ctrl + K	Command + K
Edit keywords	Ctrl + Shift + K	Command + Shift + K
Set a keyword shortcut	Ctrl + Alt + Shift + K	Command + Option + Shift + K

Add/remove keyword shortcut from selected photo	Shift + K	Shift + K
Enable painting	Ctrl + Alt + K	Command + Option + K
Add a keyword from a keyword set to selected photo	Alt + 1-9	Option + 1-9
Cycle forward / backward through keyword sets	Alt + 0 / Alt + Shift + 0	Option + 0 / Option + Shift + 0
Copy/paste metadata	Ctrl + Alt + Shift + C / Ctrl + Alt + Shift + V	Command + Option + Shift + C / Command + Option + Shift + V
Save metadata to file	Ctrl + S	Command + S
Open Spelling dialog box		Command + :
Check spelling		Command + ;
Open Character palette		Command + Option + T

Keys for Working in the Develop Module.

Result	**Windows Shortcut**	**Mac OS Shortcut**
Convert to grayscale	V	V

Auto tone	Ctrl + U	Command + U
Auto white balance	Ctrl + Shift + U	Command + Shift + U
Edit in Photoshop	Ctrl + E	Command + E
Copy/paste Develop settings	Ctrl + Shift + C / Ctrl + Shift + V	Command + Shift + C / Command + Shift + V
Paste settings from previous photo	Ctrl + Alt + V	Command + Option + V
Copy After settings to Before	Ctrl + Alt + Shift + Left Arrow	Command + Option + Shift + Left Arrow
Copy Before settings to After	Ctrl + Alt + Shift + Right Arrow	Command + Option + Shift + Right Arrow
Swap Before and After settings	Ctrl + Alt + Shift + Up Arrow	Command + Option + Shift + Up Arrow
Increase/decrease selected slider in small increments	Up Arrow / Down Arrow or + / -	Up Arrow / Down Arrow or + / -
Increase/decrease selected slider in larger increments	Shift + Up Arrow / Shift + Down Arrow or Shift + + / Shift + -	Shift + Up Arrow / Shift + Down Arrow or Shift + + / Shift + -
Cycle through Basic panel settings	. (period) / , (comma)	. (period) / , (comma)

(forward/backward)		
Reset a slider	Double-click slider name	Double-click slider name
Reset a group of sliders	Alt-click group name	Option-click group name
Reset all settings	Ctrl + Shift + R	Command + Shift + R
Sync settings	Ctrl + Shift + S	Command + Shift + S
Sync settings bypassing Synchronize Settings dialog box	Ctrl + Alt + S	Command + Option + S
Toggle Auto Sync	Ctrl-click Sync button	Command-click Sync button
Enable Auto Sync	Ctrl + Alt + Shift + A	Command + Option + Shift + A
Match total exposures	Ctrl + Alt + Shift + M	Command + Option + Shift + M
Select White Balance tool (from any module)	W	W
Select the Crop tool (from any module)	R	R
Constrain aspect ratio when Crop tool is selected	A	A

Crop to same aspect ratio as previous crop	Shift + A	Shift + A
Crop from center of photo	Alt-drag	Option-drag
Cycle Crop grid overlay	O	O
Cycle Crop grid overlay orientation	Shift + O	Shift + O
Switch crop between portrait and landscape orientation	X	X
Reset crop	Ctrl + Alt + R	Command + Option + R
Select the Guided Upright tool (also works in the Library module when a photo is selected)	Shift + T	Shift + T
Select the Spot Removal tool	Q	Q
Toggle Brush between Clone and Heal modes when Spot Removal tool is selected	Shift + T	Shift + T
Select the Adjustment	K	K

Brush tool (from any module)		
Select the Graduated Filter tool	M	M
Toggle Mask between Edit and Brush modes when the Graduated Filter or Radial Filter is selected	Shift + T	Shift + T
Increase/decrease brush size	] / [	] / [
Increase/decrease brush feathering	Shift +] / Shift + [	Shift +] / Shift + [
Switch between local adjustment brush A and B	/	/
Temporarily switch from brush A or B to Eraser	Alt-drag	Option-drag
Paint a horizontal or vertical line	Shift-drag	Shift-drag
Increase/decrease Amount	Drag adjustment pin right/left	Drag adjustment pin right/left
Show/hide local adjustment pin	H	H
Show/hide local adjustment mask overlay	O	O

Cycle local adjustment mask overlay colors	Shift + O	Shift + O
Select Targeted Adjustment tool to apply a Tone Curve adjustment	Ctrl + Alt + Shift + T	Command + Option + Shift + T
Select Targeted Adjustment tool to apply a Hue adjustment	Ctrl + Alt + Shift + H	Command + Option + Shift + H
Select Targeted Adjustment tool to apply a Saturation adjustment	Ctrl + Alt + Shift + S	Command + Option + Shift + S
Select Targeted Adjustment tool to apply a Luminance adjustment	Ctrl + Alt + Shift + L	Command + Option + Shift + L
Select Targeted Adjustment tool to apply a Grayscale Mix adjustment	Ctrl + Alt + Shift + G	Command + Option + Shift + G
Deselect Targeted Adjustment tool	Ctrl + Alt + Shift + N	Command + Option + Shift + N
Show clipping	J	J
Rotate photo right (clockwise)	Ctrl +]	Command +]

Rotate photo left (counterclockwise)	Ctrl + [	Command + [
Toggle between Loupe and 1:1 Zoom preview	Spacebar or Z	Spacebar or Z
Zoom in / zoom out	Ctrl + = / Ctrl + -	Command + = / Command + -
Play impromptu slide show	Ctrl + Enter	Command + Return
View Before and After left/right	Y	Y
View Before and After top/bottom	Alt + Y	Option + Y
View Before and After in a split screen	Shift + Y	Shift + Y
View Before only	\	\
Create a new snapshot	Ctrl + N	Command + N
Create a new preset	Ctrl + Shift + N	Command + Shift + N
Create a new preset folder	Ctrl + Alt + N	Command + Option + N
Open Develop view options	Ctrl + J	Command + J

Keys for Working in the Slideshow Module.

Result	**Windows Shortcut**	**Mac OS Shortcut**
Play slide show	Enter	Return

Play impromptu slide show	Ctrl + Enter	Command + Return
Pause slide show	Spacebar	Spacebar
Preview slide show	Alt + Enter	Option + Return
End slide show	Esc	Esc
Go to next slide	Right Arrow	Right Arrow
Go to previous slide	Left Arrow	Left Arrow
Rotate photo right (clockwise)	Ctrl +]	Command +]
Rotate photo left (counterclockwise)	Ctrl + [	Command + [
Show/hide guides	Ctrl + Shift + H	Command + Shift + H
Export PDF slide show	Ctrl + J	Command + J
Export JPEG slide show	Ctrl + Shift + J	Command + Shift + J
Export video slide show	Ctrl + Alt + J	Command + Option + J
Create a new slide show template	Ctrl + N	Command + N
Create a new slide show template folder	Ctrl + Shift + N	Command + Shift + N
Save slide show settings	Ctrl + S	Command + S

Keys for Working in the Print Module.

Result	**Windows Shortcut**	**Mac OS Shortcut**
Print	Ctrl + P	Command + P

Print one copy	Ctrl + Alt + P	Command + Option + P
Open Page Setup dialog box	Ctrl + Shift + P	Command + Shift + P
Open Print Settings dialog box	Ctrl + Alt + Shift + P	Command + Option + Shift + P
Go to first page	Ctrl + Shift + Left Arrow	Command + Shift + Left Arrow
Go to last page	Ctrl + Shift + Right Arrow	Command + Shift + Right Arrow
Go to previous page	Ctrl + Left Arrow	Command + Left Arrow
Go to next page	Ctrl + Right Arrow	Command + Right Arrow
Show/hide guides	Ctrl + Shift + H	Command + Shift + H
Show/hide rulers	Ctrl + R	Command + R
Show/hide page bleed	Ctrl + Shift + J	Command + Shift + J
Show/hide margins and gutters	Ctrl + Shift + M	Command + Shift + M
Show/hide image cells	Ctrl + Shift + K	Command + Shift + K
Show/hide dimensions	Ctrl + Shift + U	Command + Shift + U
Play impromptu slide show	Ctrl + Enter	Command + Return
Rotate photo right (clockwise)	Ctrl +]	Command +]

Rotate photo left (counterclockwise)	Ctrl + [	Command + [
Create a new print template	Ctrl + N	Command + N
Create a new print template folder	Ctrl + Shift + N	Command + Shift + N
Save print settings	Ctrl + S	Command + S

Keys for working in the Web Module.

Result	**Windows Shortcut**	**Mac OS Shortcut**
Reload web gallery	Ctrl + R	Command + R
Preview in browser	Ctrl + Alt + P	Command + Option + P
Play impromptu slide show	Ctrl + Enter	Command + Return
Export web gallery	Ctrl + J	Command + J
Create a new web gallery template	Ctrl + N	Command + N
Create a new web gallery template folder	Ctrl + Shift + N	Command + Shift + N
Save web gallery settings	Ctrl + S	Command + S

Keys for Using Help.

Result	**Windows Shortcut**	**Mac OS Shortcut**
Display current module shortcuts	Ctrl + /	Command + /

Hide current module shortcuts	Click	Click
Go to current module Help	Ctrl + Alt + /	Command + Option + Shift + /
Open Community Help	F1	F1

Applies to: *Adobe Lightroom.*

CHAPTER 6.

Tips, Tricks, Techniques, and Keyboard Shortcuts for use in Flash/Animate.

About the program: This, formerly called Adobe Flash is an application developed by Adobe Systems that is used in developing rich contents, user interfaces, web contents such as video, audio, and multimedia, and rich internet application.

A fresh topic ↳

Improving the Performance of your Adobe Flash or Animate.

By Dmitriy Yukhanov.

When developing applications with Adobe Flash Professional CS5 or later, it's important to consider strategies that can increase your application's performance and also improve the user experience. Over the past few years I've collected a series of best practices and pitfalls by working with developers on a variety of projects and also by researching the Flash documentation.

This topic offers some common Flash development rules that you may find useful in your own work. Feel free to follow these suggestions to create content more efficiently and optimize elements to ensure that your projects download quickly and run smoothly.

The tips described herein are useful not just for Flash developers but also for Flash animators and designers. Apply these approaches to your own projects to see how you can improve them.

Note: Throughout this topic, screen shots with a red border show what to avoid; green indicates what to follow.

Improving Performance.

This section includes helpful suggestions for making content play more seamlessly in Adobe Flash Player and use fewer resources.

Deactivate interactivity of unused objects with mouseChildren and mouseEnabled

If you're absolutely sure that objects in your Flash project will never be interactive (and will not contain any interactive objects), you can add the following code on the first frame of the object's containers:

mouseEnabled = false; mouseChildren = false;

This code deactivates the container and all nested containers inside it. To keep a container activated and interactive, use mouseChildren = false; only. Decreasing the number of active containers in a project helps increase performance because the movie uses fewer resources (see Figure 1).

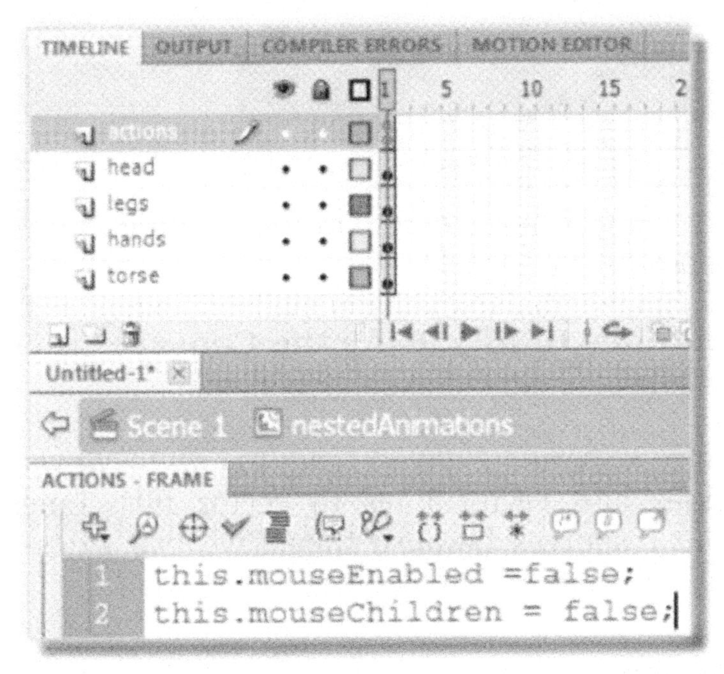

Figure 1. Use ActionScript to remove interactivity from objects on Stage.

Evaluate whether bitmaps or vectors are the best choice for each graphic asset

If the graphics in your project contain a lot of gradients, details, and colors, you may find after testing that bitmap images are the best choice to display the images on the Stage. When you use bitmap images, they are resolution-dependent and can look bad when scaled, but you may not need to scale the graphics. If they do require scaling, try using traced vector shapes to see if they can convey enough detail. Always make tests and compare the project's performance when using vector shapes and bitmap images to discover the best option in each case (see Figure 2).

Figure 2. Try using both vector and bitmap graphics to see what works best.

Convert outlines to fills using the Convert Lines to Fills option

Choose Modify > Shape > Convert Lines to Fills to convert shape outlines and vector lines to vector fills. Lines require more resources because they have two sides—compared to only one side in fills (see Figure 3).

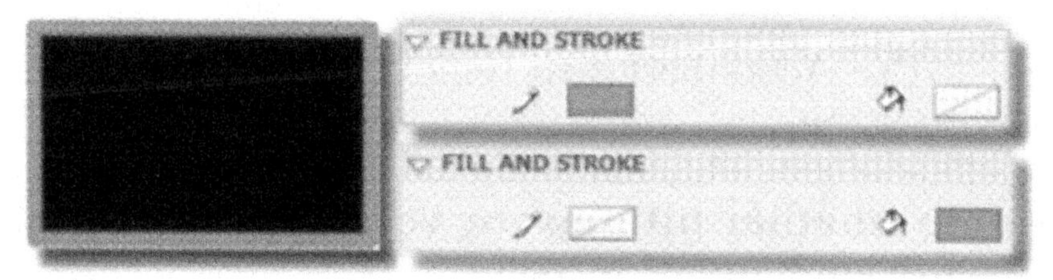

Figure 3. Use the Convert Lines to Fills option to improve performance.

Use non-solid line styles sparingly

Unless necessary, avoid adding dashed or dotted lines. Solid lines require fewer resources to draw (see Figure 4).

Figure 4. Use solid lines and strokes whenever possible.

Use lines instead of curves

When editing vector shapes, use miter joins instead of round joins. Miter joins are lines that require fewer resources compared to rendering curves. You should also use miter joins when displaying small vector shapes because rounded joins are not so noticeable and waste unneccessary resources (see Figure 5).

Figure 5. Use square miter joins for corners instead of rounded joins.

Optimize vector shapes

Complex vector shapes often contain many control points between lines and curves. By removing unneeded points, you can save resources without affecting a graphic's appearance. Choose Modify > Shape > Optimize (or use the Smooth tool) to optimize vector graphics. Strike a balance between vector complexity (shape quality) and reduced line count (see Figure 6).

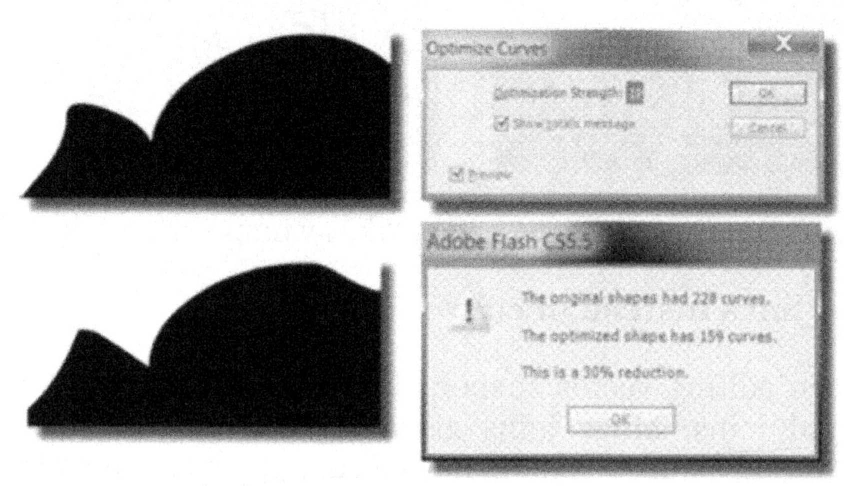

Figure 6. Reduce unnecessary points in vector artwork to save resources.

Avoid using vector gradient fills

Shapes filled with gradient fills require more resources compared to solid color fills. Whenever possible, replace gradient fills with solid fills. Although you only gain a small performance boost, this can be helpful when developing projects for mobile devices (see Figure 7).

Figure 7. Fill vector shapes with solid color fills.

Minimize the use of graphics with alpha transparencies

Alpha channel transparency really impacts performance, especially when applied to animated objects. Double-check PNG bitmap images to verify that they don't have unused alpha transparency settings when you imported them. Unless needed, don't set the alpha property on symbol instances as well—avoid creating fading animations in projects (see Figure 8).

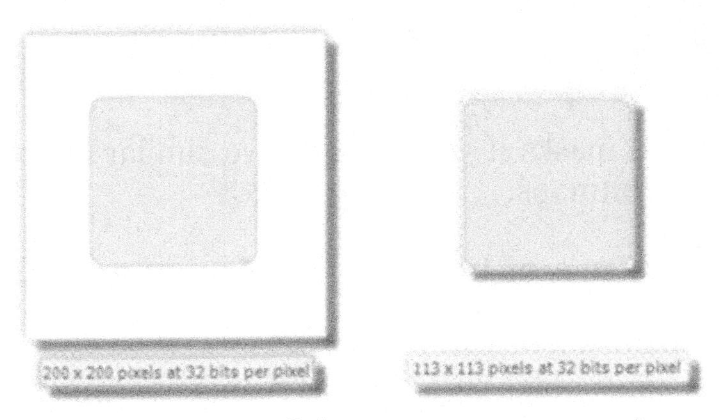

Figure 8. Remove alpha transparency settings unless they are necessary.

Only use masks when necessary

Identify situations when you must use masks, and try to use them sparingly. Whenever possible, crop images and vector graphics using an image-editing program, such as Adobe Illustrator or Adobe Fireworks, rather than cropping images with masks.

Masks require additional resources and hidden parts of the graphic increase file size unnecessarily. In some cases, you can replace rectangle masks with code functions. Programming with the scrollRect property uses fewer resources, but is not always suitable; it depends on the goal you are trying to achieve. Look for strategic ways to avoid using masks in your projects and explore new options that result in a similar appearance (see Figure 9).

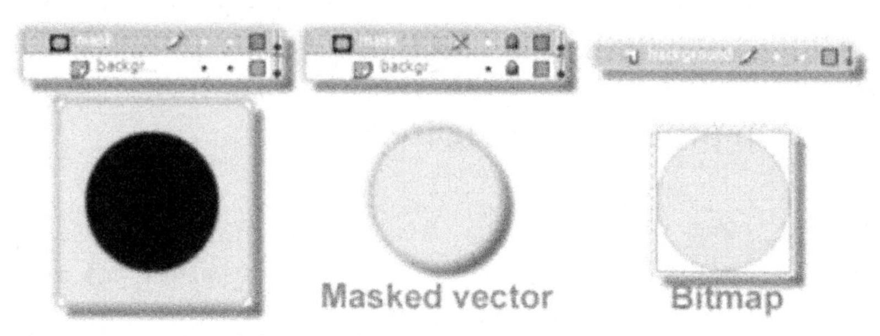

Figure 9. Avoid masks if you can achieve similar effects with shapes or bitmaps.

Try to reduce use of blending modes on graphic elements

When you apply blending, it decreases a project's performance. Use an image editing program to prepare images and graphics to avoid using blending as much as possible (see Figure 10).

Figure 10. Prepare images with blend effects before importing them into Flash.

Minimize use of filters in Flash

Try to avoid using filters unless it is necessary to achieve a specific effect. Prepare images with shadows in an image editing program instead of applying shadow filter to images in Flash. Filters impact the project's performance in some cases (see Figure 11).

Figure 11. Add filter effects, like dropshadows, before importing images.

Use the lowest filter quality setting that results in an acceptable appearance

If your project doesn't require the higher settings, don't use the High and Medium quality. Test the Low Quality setting to see if it works well enough for your requirements. When you use the higher quality settings, you increase resources consumption (see Figure 12).

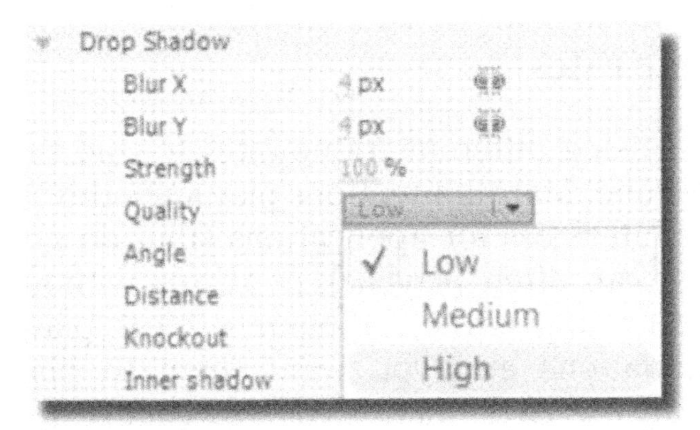

Figure 12. Use the Low Quality setting if it looks acceptable in your projects.

Resize bitmap images using even numbers if they are going to be downscaled

When scaling and cropping images in an image-editing program, to prepare them to be imported in Flash for downscaling, crop them to square dimensions using even number values.

You can also use mipmapping to calculate the optimal dimensions of the bitmaps you are creating. Mipmapping doesn't work on cached bitmap images (or bitmaps with filters applied). If you don't plan on downscaling a bitmap image, use an image-editing program to resize the bitmap graphic to the actual size needed prior to importing it into Flash.

Here are some sample dimensions:

- 1024 x 1024 pixels
- 512 x 512 pixels
- 256 x 256 pixels

Use lower frame rates

Test your project using different frame rates to find the lowest acceptable one. Many animations play smoothly at 24–30 fps. User interfaces for applications (that do not have animations) can often playback at 12 fps without noticeably affecting appearance. If your project plays intermittent animations and you want them to play smoothly, you can use ActionScript code to change the frame rate at runtime. When a project is set to use higher frame rates, Flash Player has less time to draw the elements on the Stage and process the code. Depending on the project, higher frame rates can result in decreased performance. Be sure to test the project to see what works best for your content (see Figure 13).

Figure 13. Adjust the frame rate in the Property inspector.

Avoid nesting movie clips

Use layers instead of movie clip containers to organize assets whenever possible. Decreasing the number of nested containers in a project increases its performance (see Figure 14).

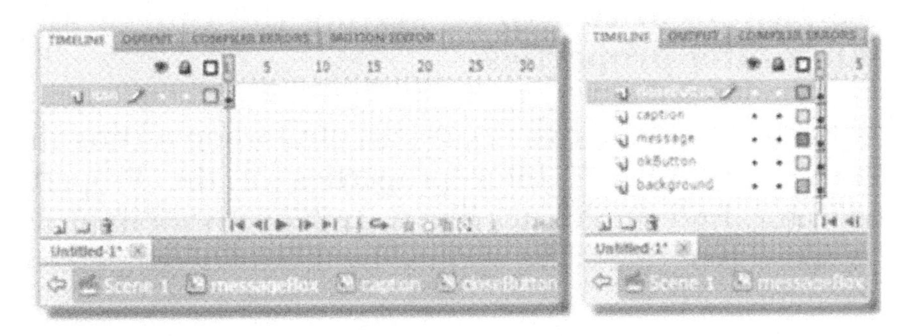

Figure 14. Rather than nesting movie clips, organize assets in the layers of the Timeline.

Avoid animating objects with applied filters

When you apply filters to objects, they automatically adopt the cacheAsBitmap behavior. Animating filters, tweening filter properties, tweening transformations, and tweening color effects forces Flash Player to recache objects on every frame and reapply their filters—which leads to the extremely high consumption of resources (see Figure 15).

Figure 15. Animated filters, transformations, and color effects require more resources.

Note: You can animate the *x* and *y* properties of objects without recaching them.

Use powers of two when setting the Blur X and Blur Y filter properties

Calculate powers of two (2^1, 2^2, 2^3, etc.) when setting the Blur X and Blur Y filter properties in the Property inspector. Entering values like 2, 4, 8, or 16 can improve the speed that filters are applied by up to 20–30 percent (see Figure 16).

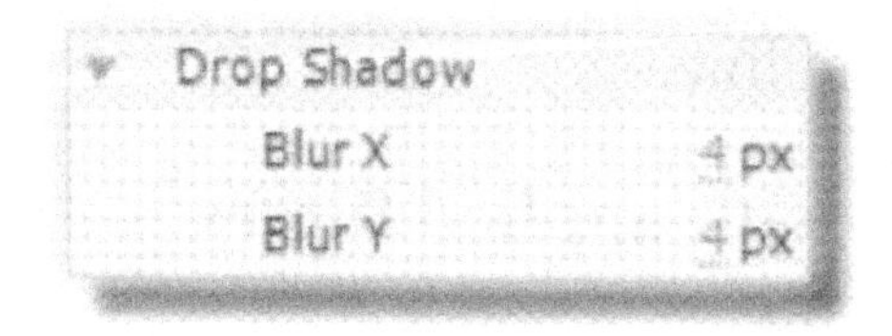

Figure 16. Enter powers of two when setting Blur X and Blur Y properties.

Cache complex vector graphics and text strategically

Use the Cache as Bitmap feature for complex vector graphics that do not contain nested animation. You can also apply it to static text fields. Use the Cache as Bitmap feature for objects that are not animated (or are animated only using the *x* and *y* properties)—including their parent containers.

If you are using ActionScript, you can also use cacheAsBitmapMatrix available in Adobe AIR only (starting with AIR 2). This enables you to scale and rotate cached objects without recaching so that the GPU (graphics card installed in the user's machine) composits and scales the transformations.

Additionally, you can use the Export as Bitmap feature introduced in Flash Professional CS5.5 to convert complex vector objects or nested objects into a bitmap graphic at the time the SWF file is compiled. Keep in mind that you have no control over the smoothing or compression settings applied to the exported bitmap images. Only use the Export as Bitmap feature on objects that do not contain nested animation. This mode has some added advantages over the classic Cache as Bitmap functionality. For example, exported images can be rotated, scaled, and animated as desired without incurring the same dramatic performance hit that occurs when working with cached objects. However, the exported bitmap images added to the SWF file do increase its file size.

If cached or exported bitmap objects have an opaque, continuous tone background fill, you should use the Opaque Bitmap background option and select a color to fill the background and gain even more performance improvements.

If a cached container includes a great deal of unused space between contained objects, make sure to cache each object individually to save extra bytes in memory. Try different strategies and compare the results to determine the best method to use (see Figure 17).

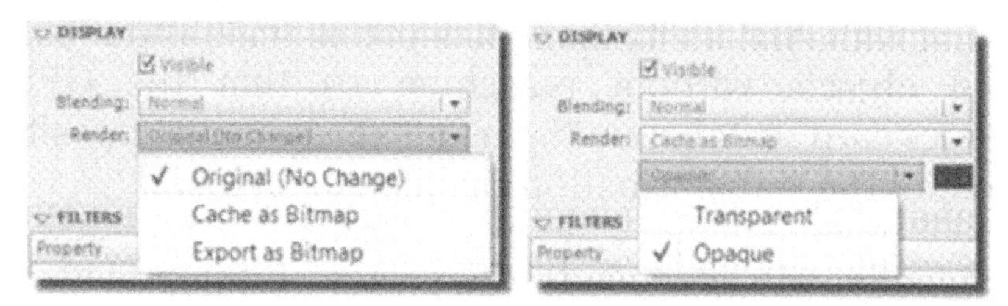

Figure 17. Choose the Display settings in the Property inspector.

Avoid using tween animations when creating very simple animations

You can use a programmatic approach to make simple animations such as movement, rotation, color changes, alpha transparency fading, and more. Explore using third-party libraries like TweenLite developed by GreenSock. This results in animations that save more resources and are more flexible to update (see Figure 18).

Figure 18. Replace tween animations with animations controlled by ActionScript.

Avoid using 2.5D in CPU mode

When you transform 3D objects using the user's computer's processor (CPU) instead of the graphics card (GPU), the project incurs the same performance issues as objects that use the Cached as Bitmap feature (see Figure 19).

Figure 19. Transformed 3D objects require greater processing resources.

Use redraw regions

You can use the option to show redraw regions in the context menu of the Debug Flash Player to see exactly which items are being drawn on the Stage (as well as when they appear). This strategy is helpful because you can find leftover invisible animations that are taking up unnecessary resources (see Figure 20).

Figure 20. Use the Show Redraw Regions option to see outlines of redrawn elements.

Strive to keep redraw areas as small as possible

Whenever possible, prevent regions from overlapping. The redraw regions of overlapping objects can merged into one larger region, which results in more empty space being redrawn. Smaller regions draw faster (see Figure 21).

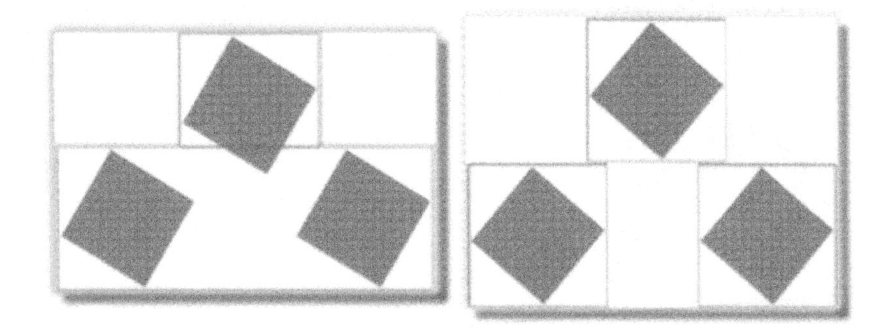

Figure 21. Overlapped elements can increase the size of redraw regions.

Always stop animations in hidden movie clips

If a movie clip contains animation that is played on demand (and not as the SWF loads) double-check that the animation is not running while the movie clip is hidden. Always stop animations when containers are hidden (or whenever you remove movie clips) to avoid using extra resources (see Figure 22).

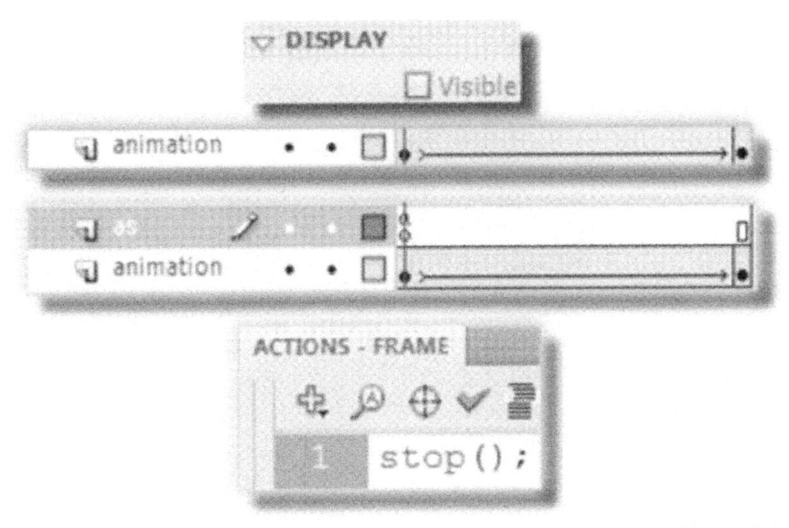

Figure 22. Add a stop action to ensure that hidden animations do not continue to play.

Avoid placing objects off the visible area of the Stage

Try not to place objects off the Stage area. If you change the Stage size and forget to remove them, the unseen graphics in the background will continue to consume resources while the SWF file plays. Also avoid keeping objects off the Stage in order to bring them onto the Stage later. It is better to use ActionScript code to set the visible property of the object to false and then set it to true—or add the object with the addChild() method—at the time you want the object to appear. Objects that are placed off the Stage, although not seen during playback, still consume resources (see Figure 23).

Figure 23. Avoid placing objects off the Stage area.

Avoid using TLF text fields unless you need specific text functionality

Use Classic text fields instead of TLF text fields unless your project specifically requires TLF text functionality. TLF text renders more slowly and adds more bytes to the SWF file compared to Classic text fields.

If you wish to add text features that are not included with Classic text fields, try using third-party TLF equivalents, such as TinyTLF. By default, imported text fields are set as TLF text fields. If you are not working with TLF text, remember to set them as Classic text fields in the Property inspector after importing them.

Choose the appropriate Preview Mode for each project

Change the document rendering quality to speed up its display. You can choose the most appropriate mode for your project by selecting View > Preview Mode (see Figure 24).

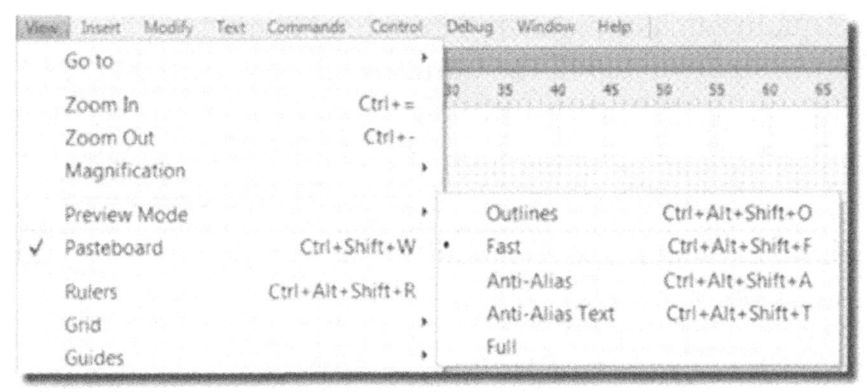

Figure 24. Experiment with using different preview modes for your projects.

Optimizing file size of project assets

Follow these suggestions to reduce the file size of the SWF files you create and improve their download times.

Set the appropriate compression on bitmap images

Carefully fine-tune the compression type and quality for every image in the Library using the Bitmap Properties dialog box, especially if you imported images created in

Adobe Photoshop. This practice decreases the resources required and reduces the file size of the SWF file. If graphics contain many details, gradients, and colors, use JPEG compression; use PNG compression for less complex images to achieve a smaller SWF file size.

Avoid applying the Allow Smoothing option if possible because smoothing requires additional resources. Try to find a good balance between image quality and file size. Click the Test button to review the image's size and quality with the selected compression settings (see Figure 25); the quality is listed on the left side of the dialog box and the file size is listed at the bottom.

Figure 25. Click the Test button to see the quality and compression settings.

Consider when to fill shapes with bitmap images

You can break an image apart (Modify > Break Apart) or use the Color panel to set a shape's Color type to Bitmap fill. If you're only using part of the bitmap image to fill a shape, remember that the entire bitmap image will be compiled into SWF file when it is published.

Even though you're using only a few small pieces of the larger image, the entire image size will be added to the resulting SWF file. It's best to use an image editing program to prepare and import the smaller pieces as separate bitmap images and then use these smaller bitmap files as is, instead of to fill shapes.

Having said that, I think bitmap filling is a great strategy if you are using the entire bitmap image (or most of it) in multiple containers. In this case, you can use the bitmap fill feature to decrease the size of the SWF file because only one bitmap image will be compiled into the SWF file when it is published (see Figure 26).

Figure 26. Determine when it is most efficient to use bitmap fills for shapes.

Avoid scaling bitmap images

Whenever possible, use an image editing program to prepare images to avoid scaling them in Flash. Images that are scaled larger require additional resources. If you reduce the size of an imported image by scaling it down, you are adding unused bytes to the file size of the SWF file.

However, there are cases when you animate bitmap images in the Timeline to scale them smaller. In this situation, it is best to import the image at its largest size, prior to scaling (see Figure 27).

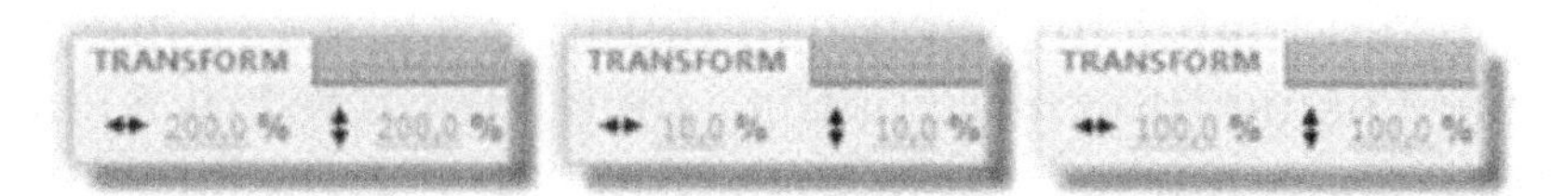

Figure 27. Resize images in an image editing program, and then import them.

Replace simple bitmap graphics with traced vector shapes

Use traced vector graphics in place of images with fewer colors, gradients, or details. When displaying simple graphics, vector shapes require fewer resources and result in a smaller SWF file size. If the source image is a bitmap image, you can convert the bitmap image to a vector shape with Illustrator. You can also choose Modify > Bitmap > Trace Bitmap in Flash. Always make tests compare performance when swapping out vector shapes for bitmap images to achieve the most efficient results (see Figure 28).

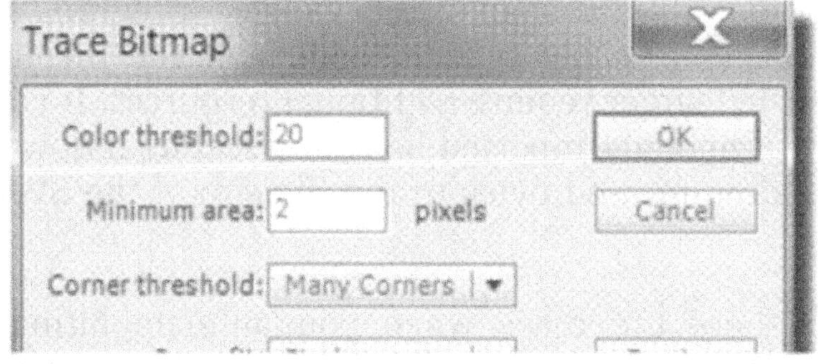

Figure 28. Use the Trace Bitmap feature in Flash to create vector shapes.

Replace frame-by-frame animations with tween animations

Whenever possible, use tween animations instead of frame-by-frame animations. In addition to saving time, the resulting SWF file may use fewer resources and result in a smaller SWF file size (see Figure 29).

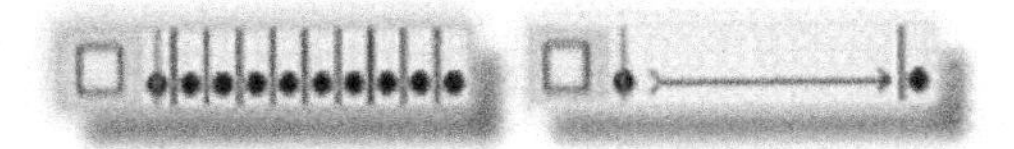

Figure 29. Use tween animations rather than frame-by-frame animations.

Check the size report to identify assets in the project with larger file sizes

In the Publish Settings dialog box, enable the Generate Size Report option to learn if some of the elements in a Flash file are larger than expected. Identify larger files and attempt to optimize them or swap them out with smaller files.

Use symbols whenever possible

Whenever possible, convert graphic objects to symbols. Always convert graphic elements to symbols if the graphic asset is used more than once in the project. You can scale and apply color effects to symbol instances to create variations of the original graphic file. This strategy reduces the file size of the published SWF file.

Embed only the characters of a font you need to display in text fields

When working with dynamic, input, or TLF text fields, don't embed the entire character set of a font. Instead, embed only the characters that are used in the Flash project. This strategy avoids adding extra bytes to the SWF file. To embed fonts, choose Text > Font Embedding and be sure to name the embedded fonts with descriptive names to make the project easy to edit later (see Figure 30).

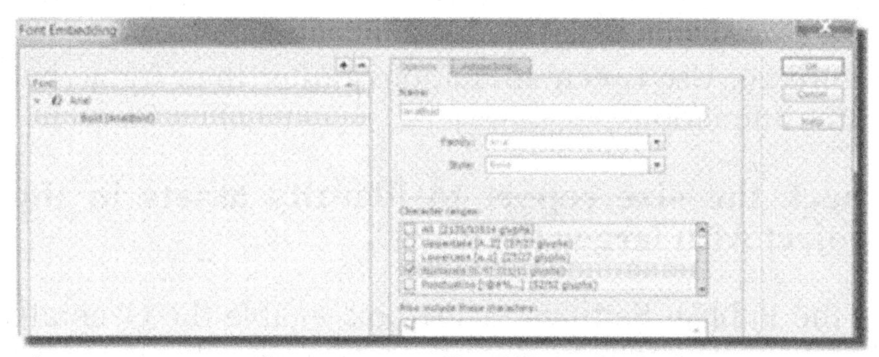

Figure 30. Use the Font Embedding dialog box to select only the characters needed to display the text in a project.

Disable the option to include XMP metadata in the Publish Settings dialog box

In the Publish Settings dialog box, disable the Include XMP Metadata option if the project does not use XMP metadata. This removes a few bytes from the published SWF file (see Figure 31).

Figure 31. Deselect the Include XMP Metadata option.

Developing Flash projects more elegantly

The suggestions described in this section improve the performance of your content. These practices facilitate changes, help you organize files, and make it easier to share your project files with other developers.

Avoid setting measurements to a twentieth of a pixel (twip)

Strive to set the *x* and *y* dimensions of every object rounded to whole integer values. This practice helps avoid various aliasing issues and also saves resources (see Figure 32).

Figure 32. Enter whole numbers for object property values.

Consider whether to use the Convert to Bitmap feature

The Convert to Bitmap feature (see Figure 33) enables you to convert vector elements and nested objects quickly into a single bitmap object. As it calculates the elements, it also takes into account any nested effects and masks. In some cases, it results in color loss or the addition of extra alpha during the conversion process. Always check the resulting bitmap after completing the conversion. If you are finding that the results are not as expected, you can also consider taking a screenshot or using external image editing products to combine the elements, and then reimport the compiled bitmap file. Bitmap images created using the Convert to Bitmap feature are set to allow smoothing and Use PNG compression by default.

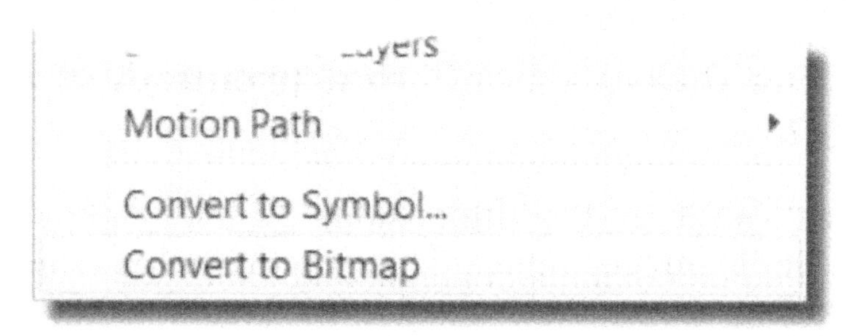

Figure 33. Always check images generated using the Convert to Bitmap option.

Use the Anti-alias for Animation font rendering option sparingly

Whenever possible, use the Anti-alias for Readability font rendering method unless you are animating a text field. The Anti-alias for Animation option results in fonts that are not as smooth as text using Anti-alias for Readability (see Figure 34).

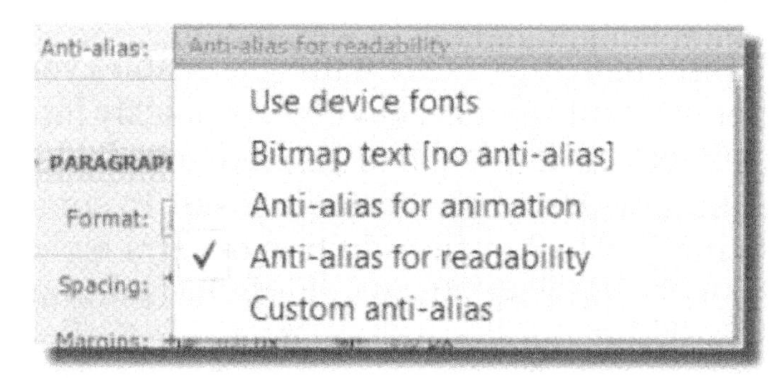

Figure 34. Set the Anti-alias for Readability option whenever possible.

Disable the Selectable option on text fields unless needed

The Selectable option on text fields is enabled by default. Disable this setting if it is not needed. It is a best practice to keep this setting enabled only if you think users will be copying the text in the text field, such as text fields that display error messages (see Figure 35).

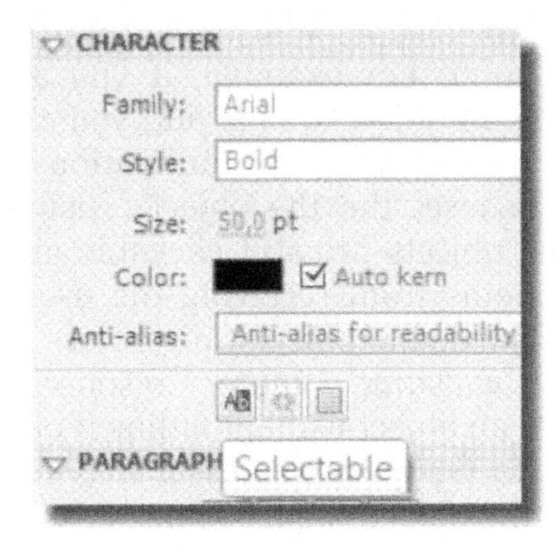

Figure 35. Remember to disable the Selectable option unless it is absolutely necessary.

Remove unused tween animations in the Timeline

Before publishing the final version of a project, review the Timeline to locate any tween animations that are not being used. Remove them using the "Remove tween" context menu and then publish the SWF file (see Figure 36).

Figure 36. Locate and delete any unused tween animations in the Timeline.

Hide objects strategically

Depending on the project goals, you can set the visible property of an instance to false as well as setting the object's alpha property to 0. For example, if you are programmatically causing an object to fade out, you can set its alpha value to 0. But once the animation is completed, be sure to also set the the object's visible property to false. Visible objects are still clickable and could block underlying items from receiving the user's mouse clicks. Additionally, visible objects, regardless of their alpha setting, consume more resources. If you simply want to hide an object without fading it out, set the visible property to false. In this case, it is not necessary to also change the object's alpha value.

To save more resources, completely remove objects from the DisplayList instead of hiding them. Programmatically show and hide them as needed, as long as the hide and show operations do not occur on every frame.

Avoid hiding objects under other objects on the Stage

If you wish to hide an object, set its visible property to false or remove it from the DisplayList. Objects hidden below other objects still wastes resources (see Figure 37).

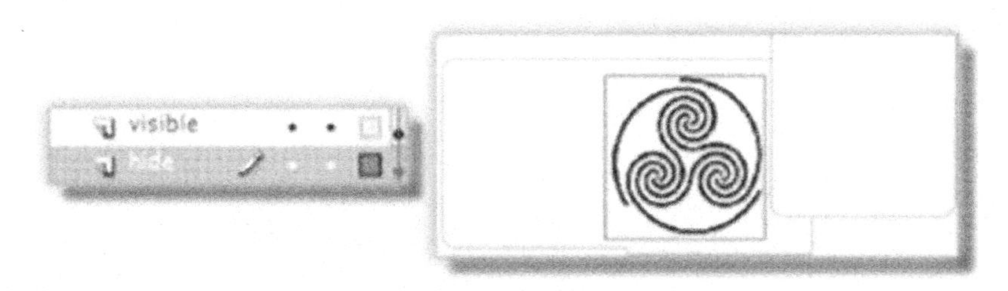

Figure 37. Set an object's visibility to false or remove it entirely; don't hide the object from view by placing it below other elements on the Stage.

Use custom UI components

Everything you can do to conserve resources and reduce file size improves the project— especially when developing for mobile devices. When you want to incorporate UI elements, such as a list menu, slider, or combo box, try using third-party components or develop custom UI elements yourself. Standard Flash components can consume too many resources to meet the requirements of some Flash applications (see Figure 38).

Figure 38. Create your own custom UI components built with ActionScript.

Name elements descriptively

Always enter meaningful, descriptive names to layers, fonts, and assets in the Library. This is a best practice because it helps you and other developers track bugs when debugging the project later (see Figure 39).

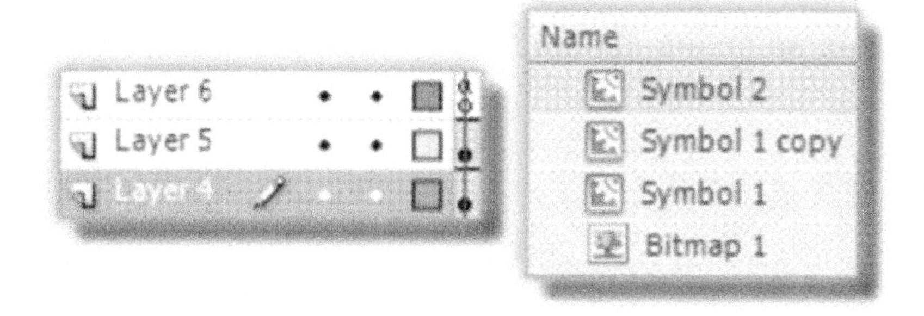

Figure 39. Don't use the default names assigned by Flash; enter names that describe each layer and element in the project.

Use only alpha-numeric characters, dashes, and underscores in names

Do not use spaces, capitalization, or special characters (even accented letters), especially from your native language (if it uses characters not used in the English alphabet). This is important because special characters in names can cause issues, including version control when using external tools.

Use consistent instance names for animated objects in the Timeline

If you've entered a name in the Instance Name field to reference an object in a tween animation on the Timeline, make sure to use the same instance name for all other instances of that object throughout the animation on the same layer. Doing so avoids several different issues that can occur if you are referencing the object with ActionScript code (see Figure 40).

Figure 40. Ensure that a named instance uses the same instance name throughout the entire layer.

Convert objects to movie clips before animating them

Always convert objects to symbols before animating them. If you don't work with symbols, the objects are automatically converted into graphic symbols (which cannot be named in the Property inspector, so they are useless when using ActionScript code). If you see items in the Library panel named "Tween1", "Tween2", and so on, this means that Flash converted objects that were not symbols into graphic symbols at the time they were tweened (see Figure 41).

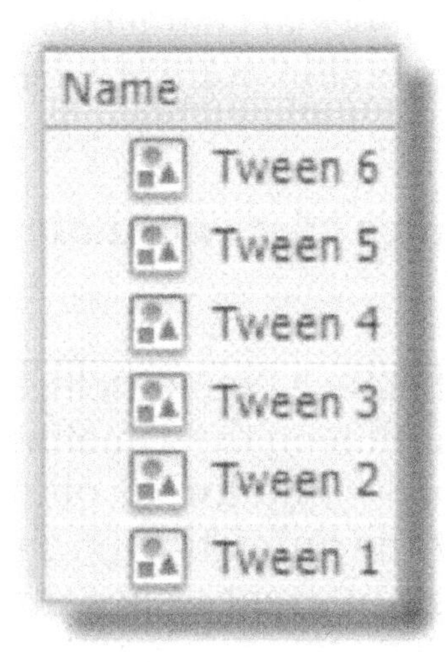

Figure 41. Always convert objects to symbols prior to animating them to avoid the automatic generation of graphic symbols.

Use the right text field type required for each situation

Consider the project requirements before choosing the type of text field to use. Choose the Static Text option if the text field does not have to be editable by the user or dynamically populated (or accessed) with ActionScript code. Use the Dynamic Text option if the text field's contents will be controlled using ActionScript. Choose the Input Text option if the text field must be editable by both the user and ActionScript code (see Figure 42).

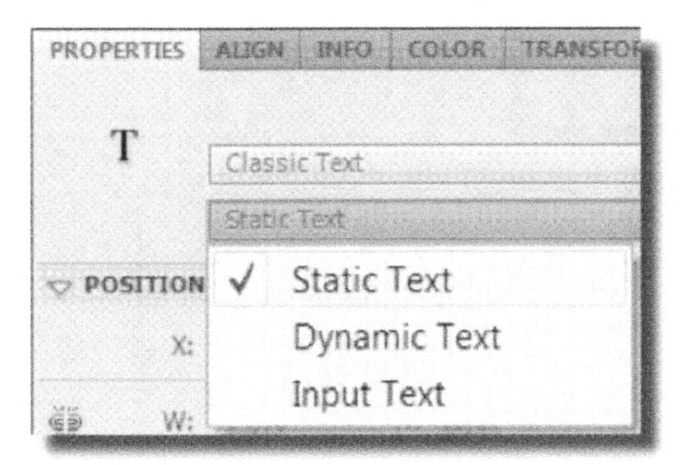

Figure 42. Choose the text field type that corresponds to your project requirements.

Choose the correct ActionScript type when creating and publishing files

If your project includes ActionScript 3 code, choose the ActionScript 3 option whenever you are creating new files or updating the Publish Settings. If you choose a different option (such as ActionScript 2) but the project contains ActionScript 3 code, it will not work and you may not immediately recognize why it appears to be broken (see Figure 43).

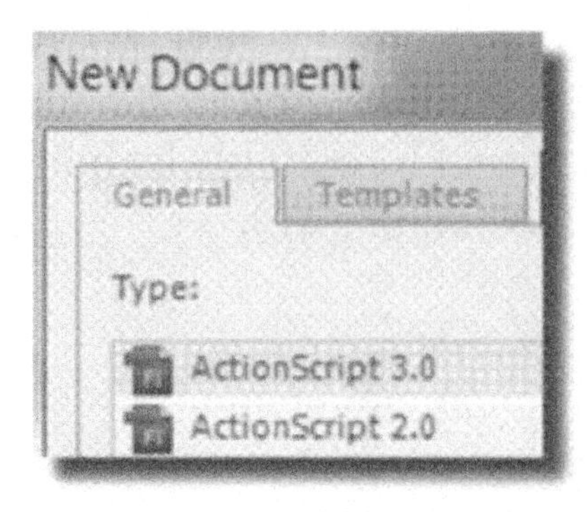

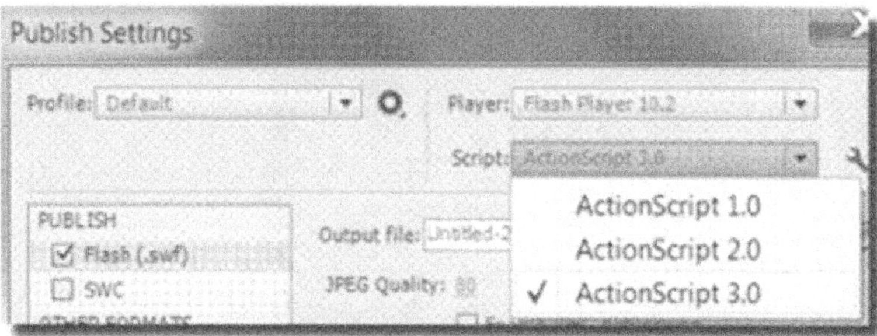

Figure 43. Choose the correct ActionScript type when creating and publishing files.

Use the publishing options that work best for each project

If a project uses an external library, consider using a SWC file instead of working with a set of AS files. Some Flash developers choose to publish their projects as both SWC and a folder of AS files.

You can configure the Publish Cache settings (introduced in Flash Professional CS5.5) to specify your hardware. To access the Publish Cache settings, choose Edit > Preferences > Publish Cache.

If your project contains a lot of code and takes a long time to compile, you can disable the Warnings Mode option in the Publish Settings. Select the Flash tab, and then click the Advanced ActionScript 3.0 Settings while ActionScript 3 is selected, and then deselect the Warnings Mode check box. This option can result in a faster publishing process. However, keep in mind that when you disable the warning messages, you won't see code tips that are helpful when debugging projects (see Figure 44).

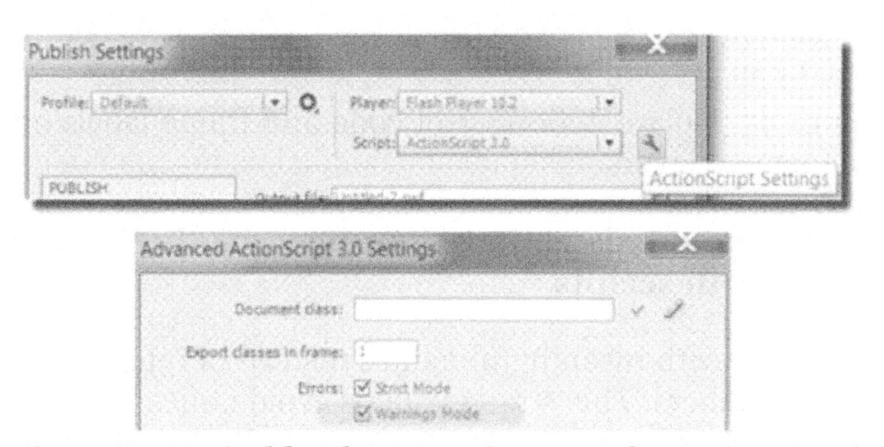

Figure 44. Disable the Warnings Mode option in the Publish Settings dialog box.

Making project files easier to update

Consider applying these best practices as you develop applications in Flash Professional. You can organize projects and set up elements to ensure that you and other team members can quickly update them later.

Place ActionScript and frame labels on the first two layers in the Timeline

Don't write your code on layers that contain project assets. If you do, you are hiding it from other developers (and yourself) when the Flash file is edited later. Place all code on its own, separate layer and place all frame labels on their own layer. Both layers should be located at the top of the layers stack in the Timeline, and locked to avoid accidentally adding assets to the layers that contain ActionScript code or frame labels (see Figure 45).

Figure 45. Isolate ActionScript code and frame labels on the first two layers.

Use frame labels rather than hard-coding frame numbers in scripts

Use labels with meaningful names instead of referring to frame numbers. This strategy helps avoid issues that can occur if an animation's length changes. It also makes it much easier to edit the Flash project later, and to help other developers understand how the project is set up (see Figure 46).

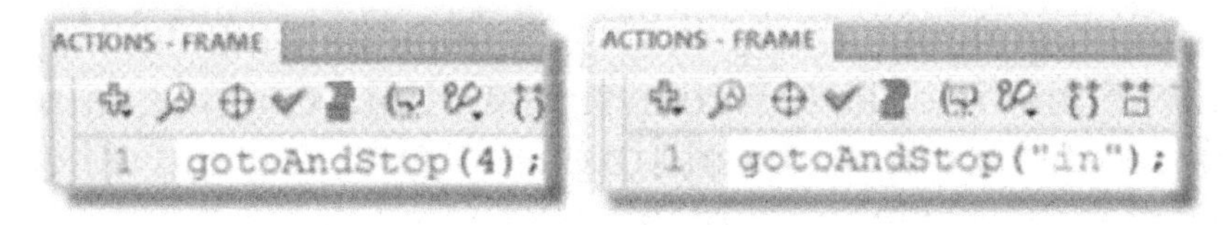

Figure 46. Use frame labels that describe the project, rather than referencing the frame by its number in the Timeline.

Avoid using bitmap images for text elements

It is much more difficult to edit text in bitmap files compared to editing text in text fields. When you import text, don't choose the Flattened Bitmap Image option; select the Editable Text option instead (see Figure 47).

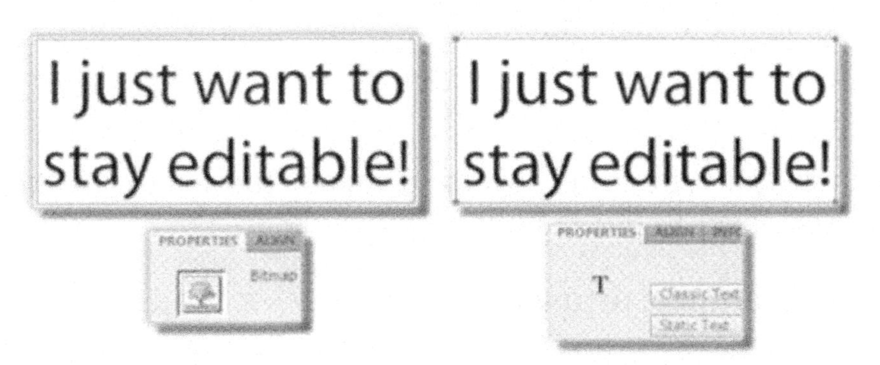

Figure 47. Use text fields, rather than bitmap images, for text elements.

Remove unnecessary keyframes from the Timeline

Keep track of unused keyframes and remove them from the Timeline. If you previously inserted keyframes, but they are no longer used to make any changes, you should remove them. In addition to wasting resources, empty keyframes can add confusion later when editing the project (see Figure 48).

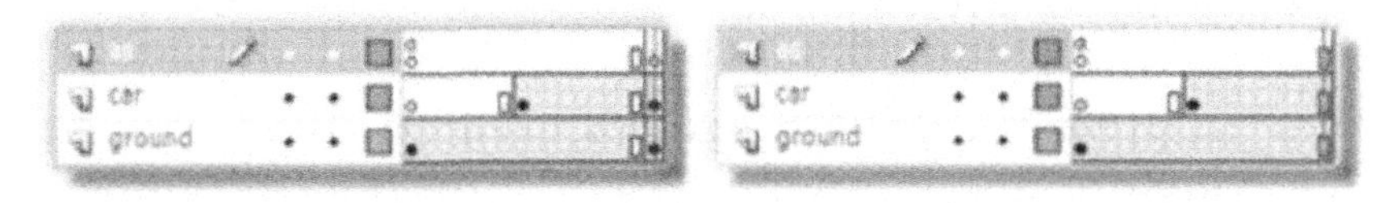

Figure 48. Delete unnecessary keyframes in layers.

Make all layers in the Timeline the same length

Press F5 to insert additional frames to shorter layers and make them the same length as the longest layer. This is a best practice and keeps the Timeline easier to read (see Figure 49).

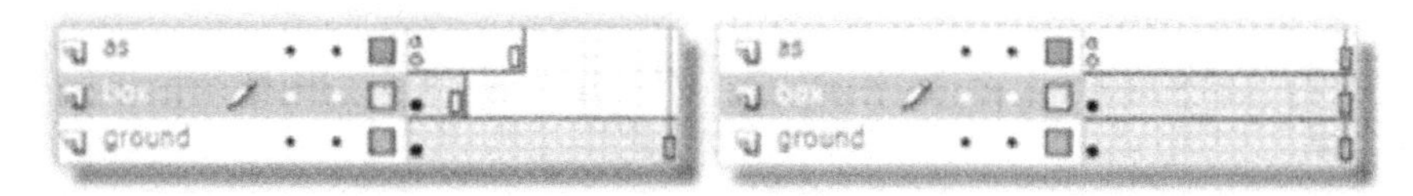

Figure 49. Extend all layers to match the length of the longest layer in the Timeline.

Delete empty, unused layers

Delete layers that do not contain any assets, ActionScript code, frame labels, audio elements, or other project elements. Empty layers can cause confusion and make editing the Timeline unnecessarily difficult (see Figure 50).

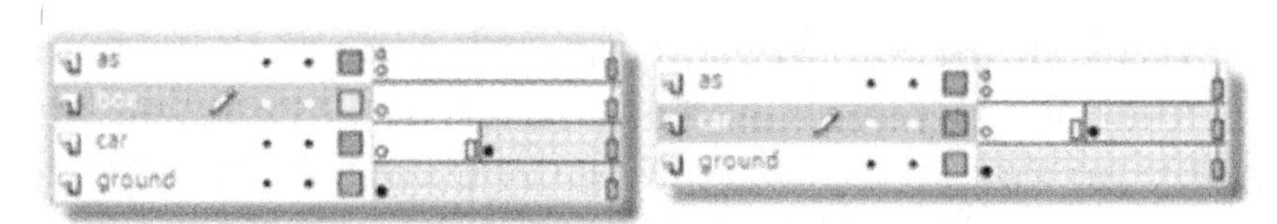

Figure 50. If layers are not needed, delete them from the Timeline.

Avoid using multiple scenes

Rather than working with scenes created in the Scenes panel, consider using movie clips or jumping to frames in the main Timeline instead. When you use multiple scenes, it can make the Flash file confusing to edit, particularly if you are sharing project files with other developers.

Additionally, multiple scenes often cause increased size in published SWF files (see Figure 51).

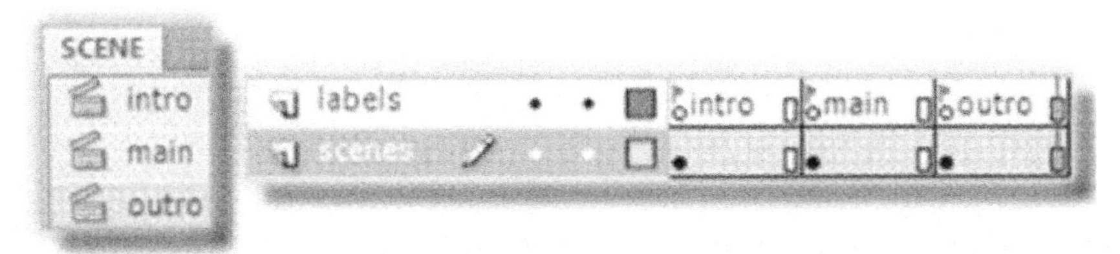

Figure 51. Use frame labels and ActionScript to jump to sections in the main Timeline.

Name and use groups consistently, and only when needed

Groups make it easy to work with multiple objects simultaneously. Grouping is helpful when achieving tasks, such as aligning a group of objects to the Stage. You can group objects without impacting the performance of projects because groups are ignored when the SWF file is published.

However, if you are working on a project with a team of developers, it is a best practice to avoid grouping objects unnecessarily. It is much more elegant to use movie clips as containers for a set of related objects, because the team members can access the elements in a movie clip more easily. Objects that are grouped together may be more difficult to edit (see Figure 52).

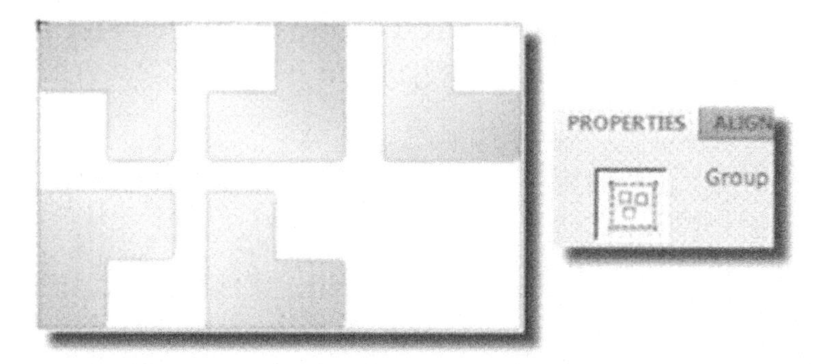

Figure 52. If you need to group objects to align them, ungroup them again after aligning the objects on the Stage.

Periodically check the Timeline to ensure tween animations remain unbroken

If a tween animation looks different in the Timeline (the solid line is now displaying a dashed line between frames), it means that the tween is broken. Usually this occurs because the objects used to create the animation are no longer on the Stage and are missing from one of the keyframes. In this case, delete the animation and recreate it (see Figure 53).

Figure 53. If you see dashed lines in the tween spans, it means the tween animation is broken.

Remove unused items from the Library panel

Make a backup copy of the FLA file and then remove all unused items (elements that are not used now and won't be used in future) to organize the Library panel and make the list of assets easier to read. This practice also ensures that the FLA project file is smaller.

In the Library panel, the Use Count feature is helpful for identifying unused elements. You can also choose Select Unused Items, but be careful when selecting this menu item because occasionally it includes files that are used in the project (see Figure 54).

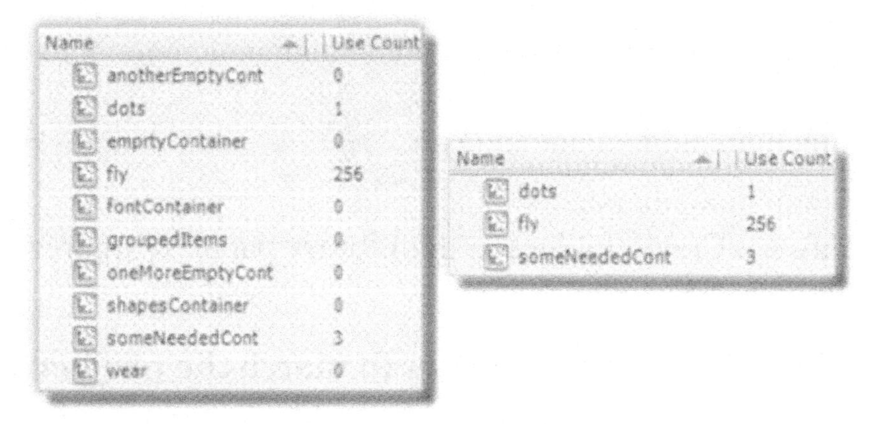

Figure 54. Review the Use Count column to identify elements that are not used in the project.

Create folders in the Library to organize related asset files

You can use folders to manage the contents of the Library panel and keep it well structured. Projects that use folders to organize assets are easier and faster to update (see Figure 55).

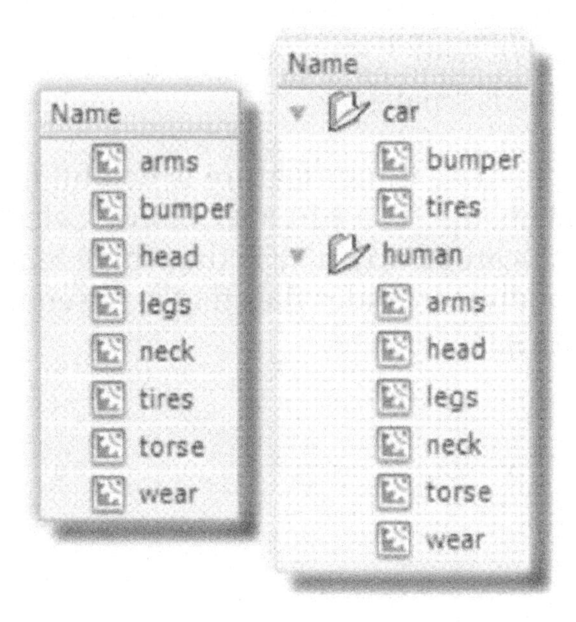

Figure 55. Create folders in the Library panel to organize project assets.

Update text field properties to match the project's design

By default, text fields are set to use a line spacing of 2 and multiline behavior. If your project only requires a single line text field with a line spacing of 0, update the options in the Property inspector to match the text field settings for your project (see Figure 56).

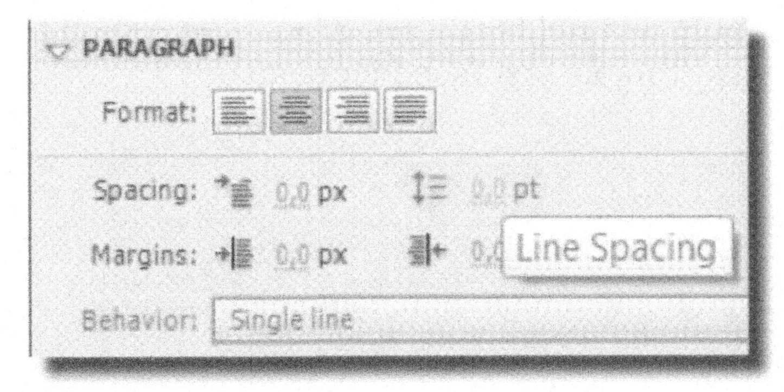

Figure 56. Use the Property inspector settings to update the selected text field

Don't break text fields apart

After you break apart text fields, they are no longer editable. If you are using the break apart feature to animate characters in a text field, consider using ActionScript to achieve the same effect. If you programmatically animate the text characters, the text field remains editable and is much easier to change when needed (see Figure 57).

Figure 57. Avoid breaking apart text fields because they cannot be edited.

Maintain the editability of text fields during the import process

When you import text fields, always choose the option to import them as Editable text (see Figure 58).

Figure 58. Choose the Editable text option in the Import dialog box.

Resize text field elements to match the size of their contents

Avoid leaving static text fields larger than the text contents inside them. Unless you have a specific reason—such as using text fields to display button labels—it's a best practice to use centered text alignment. It is much easier to edit text content later if the text is center-aligned and the text field's dimensions fit the text content inside.

To set the text field's dimensions to match the text content, click the white square icon in the top-right corner of the text field while editing the text. If a circle icon is displayed instead of a square icon, it means that the dimensions of the text field already match the text content that it contains (see Figure 59).

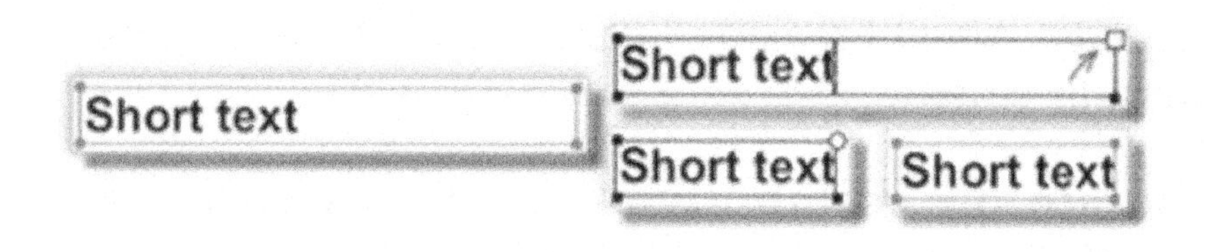

Figure 59. Resize the text field to match the text content and set the alignment of the text to align center.

Never attach ActionScript 2 code to buttons and movie clips

If you're working with a project that uses ActionScript 2 code, avoid attaching the code to objects. Always add the code as frame scripts because it is much easier to locate later (see Figure 60). You can identify frames that contain code because they display a lowercase character in the Timeline.

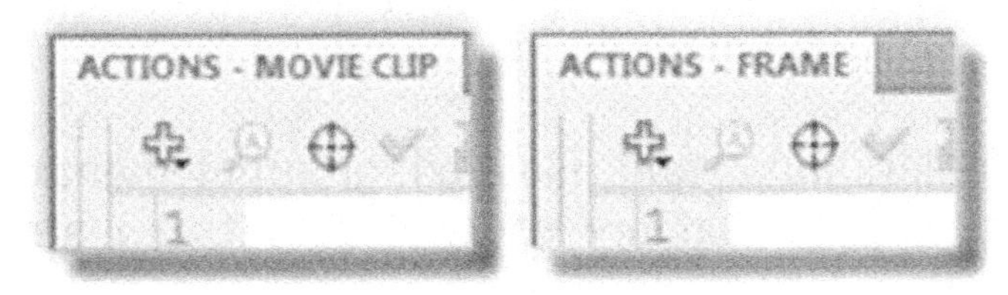

Figure 60. Add ActionScript 2 code to frame scripts.

Note: When you develop using ActionScript 3, you can only add the code to frames.

Organize project assets to keep font files easy to access

Always store font files in the project folder. When you need to share project files, be sure to include all the necessary files, including the font files used in the project.

Include all project libraries and third-party classes when you share a project

Don't forget to attach all external libraries and class files that are used in the project. Double-check that you are using global paths to link to external files.

Add ActionScript code to one centralized location in the project file

When adding ActionScript code to frames, try to organize all of the important scripts (needed for Stage resize handling, Stage setup, and more) in a location that is easy to access. This strategy makes it much easier to update the project file later. Generally speaking, it is a best practice to place important code on Frame 1 of the Actions layer so that any developer who works with the project in the future can quickly find it.

You can add the less important, isolated, or supplemental code in other locations that are controlled by this main script on Frame 1.

Use relative paths to external files

Use relative paths to classes, libraries, and output files. This makes your project portable and simple to share with other developers. If you always follow this rule, other team members won't have to change the paths later (see Figure 61).

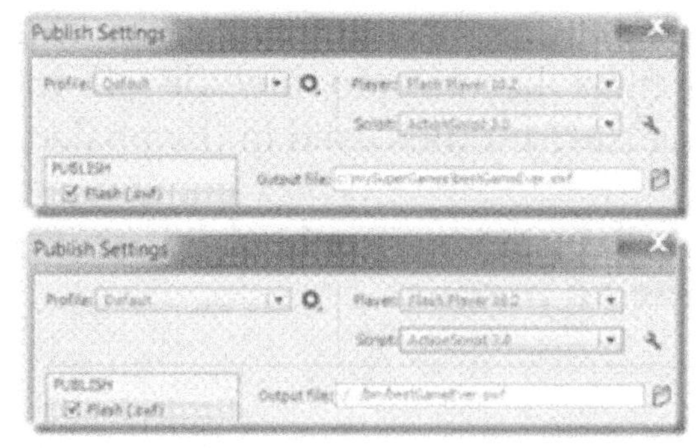

Figure 61. Use relative paths when linking to external files.

Where to go from here

I hope that the tips provided in this topic will help you create optimized Flash projects. By applying these suggestions to your development workflow, you can improve the performance of Flash animations and provide better user experiences on both desktop and mobile devices.

Additionally, by incorporating these best practices, you can ensure that your files are easier to update and manage in the future. This is especially helpful when working within a team.

If you have other Flash tips to share, especially if they solve a specific problem, please add them to the Flash cookbook.

This was by Dmitriy Yukhanov.

End of Topic.

A fresh topic

Keyboard Shortcuts in Flash/Animate.

You can create and modify keyboard shortcuts in Animate.

Customize keyboard shortcuts

1. Select (Windows) Edit > Keyboard Shortcuts or (Macintosh) Animate > Keyboard Shortcuts.

   The Keyboard Shortcuts dialog box appears.

2. Use the following options to add, delete, or edit keyboard shortcuts:

   Keyboard Layout Presets

   Lets you choose a preset of predetermined shortcuts from the drop-down, or any custom set you may have defined.

   Search

   Lets you search for any command whose shortcut you want to set or modify. Alternatively, you may drill-down the command within the tree view of commands.

   Match Case

   Lets you perform a case-sensitive search of the command.

   Add

Adds a new shortcut to the selected command. To add a new keyboard shortcut for the selected command, click Add and enter a new key combination. Each command can one keyboard shortcut each; if a shortcut is already assigned to a command, the Add button is disabled.

Undo

Undo the last set shortcut for a command.

Copy to clipboard

Copy the entire list of keyboard shortcuts to clipboard of your Operating System.

Go To Conflict

Navigates to conflicting command. In case of a conflict when setting up a shortcut, a warning message is displayed.

Save shortcuts to a preset

Save the entire set of shortcuts to a preset. Presets can then be selected from the Keyboard Layout Presets drop-down.

Delete Shortcut

Deletes a selected shortcut.

Note:

You cannot use single keys such as delete or page up, ones that are pre-defined for some generic tasks such as deleting content, page scrolling, etc.

3. Click OK.

Remove a shortcut from a command

1. From the Commands pop-up menu, select a command category, select a command from the Commands list.
2. Click the X mark beside the shortcut.

Add a shortcut to a command

1. From the Commands pop-up menu, select a command category and select a command.
2. Click the Add button.
3. Press a key combination.

   Note:

   If a conflict occurs with the key combination (for example, if the key combination is already assigned to another command), an explanatory message appears just below the Commands list. Click the Go To Conflict button to quickly navigate to the conflicting command, and change the shortcut.

4. Click Ok.

Edit an existing shortcut

1. From the Commands pop-up menu, select a command category, select a command from the Commands list.
2. Double-click the shortcut.
3. Press a new key combination.

   Note:

   If a conflict occurs with the key combination (for example, if the key combination is already assigned to another command), an explanatory message appears just below the Commands list. Click the Go To Conflict button to quickly navigate to the conflicting command, and change the shortcut.

Use the following list of keyboard shortcuts to enhance your productivity in Adobe Animate.

File.

Result	Mac Shortcut	Windows Shortcut
Import Image/Sound/etc...	Command + R	Ctrl + R
Export to .swf/.spl/.gif/, and so on	Command + Shift + R	Ctrl + Shift + R
Open as Library	Command + Shift + O	Ctrl + Shift + O

View.

Result	Mac Shortcut	Windows Shortcut
View movie at 100% size	Command + 1	Ctrl + 1
Show Frame	Command + 2	Ctrl + 2
Show All	Command + 3	Ctrl + 3

Windows.

Result	Mac Shortcut	Windows Shortcut
Show/Hide Library	Command + L	Ctrl + L
Modify Movie Properties	Command + M	Ctrl + M
Toggle between Edit Movie and Edit Symbol Mode	Command + E	Ctrl + E
Show/Hide Work Area	Command + Shift + L	Ctrl + Shift + L
Show/Hide Timeline	Command + Shift + W	Ctrl + Shift + W

Edit and Modify.

Result	Mac Shortcut	Windows Shortcut
Group	Command + G	Ctrl + G

Ungroup	Command + U	Ctrl + U
Break Apart	Command + B	Ctrl + B
Paste in Place	Command + Shift + V	Ctrl + Shift + V
Duplicate	Command + D	Ctrl + D
Select All	Command + A	Ctrl + A
Deselect All	Command + Shift + A	Ctrl + Shift + A
Optimize Curves	Command + Shift + O	Ctrl + Shift + O
Align Window	Command + D	Ctrl + D
Scale and Rotate	Command + Shift + S	Ctrl + Shift + S
Remove Transform	Command + Shift + Z	Ctrl + Shift + Z
Move Ahead	Command + Arrrow up	Ctrl + Arrrow up
Move Behind	Command + Arrrow down	Ctrl + Arrrow down
Bring to Front	Command + Shift+ Arrrow up	Ctrl + Shift + Arrrow up
Send to Back	Command + Arrrow down	Ctrl + Shift + Arrrow down
Modify Font	Command + T	Ctrl + T
Modify Paragraph	Command + Shift + T	Ctrl + Shift + T
Narrower letter spacing (kerning)	Command + Arrrow left	Ctrl + Arrrow left

Wider letterspacing (kerning)	Command + Arrrow right	Ctrl + Arrrow right

Miscellaneous Actions.

Result	**Mac Shortcut**	**Windows Shortcut**
Remove rotation or scaling from the selected objects	Command + Shift + Z	Ctrl + Shift + Z
Rotate the selection to 90 degrees left	Command + Shift + 7	Ctrl + Shift + 7
Scale and/or rotate the selection using numeric values	Command + Shift + S	Ctrl + Shift + S
Auto formats the editor code	Command + Shift + F	Ctrl + Shift + F
Show hidden characters	Command + Shift + 8	Ctrl + Shift + 8

suppresses highlighting of selected items	Command + Shift + E	Ctrl + Shift + E
Show or hide the pasteboard that surrounds the stage	Command + Shift + W	Ctrl + Shift + W
Show or hide the rulers	Command + Shift + Alt + R	Ctrl + Shift + Alt + R
Show Frame Script Navigator	Command + Alt + [	Ctrl + Alt + [
Show or hide the tweening shape hints	Command + Alt + I	Ctrl + Alt + I
Show a smaller area of the drawing with more detail	Command + =	Ctrl + =
Show a larger area of the drawing with less detail	Command + -	Ctrl + -

Show or hide the Align panel	Command + K	Ctrl + K
Show or hide the Color panel	Command + Shift + 5	Ctrl + Shift + 5
Show or hide the Compiler Errors panel	Command +Alt + 8	Ctrl +Alt + 8
Add Component Widgets	Command + 3	Ctrl + 3
Open a new window in the front most simulation that is a duplicate of the active window	Command + Alt + K	Ctrl + Alt + K
Show or hide the History panel	Command + T	Ctrl + T
Show or change the properties and position of	Command + I	Ctrl + I

the selected object		
Show or hide the Library panel for this document	Command + L	Ctrl + L
Show or hide the Property Inspector	Command + 9	Ctrl + 9
Show or change a list of the scenes in the current movie	Command + Shift	Ctrl + Shift
Select colors from swatches and manage swatches	Command + 5	Ctrl + 5
Show or hide the animation timeline and layers controls	Command + Alt + T	Ctrl + Alt + T
Show or hide the drawing toolbar	Command + 8	Ctrl + 8

Scale and/or rotate the selection using numeric values	Command + T	Command + T
Shifts the entire range of onion skin markers to the left	Command + drag towards left	Shift + drag towards left
Shifts the entire range of onion skin markers to the right	Command + drag towards right	Shift + drag towards right

Applies to: *Adobe Animate.*

CHAPTER 7.

Tips, Tricks, Techniques, and Keyboard Shortcuts for use in Illustrator.

About the program: This is a program used by graphics designers and artists for the creation of vector images, developed by Adobe Systems.

A fresh topic

Tools Panel Overview.

The first time you start the application, the Tools panel appears at the left side of the screen. You can move the Tools panel by dragging its title bar. You can also show or hide the Tools panel by choosing Window > Tools.

You use tools in the Tools panel to create, select, and manipulate objects in Illustrator. Some tools have options that appear when you double-click a tool. These include tools that let you use type, and select, paint, draw, sample, edit, and move images.

You can expand some tools to show hidden tools beneath them. A small triangle at the lower-right corner of the tool icon signals the presence of hidden tools. To see the name of a tool, position the pointer over it.

You can also use the Tools panel to change the drawing mode from Draw Normal to Draw Behind or Draw Inside.

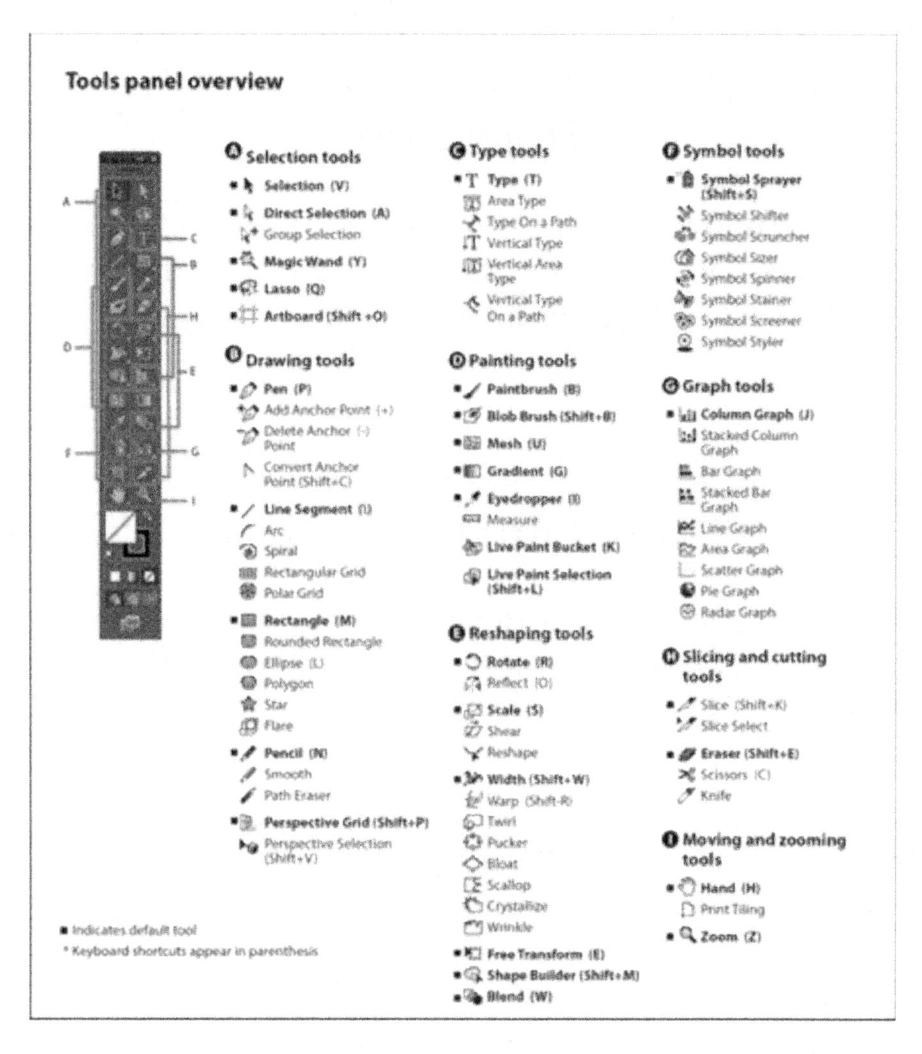

Tools panel overview

View hidden tools.

- Hold down the mouse button on the visible tool.

View tool options

- Double-click a tool in the Tools panel.

Move the Tools panel

- Drag its title bar.

View the Tools panel in double-stack or single-column

- Click the double-arrow on the title bar to toggle between double-stack and single-column view of the Tools panel.

Hide the Tools panel

- Choose Window > Tools.

Tear off hidden tools into a separate panel

- Drag the pointer over the arrow at the end of the hidden tools panel and release the mouse button.

Close a separate tool panel

- Click the close button on the panel's title bar. The tools return to the Tools panel.

Select a tool

- Do one of the following:
    - Click a tool in the Tools panel. If there is a small triangle at a tool's lower-right corner, hold down the mouse button to view the hidden tools, and then click the tool you want to select.
    - Hold down Alt (Windows) or Option (Mac OS), and then click a tool to cycle through and select hidden tools.
    - Press the tool's keyboard shortcut. The keyboard shortcut is displayed in its tool tip. For example, you can select the Move tool by pressing the V key.

      ***Tip**: To hide tool tips, choose Edit > Preferences > General (Windows) or Illustrator > Preferences > General (Mac OS), and deselect Show Tool Tips.*

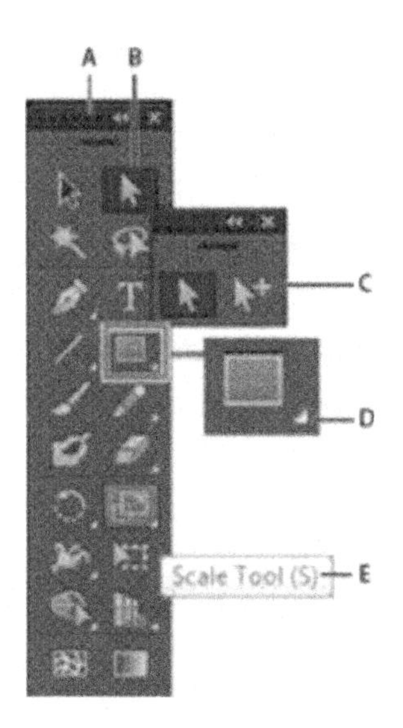

- Selecting a hidden tool

A. Tools panel **B.** Active tool **C.** Tear off panel with hidden tools **D.** Hidden tool triangle **E.** Tool name and shortcut

Change Tool Pointers.

The mouse pointer for most tools matches the tool's icon. Each pointer has a different hotspot, where an effect or action begins. With most tools, you can switch to precise cursors, which appear as cross hairs centered around the hotspot, and provide for greater accuracy when working with detailed artwork.

- Choose Edit > Preferences > General (Windows) or Illustrator > Preferences > General (Mac OS), and select Use Precise Cursors. Alternatively, press Caps Lock on the keyboard.

-by Adobe Systems Inc. experts.

A fresh topic

Default Keyboard Shortcuts in Adobe Illustrator.

Use the following list of keyboard shortcuts to enhance your productivity in Adobe Illustrator.

Keys for Selecting Tools.

Result	Windows Shortcut	Mac OS Shortcut
Artboard tool	Shift + O	Shift + O
Selection tool	V	V
Direct Selection tool	A	A
Magic Wand tool	Y	Y
Lasso tool	Q	Q
Pen tool	P	P
Blob Brush tool	Shift + B	Shift + B
Add Anchor Point tool	+ (plus)	+ (plus)
Delete Anchor Point tool	- (minus)	- (minus)
Convert Anchor Point tool	Shift + C	Shift + C
Type tool	T	T
Line Segment tool	\ (backslash)	\ (backslash)
Rectangle tool	M	M
Ellipse tool	L	L
Paintbrush tool	B	B
Pencil tool	N	N
Rotate tool	R	R
Reflect tool	O	O
Scale tool	S	S
Warp tool	Shift + R	Shift + R
Width Tool	Shift+W	Shift+W
Free Transform tool	E	E
Shape Builder Tool	Shift+M	Shift+M
Perspective Grid Tool	Shift+P	Shift+P
Perspective Selection Tool	Shift+V	Shift+V

Symbol Sprayer tool	Shift + S	Shift + S
Column Graph tool	J	J
Mesh tool	U	U
Gradient tool	G	G
Eyedropper tool	I	I
Blend tool	W	W
Live Paint Bucket tool	K	K
Live Paint Selection tool	Shift + L	Shift + L
Slice tool	Shift + K	Shift + K
Eraser tool	Shift + E	Shift + E
Scissors tool	C	C
Hand tool	H	H
Zoom tool	Z	Z
Switch to Smooth tool while using Blob Brush tool	Press Alt	Press Option

Keys for Viewing Artwork.

This is not a complete list of keyboard shortcuts. This table lists only those shortcuts that are not displayed in menu commands or tool tips.

Result	**Windows Shortcut**	**Mac OS Shortcut**
Toggle between screen modes: Normal Screen	F	F

Mode, Full Screen Mode with Menu Bar, Full Screen Mode		
Fit imageable area in window	Double-click Hand tool	Double-click Hand tool
Magnify 100%	Double-click Zoom tool	Double-click Zoom tool
Switch to Hand tool (when not in text-edit mode)	Spacebar	Spacebar
Switch to Zoom tool in magnify mode	Ctrl + Spacebar	Spacebar + Command
Switch to Zoom tool in reduce mode	Ctrl + Alt + Spacebar	Spacebar + Command + Option
Move Zoom marquee while dragging	Spacebar	Spacebar

with the Zoom tool		
Hide unselected artwork	Control + Alt + Shift + 3	Command + Option + Shift + 3
Convert between horizontal and vertical guide	Alt-drag guide	Option-drag guide
Release guide	Ctrl + Shift-double-click guide	Command + Shift-double-click guide
Show/Hide artboards	Ctrl + Shift + H	Command + Shift + H
Show/Hide artboard rulers	Ctrl + Alt + R	Command + Option + R
View all artboards in window	Ctrl + Alt + 0 (zero)	Command + Option + 0 (zero)
Paste in place on the active artboard	Ctrl+Shift+V	Command+Shift+V
Exit Artboard tool mode	Esc	Esc
Create artboard inside	Shift-drag	Shift-drag

another artboard		
Select multiple artboards in the Artboards panel	Ctrl+click	Command+click
Navigate to next document	Ctrl + F6	Command+F6
Navigate to previous document	Ctrl + Shift + F6	Command+Shift+F6
Navigate to next document group	Ctrl + Alt + F6	Command+Option+F6
Navigate to previous document group	Ctrl + Alt + Shift + F6	Command+Option+Shift+F6
Exit Full Screen mode	Esc	Esc
Save multiple artboards to Illustrator CS3 or	Alt + v	

earlier format		

Keys for Drawing.

This is not a complete list of keyboard shortcuts. This table lists only those shortcuts that are not displayed in menu commands or tool tips.

Result	Windows Shortcut	Mac OS Shortcut
Constrain a shape's proportions or orientation to: • equal height and width for rectangles, rounded rectangles, ellipses, and grids • Increments of 45° for line and	Shift-drag	Shift-drag

arc segments • Original orientation for polygons, stars, and flares		
Move a shape while drawing it	spacebar-drag	spacebar-drag
Draw from the center of a shape (except for polygons, stars, and flares)	Alt-drag	Option-drag
Increase or decrease polygon sides, star points, arc angle, spiral winds, or flare rays	Start dragging, then press the Up Arrow or Down Arrow	Start dragging, then press the Up Arrow or Down Arrow
Keep the inner radius of a star constant	Start dragging, then hold down Ctrl	Start dragging, then hold down Command
Keep the sides of a star straight	Alt-drag	Option-drag

Switch between an open and closed arc	Start dragging, then hold down C	Start dragging, then hold down C
Flip an arc, keeping the reference point constant	Start dragging, then hold down F	Start dragging, then hold down SF
Add or subtract winds from a spiral while increasing the length of the spiral	Start dragging, then Alt-drag	Start dragging then Option-drag
Change the decay rate of a spiral	Start dragging then Ctrl-drag	Start dragging then Command-drag
Add or remove horizontal lines from a rectangular grid or concentric lines from a polar grid	Start dragging, then press the Up Arrow or Down Arrow	Start dragging, then press the Up Arrow or Down Arrow
Add or remove vertical lines from a rectangular grid or radial lines from a polar grid	Start dragging, then press the Right Arrow or Left Arrow	Start dragging, then press the Right Arrow or Left Arrow

Decrease the skew value for horizontal dividers in a rectangular grid or radial dividers in a polar grid by 10%	Start dragging, then press F	Start dragging, then press F
Increase the skew value for horizontal dividers in a rectangular grid or radial dividers in a polar grid by 10%	Start dragging, then press V	Start dragging, then press V
Decrease the skew value for vertical dividers in a rectangular grid or concentric dividers in a polar grid by 10%	Start dragging, then press X	Start dragging, then press X
Increase the skew value for vertical dividers in a rectangular grid or	Start dragging, then press C	Start dragging, then press C

concentric dividers in a polar grid by 10%		
Create and expand a Live Trace object in one step	Alt-click Live Trace in the Control panel, or hold down Alt and select a tracing preset.	Option-click Live Trace in the Control panel, or hold down Option and select a tracing preset.
Increase size of Blob Brush	] (right square bracket)	] (right square bracket)
Decrease size of Blob Brush	[(left square bracket)	[(left square bracket)
Constrain Blob Brush path horizontally or vertically	Shift	Shift
Switch through drawing modes	Shift+D	Shift+D
Join two or more paths	Select the paths, then press Ctrl+J	Select the paths, then press Command+J
Create corner or smooth join	Select the paths, then press	Select the anchor point, then press Shift+Command+Option+j

	Shift+Ctrl+Alt+j	

Keys for Drawing in Perspective.

This is not a complete list of keyboard shortcuts. This table lists only those shortcuts that are not displayed in menu commands or tool tips.

Results	Windows Shortcut	Mac OS Shortcut
Perspective Grid Tool	Shift+P	Shift+P
Perspective Selection Tool	Shift+V	Shift+V
Perspective Grid	Ctrl+Shift+I	Command+Shift+I
Moving objects perpendicularly	Press the number 5 key, then click and drag the object	Press the number 5 key, then click and drag the object
Switching perspective planes	Use the Perspective Selection tool and then press 1 for left grid, 2 for horizontal grid, 3 for right grid, or 4	Use the Perspective Selection tool and then press 1 for left grid, 2 for horizontal grid, 3 for right grid, or 4 for no active grid

	for no active grid	
Copying objects in perspective	Ctrl+Alt+drag	Command+Alt+drag
Repeat transforming objects in perspective	Ctrl+D	Command+D
Switching between drawing modes	Shift+D	Shift+D

Keys for Selecting.

This is not a complete list of keyboard shortcuts. This table lists only those shortcuts that are not displayed in menu commands or tool tips.

Result	**Windows Shortcut**	**Mac OS Shortcut**
Switch to last-used selection tool (Selection tool, Direct Selection tool, or Group Selection tool)	Ctrl	Command
Switch between Direct Selection tool and Group Selection tool	Alt	Option
Add to a selection with Selection tool, Direct Selection tool,	Shift-click	Shift-click

Group Selection tool, Live Paint Selection tool, or Magic Wand tool		
Subtract a selection with Selection tool, Direct Selection tool, Group Selection tool, or LIve Paint Selection tool	Shift-click	Shift-click
Subtract from selection with Magic Wand tool	Alt-click	Option-click
Add to selection with Lasso tool	Shift-drag	Shift-drag
Subtract from selection with Lasso tool	Alt-drag	Option-drag
Change pointer to cross hair for Lasso tool	Caps Lock	Caps Lock
Select artwork in active artboard	Ctrl + Alt + A	Command + Option + A
Create crop marks around selected object	Alt + c + o	
Select behind an object	Press Ctrl+click twice	Press Command+click twice
Select behind in isolation mode	Ctrl+click twice	Command+click twice

Keys for Moving Selections.

This is not a complete list of keyboard shortcuts. This table lists only those shortcuts that are not displayed in menu commands or tool tips.

Result	Windows Shortcut	Mac OS Shortcut
Move selection in user-defined increments	Right Arrow, Left Arrow, Up Arrow, or Down Arrow	Right Arrow, Left Arrow, Up Arrow, or Down Arrow
Move selection in 10x user-defined increments	Shift + Right Arrow, Left Arrow, Up Arrow, or Down Arrow	Shift + Right Arrow, Left Arrow, Up Arrow, or Down Arrow
Lock all deselected artwork	Ctrl + Alt + Shift + 2	Command + Option + Shift + 2
Constrain movement to 45° angle (except when using Reflect tool)	Hold down Shift	Hold down Shift

Note:

Set keyboard increments in General Preferences

Keys for Editing Shapes.

This is not a complete list of keyboard shortcuts. This table lists only those shortcuts that are not displayed in menu commands or tool tips.

Result	**Windows Shortcut**	**Mac OS Shortcut**
Switch Pen tool to Convert Anchor Point tool	Alt	Option
Switch between Add Anchor Point tool and Delete Anchor Point tool	Alt	Option
Switch Scissors tool to Add Anchor Point tool	Alt	Option
Switch Pencil tool to Smooth tool	Alt	Option
Move current anchor point while drawing with Pen tool	Spacebar-drag	Spacebar-drag
Cut a straight line with Knife tool	Alt-drag	Option-drag
Cut at 45° or 90° with Knife tool	Shift + Alt-drag	Shift + Option-drag
Use shape mode buttons in	Alt + Shape mode	Option + Shape mode

Pathfinder panel to create compound paths		
Erase unwanted closed regions created using Shape Builder tool	Alt+click the closed region	Option+click the closed region
Select the Shape Builder tool	Shift+M	Shift+M
Display rectangular marquee to easily merge multiple paths (when using Shape Builder tool)	Shift+click+drag	Shift+click+drag

Keys for Painting Objects.

This is not a complete list of keyboard shortcuts. This table lists only those shortcuts that are not displayed in menu commands or tool tips.

Result	Windows Shortcut	Mac OS Shortcut
Toggle between fill and stroke	X	X
Set fill and stroke to default	D	D

Swap fill and stroke	Shift + X	Shift + X
Select gradient fill mode	>	>
Select color fill mode	<	<
Select no stroke/fill mode	/ (forward slash)	/ (forward slash)
Sample color from an image or intermediate color from gradient	Shift + Eyedropper tool	Shift + Eyedropper tool
Sample style and append appearance of currently selected item	Alt + Shift-click + Eyedropper tool	Option + Shift-click + Eyedropper tool
Add new fill	Ctrl + / (forward slash)	Command + / (forward slash)
Add new stroke	Ctrl + Alt + / (forward slash)	Command + Option + / (forward slash)
Reset gradient to black and white	Ctrl-click gradient button in Tools panel or Gradient panel	Command-click gradient button in Tools panel or Gradient panel
Open Mosaic options for selected raster object	Alt + o + j	
Decrease Bristle brush size	[	[

Increase Bristle brush size	]	]
Set Bristle brush paint opacity value	Number keys 1 - 0. Number key 1 increases the value to 10% Number key 0 increases the value to 100%	Number keys 1 - 0. Number key 1 increases the value to 10% Number key 0 increases the value to 100%

Keys for Working with Live Paint Groups.

This is not a complete list of keyboard shortcuts. This table lists only those shortcuts that are not displayed in menu commands or tool tips.

Result	**Windows Shortcut**	**Mac OS Shortcut**
Switch to Eyedropper tool and sample fill and/or stroke	Alt-click + Live Paint Bucket tool	Option-click + Live Paint Bucket tool
Switch to Eyedropper tool and sample color from an image or intermediate color from a gradient	Alt + Shift-click + Live Paint Bucket tool	Option + Shift-click + Live Paint Bucket tool
Select opposite Live Paint Bucket tool options (if Paint Fills	Shift + Live Paint Bucket tool	Shift + Live Paint Bucket tool

and Paint Strokes are currently selected, switch to Paint Fills only)		
Fill across unstroked edges into adjacent faces	Double-click + Live Paint Bucket tool	Double-click + Live Paint Bucket tool
Fill all faces that have same fill and stroke all edges that have same stroke	Triple-click + Live Paint Bucket tool	Triple-click + Live Paint Bucket tool
Switch to Eyedropper tool and sample fill and/or stroke	Alt-click + Live Paint Selection tool	Option-click + Live Paint Selection tool
Switch to Eyedropper tool and sample color from an image or intermediate color from a gradient	Alt + Shift-click + Live Paint Selection tool	Option + Shift-click + Live Paint Selection tool
Add to/subtract from a selection	Shift-click + Live Paint Selection tool	Shift-click + Live Paint Selection tool
Select all connected faces /edges with same fill/stroke	Double-click + Live Paint Selection tool	Double-click + Live Paint Selection tool
Select all faces/edges with same fill/stroke	Triple-click + Live Paint Selection tool	Triple-click + Live Paint Selection tool

Keys for Transforming Objects.

This is not a complete list of keyboard shortcuts. This table lists only those shortcuts that are not displayed in menu commands or tool tips.

Result	**Windows Shortcut**	**Mac OS Shortcut**
Set origin point and open dialog box when using Rotate tool, Scale tool, Reflect tool, or Shear tool	Alt-click	Option-click
Duplicate and transform selection when using Selection tool, Scale tool, Reflect tool, or Shear tool	Alt-drag	Option-drag
Transform pattern (independent of object) when using Selection tool, Scale tool, Reflect tool, or Shear tool	Tilde (~)-drag	Tilde (~)-drag

Keys for Creating Variable Width Points.

This is not a complete list of keyboard shortcuts. This table lists only those shortcuts that are not displayed in menu commands or tool tips.

Results	**Windows Shortcut**	**Mac OS Shortcut**
Select multiple width points	Shift+click	Shift+click
Create non-uniform widths	Alt+drag	Option+drag

Create a copy of the width point	Alt+drag the width point	Options+drag the width point
Change the position of multiple width points	Shift+drag	Shift+drag
Delete selected width point	Delete	Delete
Deselect a width point	Esc	Esc

Keys for Working with Type.

This is not a complete list of keyboard shortcuts. This table lists only those shortcuts that are not displayed in menu commands or tool tips.

Result	**Windows Shortcut**	**Mac OS Shortcut**
Move one character right or left	Right Arrow or Left Arrow	Right Arrow or Left Arrow
Move up or down one line	Up Arrow or Down Arrow	Up Arrow or Down Arrow
Move one word right or left	Ctrl + Right Arrow or Left Arrow	Command + Right Arrow or Left Arrow
Move up or down one paragraph	Ctrl + Up Arrow or Down Arrow	Command + Up Arrow or Down Arrow
Select one word right or left	Shift + Ctrl + Right Arrow or Left Arrow	Shift + Command +

		Right Arrow or Left Arrow
Select one paragraph before or after	Shift + Ctrl + Up Arrow or Down Arrow	Shift + Command + Up Arrow or Down Arrow
Extend existing selection	Shift-click	Shift-click
Align paragraph left, right, or center	Ctrl + Shift + L, R, or C	Command + Shift + L, R, or C
Justify paragraph	Ctrl + Shift + J	Command + Shift + J
Insert soft return	Shift + Enter	Shift + Return
Highlight kerning	Ctrl + Alt + K	Command + Option + K
Reset horizontal scale to 100%	Ctrl + Shift + X	Command + Shift + X
Increase or decrease type size	Ctrl + Shift + > or <	Command + Shift + > or <
Increase or decrease leading	Alt + Up or Down Arrow (horizontal text) or Right or Left Arrow (vertical text)	Option + Up or Down Arrow (horizontal text) or Right or Left Arrow (vertical text)
Reset tracking/kerning to 0	Ctrl + Alt + Q	Command + Option + Q
Increase or decrease kerning and tracking	Alt + Right or Left Arrow (horizontal text) or Up or	Option + Right or Left Arrow (horizontal text) or Up or

	Down Arrow (vertical text)	Down Arrow (vertical text)
Increase or decrease kerning and tracking by five times	Ctrl + Alt + Right or Left Arrow (horizontal text) or Up or Down Arrow (vertical text)	Command + Option + Right or Left Arrow (horizontal text) or Up or Down Arrow (vertical text)
Increase or decrease baseline shift	Alt + Shift + Up or Down Arrow (horizontal text) or Right or Left Arrow (vertical text)	Option + Shift + Up or Down Arrow (horizontal text) or Right or Left Arrow (vertical text)
Switch between Type and Vertical Type, Area Type and Vertical Area Type, and Path Type and Vertical Path Type tools	Shift	Shift
Switch between Area Type and Path Type, Vertical Area Type and Vertical Path Type tools	Alt	Option

Note:

To change the increment value for type shortcuts, choose Edit > Preferences >Type (Windows) or Illustrator > Preferences >Type (Mac OS). Enter the values you want in the Size/Leading, Baseline Shift, and Tracking text boxes, and click OK.

Keys for Using Panels.

This is not a complete list of keyboard shortcuts. This table lists only those shortcuts that are not displayed in menu commands or tool tips.

Result	Windows Shortcut	Mac OS Shortcut
Set options (except for Actions, Brushes, Swatches, and Symbols panels)	Alt-click New button	Option-click New button
Delete without confirmation (except for Layers panel)	Alt-click Delete button	Option-click Delete button
Apply value and keep text box active	Shift + Enter	Shift + Return
Select range of actions, brushes, layers, links, styles, or swatches	Shift-click	Shift-click
Select noncontiguous actions, brushes, layers (same level only), links, styles, or swatches	Ctrl-click	Command-click
Show/Hide all panels	Tab	Tab
Show/Hide all panels except the Tools panel and Control panel	Shift + Tab	Shift + Tab

Keys for the Actions Panel.

This is not a complete list of keyboard shortcuts. This table lists only those shortcuts that are not displayed in menu commands or tool tips.

Result	Windows Shortcut	Mac OS Shortcut
Expand/Collapse entire hierarchy for action set	Alt-click expansion triangle	Option-click expansion triangle
Set options for action set	Double-click folder icon	Double-click folder icon
Play a single command	Ctrl-click Play Current Selection button	Command-click Play Current Selection button
Begin recording actions without confirmation	Alt-click New Action button	Option-click New Action button

Keys for the Brushes Panel.

This is not a complete list of keyboard shortcuts. This table lists only those shortcuts that are not displayed in menu commands or tool tips.

Result	Windows Shortcut	Mac OS Shortcut

Open Brush Options dialog box	Double-click brush	Double-click brush
Duplicate brush	Drag brush to New Brush button	Drag brush to New Brush button

Keys for the Character and Paragraph Panels.

This is not a complete list of keyboard shortcuts. This table lists only those shortcuts that are not displayed in menu commands or tool tips.

Result	Windows Shortcut	Mac OS Shortcut
Increase/decrease the selected value by a small increment	Up Arrow or Down Arrow	Up Arrow or Down Arrow
Increase/decreases the selected value by a large increment	Shift + Up Arrow or Down Arrow	Shift + Up Arrow or Down Arrow
Highlight the font name field in the Character panel	Ctrl + Alt + Shift + F	Command + Option + Shift + F

Keys for the Color Panel.

This is not a complete list of keyboard shortcuts. This table lists only those shortcuts that are not displayed in menu commands or tool tips.

Result	Windows Shortcut	Mac OS Shortcut
Select the complement for the current color fill/stroke	Ctrl-click color bar	Command-click color bar
Change the nonactive fill/stroke	Alt-click color bar	Option-click color bar
Select the complement for the nonactive fill/stroke	Ctrl + Alt-click color bar	Command + Option-click color bar
Select the inverse for the current fill/stroke	Ctrl + Shift-click color bar	Command + Shift-click color bar
Select the inverse for the nonactive fill/stroke	Ctrl + Shift + Alt-click color bar	Command + Shift + Option-click color bar
Change the color mode	Shift-click color bar	Shift-click color bar
Move color sliders in tandem	Shift-drag color slider	Shift-drag color slider
Switch between percentage and 0-255 values for RGB	Double-click to right of a numerical field	Double-click to right of a numerical field

Keys for the Gradient Panel.

This is not a complete list of keyboard shortcuts. This table lists only those shortcuts that are not displayed in menu commands or tool tips.

Result	Windows Shortcut	Mac OS Shortcut
Duplicate color stops	Alt-drag	Option-drag
Swap color stops	Alt-drag color stop onto another stop	Option-drag color stop onto another color stop
Apply swatch color to active (or selected) color stop	Alt-click swatch in the Swatches panel	Option-click swatch in the Swatches panel
Reset the gradient fill to default black and white linear gradient	Ctrl-click Gradient Fill box in the Gradient panel	Command-click Gradient Fill box in the Gradient panel
Show/Hide gradient arrow	Ctrl + Alt + G	Command + Option + G
Modify angle and end-point together	Alt-drag end point of gradient annotator	Option-drag end point of gradient annotator
Constrain Gradient tool or Gradient annotator while dragging	Shift-drag	Shift-drag
View Gradient annotator in selected gradient filled object	G	G

Keys for the Layers Panel.

This is not a complete list of keyboard shortcuts. This table lists only those shortcuts that are not displayed in menu commands or tool tips.

Result	Windows Shortcut	Mac OS Shortcut
Select all objects on the layer	Alt-click layer name	Option-click layer name
Show/hide all layers but the selected one	Alt-click eye icon	Option-click eye icon
Select Outline/Preview view for the selected layer	Ctrl-click eye icon	Command-click eye icon
Selects Outline/Preview view for all other layers	Ctrl + Alt-click eye icon	Command + Option-click eye icon
Lock/unlock all other layers	Alt-click lock icon	Option-click lock icon
Expand all sublayers to display entire hierarchy	Alt-click expansion triangle	Option-click expansion triangle
Set options as you create new layer	Alt-click New Layer button	Option-click New Layer button
Set options as you create new sublayer	Alt-click New Sublayer button	Option-click New Sublayer button
Place new sublayer at bottom of layer list	Ctrl + Alt-click New	Command + Option-click

	Sublayer button	New Sublayer button
Place layer at top of layer list	Ctrl-click New Layer button	Command-click New Layer button
Place layer below selected layer	Ctrl + Alt-click New Layer button	Command + Option-click New Layer button
Copy the selection to a layer, sublayer, or group	Alt-drag selection	Option-drag selection

Keys for the Swatches Panel.

This is not a complete list of keyboard shortcuts. This table lists only those shortcuts that are not displayed in menu commands or tool tips.

Result	Windows Shortcut	Mac OS Shortcut
Create new spot color	Ctrl-click New Swatch button	Command-click New Swatch button
Create new global process color	Ctrl + Shift-click New Swatch button	Command + Shift-click New Swatch button
Replace swatch with another	Alt-drag a swatch over another	Option-drag a swatch over another

Keys for the Transform Panel.

This is not a complete list of keyboard shortcuts. This table lists only those shortcuts that are not displayed in menu commands or tool tips.

Result	Windows Shortcut	Mac OS Shortcut
Apply a value and keep focus in edit field	Shift + Enter	Shift + Return
Apply a value and copy object	Alt + Enter	Option + Return
Apply a value and scale option proportionately for width or height	Ctrl + Enter	Command + Return

Keys for the Transparency Panel.

This is not a complete list of keyboard shortcuts. This table lists only those shortcuts that are not displayed in menu commands or tool tips.

Result	Windows Shortcut	Mac OS Shortcut
Change mask to grayscale image for editing	Alt-click on mask thumbnail	Option-click on mask thumbnail
Disable opacity mask	Shift-click on mask thumbnail	Shift-click on mask thumbnail
Re-enable opacity mask	Shift-click on disabled mask thumbnail	Shift-click on disabled mask thumbnail

Increase/decrease opacity in 1% increments	Click opacity field + Up Arrow or Down Arrow	Click opacity field + Up Arrow or Down Arrow
Increase/decrease opacity in 10% increments	Shift-click opacity field + Up Arrow or Down Arrow	Shift-click opacity field + Up Arrow or Down Arrow

Function Keys.

This is not a complete list of keyboard shortcuts. This table lists only those shortcuts that are not displayed in menu commands or tool tips.

Result	**Windows Shortcut**	**Mac OS Shortcut**
Invoke Help	F1	F1
Cut	F2	F2
Copy	F3	F3
Paste	F4	F4
Show/hide Brushes panel	F5	F5
Show/hide Color panel	F6	F6
Show/hide Layers panel	F7	F7
Create new symbol	F8	F8
Show/hide Info panel	Ctrl + F8	Command + F8

Show/hide Gradient panel	Ctrl + F9	Command + F9
Show/hide Stroke panel	Ctrl + F10	Command + F10
Show/hide Attributes panel	Ctrl + F11	Command + F11
Revert	F12	F12
Show/hide Graphic Styles panel	Shift + F5	Shift + F5
Show/hide Appearance panel	Shift + F6	Shift + F6
Show/hide Align panel	Shift + F7	Shift + F7
Show/hide Transform panel	Shift + F8	Shift + F8
Show/hide Pathfinder panel	Shift + Ctrl + F9	Shift + Command + F9
Show/hide Transparency panel	Shift + Ctrl + F10	Shift + Command + F10
Show/hide Symbols panel	Shift + Ctrl + F11	Shift + Command + F11
Show/hide perspective grid	Ctrl+Shift+I	Command+Shift+I

Applies to: *Adobe Illustrator.*

CHAPTER 8.

Keyboard Shortcuts for use in Adobe Premiere Pro.

About the program: This is a timeline video editing software application used by videographers to edit, manipulate, and export their video works.

A fresh topic

Visual Keyboard Layout for Assigning Keyboard Shortcuts.

You can use the keyboard GUI to see which keys have been assigned and which are available for assignment. A tool tip reveals the full command name when you hover over a key in the Keyboard layout. When you select a modifier key on the keyboard layout, the keyboard displays all the shortcuts which require that modifier. You can also press the modifier key on the hardware keyboard to achieve this result.

When you select a key on the Keyboard Layout, you can view all the commands that are assigned to that unmodified key and all other modifier combinations.

- Premiere Pro detects the keyboard hardware and the appropriate keyboard layout is displayed accordingly.
- When Premiere Pro detects a non-supported keyboard, the default view is to display the U.S. English keyboard. By default, the Adobe Premiere Pro Default preset is displayed.
- When you change a shortcut, the preset pop-up menu gets changed to Custom. After you make the required changes, you can choose Save As to save the customized shortcut set as a preset.

Color coding

- Keys shaded in purple are application-wide shortcuts.
- Keys shaded in green are panel-specific shortcuts.
- Keys shaded in both purple and green represent the panel commands that have been assigned to keys that also have an application command already assigned to them.

Application shortcuts and panel shortcuts

- Commands can be assigned for application shortcuts and command shortcuts.
- Application shortcuts function regardless of panel focus (with some exceptions) and panel shortcuts function only when the panel is in focus.
- Certain keyboard shortcuts work only in specific panels. This means that you can have more than once shortcut assigned to the same key. You can also make use of the pop-up window that shows only a certain batch of panel shortcuts (for example, only for the timeline).
- When a Panel Shortcut has the same assigned shortcut as an application Shortcut, the application shortcut does not function when that panel has focus.
- You can search for commands in the Command List, which is filtered by the search criteria. You can also assign shortcuts by clicking in the shortcut column and tapping keys on their keyboard to create the shortcut (including adding modifiers).

A warning indicating a shortcut conflict appears when:

1. An application shortcut already in use by another application shortcut.
2. A panel shortcut is already in use by another command in the same panel.
3. A panel shortcut overrides an application shortcut when that panel has focus.

You can also click drag to assign commands to keys on the keyboard layout or the Key modifier list.

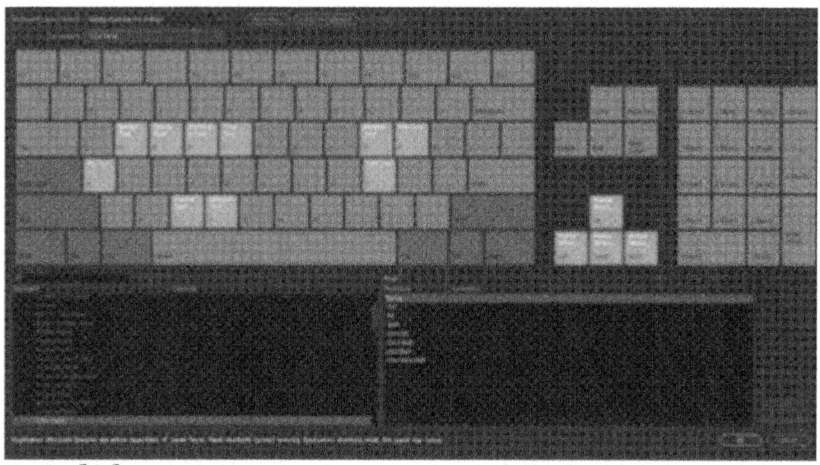

Panel shortcuts

Shortcut assignment using Drag-and-Drop

You can also assign shortcuts by dragging a command from the command List onto a key in the Keyboard Layout, or onto a modifier combination for the currently selected key displayed in the Key Modifier List. To assign a command to a key along with a modifier, hold down the modifiers during drag-and-drop.

Conflict resolution

When there is a conflict with a shortcut that is already in use with another command:

- A warning appears at the bottom of the editor
- Undo and Clear buttons in the lower right corner are enabled.

- The command in conflict is highlighted in blue, and clicking this automatically selects the command in the command list.
- This allows users to easily change the assignment for the conflicting command.

Note:

Use this instead of the 'Go To' button used in former releases.

A fresh topic

Default Keyboard Shortcuts in Adobe Premiere Pro CC.

Many commands have keyboard shortcut equivalents, so you can complete tasks with minimal use of the mouse. You can also create or edit keyboard shortcuts.

Now use the following list of keyboard shortcuts to enhance your productivity in Adobe Premiere Pro.

Results	Windows Shortcut	Mac OS Shortcut
Project/Production...	Ctrl+Alt+N	Opt+Cmd+N

Sequence...	Ctrl+N	Cmd+N
Bin		Cmd+/
Title...	Ctrl+T	Cmd+T
Open Project/Production...	Ctrl+O	Cmd+O
Browse in Adobe Bridge...	Ctrl+Alt+O	Opt+Cmd+O
Close Project	Ctrl+Shift+W	Shift+Cmd+W
Close	Ctrl+W	Cmd+W
Save	Ctrl+S	Cmd+S
Save As...	Ctrl+Shift+S	Shift+Cmd+S
Save a Copy...	Ctrl+Alt+S	Opt+Cmd+S
Capture...	F5	F5
Batch Capture...	F6	F6
Import from Media Browser	Ctrl+Alt+I	Opt+Cmd+I
Import...	Ctrl+I	Cmd+I
Export		
Media...	Ctrl+M	Cmd+M
Get Properties for		
Selection...	Ctrl+Shift+H	Shift+Cmd+H
Exit	Ctrl+Q	

Edit.

Results	**Windows Shortcut**	**Mac OS Shortcut**
Undo	Ctrl+Z	Cmd+Z
Redo	Ctrl+Shift+Z	Shift+Cmd+Z
Cut	Ctrl+X	Cmd+X
Copy	Ctrl+C	Cmd+C
Paste	Ctrl+V	Cmd+V

Paste Insert	Ctrl+Shift+V	Shift+Cmd+V
Paste Attributes	Ctrl+Alt+V	Opt+Cmd+V
Clear	Delete	Forward Delete
Ripple Delete	Shift+Delete	Shift+Forward Delete
Duplicate	Ctrl+Shift+/	Shift+Cmd+/
Select All	Ctrl+A	Cmd+A
Deselect All	Ctrl+Shift+A	Shift+Cmd+A
Find...	Ctrl+F	Cmd+F
Edit Original	Ctrl+E	Cmd+E
Keyboard Shortcuts	Ctrl+Alt+K	Cmd+Opt+K

Clip.

Results	Windows Shortcut	Mac OS Shortcut
Make Subclip...		Cmd+U
Audio Channels...		Shift+G
Speed/Duration...	Ctrl+R	Cmd+R
Insert	,	,
Overwrite	.	.
Enable		Shift+Cmd+E
Link		Cmd+l
Group	Ctrl+G	Cmd+G
Ungroup	Ctrl+Shift+G	Shift+Cmd+G

Sequence.

Results	Windows Shortcut	Mac OS Shortcut
Render Effects in Work Area/In to Out	Enter	Return
Match Frame	F	F
Reverse Match Frame	Shift+R	Shift+R
Add Edit	Ctrl+K	Cmd+K
Add Edit to All Tracks	Ctrl+Shift+K	Shift+Cmd+K
Trim Edit	T	T
Extend Selected Edit to Playhead	E	E
Apply Video Transition	Ctrl+D	Cmd+D
Apply Audio Transition	Ctrl+Shift+D	Shift+Cmd+D
Apply Default Transitions to Selection		Shift+D
Lift	;	;
Extract	'	'
Zoom In	=	=
Zoom Out	-	-
Go to Gap		
Next in Sequence		Shift+;
Previous in Sequence		Opt+;
Snap	S	S

Marker.

Results	Windows Shortcut	Mac OS Shortcut
Mark In	I	I
Mark Out	O	O
Mark Clip	X	X
Mark Selection	/	/
Go to In	Shift+I	Shift+I
Go to Out	Shift+O	Shift+O
Clear In	Ctrl+Shift+I	Opt+I
Clear Out	Ctrl+Shift+O	Opt+O
Clear In and Out	Ctrl+Shift+X	Opt+X
Add Marker	M	M
Go to Next Marker	Shift+M	Shift+M
Go to Previous Marker	Ctrl+Shift+M	Shift+Cmd+M
Clear Current Marker	Ctrl+Alt+M	Opt+M
Clear All Markers	Ctrl+Alt+Shift+M	Opt+Cmd+M
Type Alignment		
Left	Ctrl+Shift+L	Shift+Cmd+L
Center	Ctrl+Shift+C	Shift+Cmd+C
Right	Ctrl+Shift+R	Shift+Cmd+R
Tab Stops...	Ctrl+Shift+T	Shift+Cmd+T
Templates...	Ctrl+J	Cmd+J
Select		
Next Object Above	Ctrl+Alt+]	Opt+Cmd+]

Next Object Below	Ctrl+Alt+[	Opt+Cmd+[
Arrange		
Bring to Front	Ctrl+Shift+]	Shift+Cmd+]
Bring Forward	Ctrl+]	Cmd+]
Send to Back	Ctrl+Shift+[	Shift+Cmd+[
Send Backward	Ctrl+[	Cmd+[

Window.

Workspace

Results	Windows Shortcut	Mac OS Shortcut
Reset Current Workspace...		Opt+Shift +0
Audio Clip Mixer	Shift+9	Shift+9
Audio Track Mixer	Shift+6	Shift+6
Effect Controls	Shift+5	Shift+5
Effects	Shift+7	Shift+7
Media Browser	Shift+8	Shift+8
Program Monitor	Shift+4	Shift+4
Project	Shift+1	Shift+1
Source Monitor	Shift+2	Shift+2
Timelines	Shift+3	Shift+3
Show/hide application title	Ctrl+	Cmd+

Help.

Results	Windows Shortcut	Mac OS Shortcut
Adobe Premiere Pro Help...	F1	F1
Clear Poster Frame	Cmd+Shift+P	Opt+P
Cut to Camera 1	Cmd+1	Ctrl+1
Cut to Camera 2	Cmd+2	Ctrl+2
Cut to Camera 3	Cmd+3	Ctrl+3
Cut to Camera 4	Cmd+4	Ctrl+4
Cut to Camera 5	Cmd+5	Ctrl+5
Cut to Camera 6	Cmd+6	Ctrl+6
Cut to Camera 7	Cmd+7	Ctrl+7
Cut to Camera 8	Cmd+8	Ctrl+8
Cut to Camera 9	Cmd+9	Ctrl+9
Decrease Clip Volume		[
Decrease Clip Volume Many		Shift+[
Expand All Tracks		Shift+=
Export Frame	Ctrl+Shift+E	Shift+E
Extend Next Edit To Playhead		Shift+W
Extend Previous Edit To Playhead		Shift+Q

Panels.

Audio Mixer Panel Menu

Results	Windows Shortcut	Mac OS Shortcut
Show/Hide Tracks...	Ctrl+Alt+T	Opt+Cmd+T
Loop		Cmd+L
Meter Input Only	Ctrl+Shift+I	Ctrl+Shift+I
Capture Panel		
Record Video	V	V
Record Audio	A	A
Eject	E	E
Fast Forward	F	F
Go to In point	Q	Q
Go to Out point	W	W
Record	G	G
Rewind	R	R
Step Back	Left	Left
Step Forward	Right	Right
Stop	S	S
Effect Controls Panel Menu		
Remove Selected Effect	Backspace	Delete
Effects Panel Menu		
New Custom Bin	Ctrl+/	Cmd+/

Delete Custom Item	Backspace	Delete
History Panel Menu		
Step Backward	Left	Left
Step Forward	Right	Right
Delete	Backspace	Delete
Open in Source Monitor	Shift+O	Shift+O
Parent Directory	Ctrl+Up	Cmd+Up
Select Directory List		Shift+Left
Select Media List		Shift+Right
Loop		Cmd+L
Play	Space	Space
Go to Next Edit Point	Down	Down
Go to Previous Edit Point	Up	Up
Play/Stop Toggle	Space	Space
Record On/Off Toggle	0	0
Step Back	Left	Left
Step Forward	Right	Right
Loop		Cmd+L

Tools.

Results	**Windows Shortcut**	**Mac OS Shortcut**
Selection Tool	**V**	V

Track Select Tool	A	A
Ripple Edit Tool	B	B
Rolling Edit Tool	N	N
Rate Stretch Tool	R	R
Razor Tool	C	C
Slip Tool	Y	Y
Slide Tool	U	U
Pen Tool	P	P
Hand Tool	H	H
Zoom Tool	Z	Z

Multi-camera.

Result	Windows Shortcut	Mac OS Shortcut
Go to Next Edit Point	Down	Down
Go to Next Edit Point on Any Track	Shift+Down	Shift+Down
Go to Previous Edit Point	Up	Up
Go to Previous Edit Point on Any Track	Shift+Up	Shift+Up
Go to Selected Clip End	Shift+End	Shift+End
Go to Selected Clip Start	Shift+Home	Shift+Home

Go to Sequence-Clip End	End	End
Go to Sequence-Clip Start	Home	Home
Increase Clip Volume	]	]
Increase Clip Volume Many	Shift+]	Shift+]
Maximize or Restore Active Frame	Shift+`	Shift+`
Maximize or Restore Frame Under Cursor	`	`
Minimize All Tracks	Shift+-	Shift+-
Play Around	Shift+K	Shift+K
Play In to Out	Ctrl+Shift+Space	Opt+K
Play In to Out with Preroll/Postroll	Shift+Space	Shift+Space
Play from Playhead to Out Point	Ctrl+Space	Ctrl+Space
Play-Stop Toggle	Space	SpaceRecord Voiceover
Reveal Nested Sequence	Ctrl+Shift+F	Shift+T
Ripple Trim Next Edit To Playhead	W	W

Ripple Trim Previous Edit To Playhead	Q	Q
Select Camera 1	1	1
Select Camera 2	2	2
Select Camera 3	3	3
Select Camera 4	4	4
Select Camera 5	5	5
Select Camera 6	6	6
Select Camera 7	7	7
Select Camera 8	8	8
Select Camera 9	9	9
Select Find Box	Shift+F	Shift+F
Select Clip at Playhead	D	D
Select Next Clip	Ctrl+Down	Cmd+Down
Select Next Panel	Ctrl+Shift+.	Ctrl+Shift+.
Select Previous Clip	Ctrl+Up	Cmd+Up
Select Previous Panel	Ctrl+Shift+,	Ctrl+Shift+,
Set Poster Frame	Shift+P	Cmd+P
Shuttle Left	J	J

Shuttle Right	L	L
Shuttle Slow Left	Shift+J	Shift+J
Shuttle Slow Right	Shift+L	Shift+L
Shuttle Stop	K	K
Step Back	Left	Left
Step Back Five Frames - Units	Shift+Left	Shift+Left
Step Forward	Right	Right
Step Forward Five Frames - Units	Shift+Right	Shift+Right
Toggle All Audio Targets	Ctrl+9	Cmd+9
Toggle All Source Audio	Ctrl+Alt+9	Opt+Cmd+9
Toggle All Source Video	Ctrl+Alt+0	Opt+Cmd+0
Toggle All Video Targets	Ctrl+0	Cmd+0
Toggle Audio During Scrubbing	Shift+S	Shift+S
Toggle Control Surface Clip Mixer Mode		
Toggle Full Screen	Ctrl+`	Ctrl+`
Toggle Multi-Camera View	Shift+0	Shift+0
Toggle Trim Type	Shift+T	Ctrl+T

Trim Backward	Ctrl+Left	Opt+Left
Trim Backward Many	Ctrl+Shift+Left	Opt+Shift+Left
Trim Forward	Ctrl+Right	Opt+Right
Trim Forward Many	Ctrl+Shift+Right	Opt+Shift+Right
Trim Next Edit to Playhead	Ctrl+Alt+W	Opt+W
Trim Previous Edit to Playhead	Ctrl+Alt+Q	Opt+Q

Project Panel.

Result	Windows Shortcut	Mac OS Shortcut
Workspace 1	Alt+Shift+1	Opt+Shift+1
Workspace 2	Alt+Shift+2	Opt+Shift+2
Workspace 3	Alt+Shift+3	Opt+Shift+3
Workspace 4	Alt+Shift+4	Opt+Shift+4
Workspace 5	Alt+Shift+5	Opt+Shift+5
Workspace 6	Alt+Shift+6	Opt+Shift+6
Workspace 7	Alt+Shift+7	Opt+Shift+7
Workspace 8	Alt+Shift+8	Opt+Shift+8
Workspace 9	Alt+Shift+9	Opt+Shift+9
Zoom to Sequence	\	\
Extend Selection Up	Shift+Up	Shift+Up
Move Selection Down	Down	Down
Move Selection End	End	End
Move Selection Home	Home	Home

Move Selection Left	Left	Left
Move Selection Page Down	Page Down	Page Down
Move Selection Page Up	Page Up	Page Up
Move Selection Right	Right	Right
Move Selection Up	Up	Up
Next Column Field	Tab	Tab
Next Row Field	Enter	Return
Open in Source Monitor	Shift+O	Shift+O
Previous Column Field	Shift+Tab	Shift+Tab
Previous Row Field	Shift+Enter	Shift+Return
Thumbnail Size Next	Shift+]	Shift+]
Thumbnail Size Previous	Shift+[	Shift+[
Toggle View	Shift+\	Shift+\

Timeline Panel.

Result	**Windows Shortcut**	**Mac OS Shortcut**
Add Clip Marker	Ctrl+1	
Clear Selection	Backspace	Delete

Decrea se Audio Tracks Height	Alt+-	Opt+-
Decrea se Video Tracks Height	Ctrl+-	Cmd+-
Increase Audio Tracks Height	Alt+=	Opt+=
Increase Video Tracks Height	Ctrl+=	Cmd+=
Nudge Clip Selection Left Five Frames	Alt+Shift+Left	Shift+Cmd+Left
Nudge Clip Selection Left One Frame	Alt+Left	Cmd+Left
Nudge Clip Selection Right Five Frames	Alt+Shift+Right	Shift+Cmd+Right
Nudge Clip	Alt+Right	Cmd+Right

Selection Right One Frame		
Ripple Delete	Alt+Backspace	Opt+Delete
Set Work Area Bar In Point	Alt+[	Opt+[
Set Work Area Bar Out Point	Alt+]	Opt+]
Show Next Screen	Page Down	Page Down
Show Previous Screen	Page Up	Page Up
Slide Clip Selection Left Five Frames	Alt+Shift+,	Opt+Shift+,
Slide Clip Selection Left One Frame	Alt+,	Opt+,
Slide Clip Selection	Alt+Shift+.	Opt+Shift+.

Right Five Frames		
Slide Clip Selection Right One Frame	Alt+.	Opt+.
Slip Clip Selection Left Five Frames	Ctrl+Alt+Shift+Left	Opt+Shift+Cmd+Left
Slip Clip Selection Left One Frame	Ctrl+Alt+Left	Opt+Cmd+Left
Slip Clip Selection Right Five Frames	Ctrl+Alt+Shift+Right	Opt+Shift+Cmd+Right
Slip Clip Selection Right One Frame	Ctrl+Alt+Right	Opt+Cmd+Right

Titler.

Result	Windows Shortcut	Mac OS Shortcut
Arc Tool	A	A
Bold	Ctrl+B	Cmd+B
Decrease Kerning by Five Units	Alt+Shift+Left	Opt+Shift+Left

Decrease Kerning by One Unit	Alt+Left	Opt+Left
Decrease Leading by Five Units	Alt+Shift+Down	Opt+Shift+Down
Decrease Leading by One Unit	Alt+Down	Opt+Down
Decrease Text Size by Five Points	Ctrl+Alt+Shift+Le ft	Opt+Shift+Cmd+Le ft
Decrease Text Size by One Point	Ctrl+Alt+Left	Opt+Cmd+Left
Ellipse Tool	E	E
Increase Kerning by Five Units	Alt+Shift+Right	Opt+Shift+Right
Increase Kerning by One Unit	Alt+Right	Opt+Right
Increase Leading by Five Units	Alt+Shift+Up	Opt+Shift+Up
Increase Leading by One Unit	Alt+Up	Opt+Up
Increase Text Size by Five Points	Ctrl+Alt+Shift+Ri ght	Opt+Shift+Cmd+Ri ght

Increase Text Size by One Point	Ctrl+Alt+Right	Opt+Cmd+Right
Insert Copyright Symbol	Ctrl+Alt+Shift+C	Opt+Shift+Cmd+C
Insert Registered Symbol	Ctrl+Alt+Shift+R	Opt+Shift+Cmd+R
Italic	Ctrl+I	Cmd+I
Line Tool	L	L
Nudge Selected Object Down by Five Pixels	Shift+Down	Shift+Down
Nudge Selected Object Down by One Pixel	Down	Down
Nudge Selected Object Left by Five Pixels	Shift+Left	Shift+Left
Nudge Selected Object Left by One Pixel	Left	Left
Nudge Selected	Shift+Right	Shift+Right

Object Right by Five Pixels		
Nudge Selected Object Right by One Pixel	Right	Right
Nudge Selected Object Up by Five Pixels	Shift+Up	Shift+Up
Nudge Selected Object Up by One Pixel	Up	Up
Path Type Tool		
Pen Tool	P	P
Position Objects to Bottom Title Safe Margin	Ctrl+Shift+D	Shift+Cmd+D
Position Objects to Left Title Safe Margin	Ctrl+Shift+F	Shift+Cmd+F
Position Objects to	Ctrl+Shift+O	Shift+Cmd+O

Top Title Safe Margin		
Rectangle Tool	R	R
Rotation Tool	O	O
Selection Tool	V	V
Type Tool	T	T
Underline	Ctrl+U	Cmd+U
Vertical Type Tool	C	C
Wedge Tool	W	W

Trim Monitor Panel.

Result	Windows Shortcut	Mac OS Shortcut
Focus Both Outgoing and Incoming	Alt+1	Opt+1
Focus on Incoming Side	Alt+3	Opt+3
Focus on Outgoing Side	Alt+2	Opt+2
Loop	Ctrl+L	Cmd+L
Trim Backward by	Alt+Shift+Left	Opt+Shift+Left

Large Trim Offset		
Trim Backward by One Frame	Alt+Left	Opt+Left
Trim Forward by Large Trim Offset	Alt+Shift+Right	Opt+Shift+Right
Trim Forward by One Frame	Alt+Right	Opt+Right

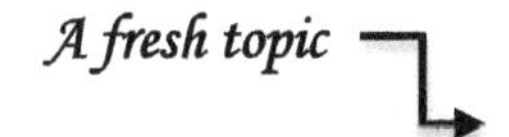

Finding Keyboard Shortcuts.

Find the keyboard shortcuts for a tool, button, or menu command by doing any of the following:

- For a tool or button, hold the pointer over the tool or button until its tool tip appears. If available, the keyboard shortcut appears in the tool tip after the tool description.
- For menu commands, look for the keyboard shortcut at the right of the command.

- For the most-used keyboard shortcuts not shown in tool tips or on menus, see the tables in this article. For a complete list of default and current shortcuts, choose Edit > Keyboard Shortcuts (Windows) or Premiere Pro > Keyboard Shortcuts (Mac OS)
- Use the search field in the Keyboard Customization dialog box to find specific commands quickly.

Customize or Load Keyboard Shortcuts.

You can set shortcuts to match shortcuts in other software you use. If other sets are available, you can choose them from the Set menu in the Keyboard Customization dialog box.

1. For customizing keyboard shortcuts, choose one of the following:
    - In Windows, choose Edit > Keyboard Shortcuts
    - In Mac OS, choose Premiere Pro > Keyboard Shortcuts
2. In the Keyboard Customization dialog box, choose an option from the menu:

    Application

    Displays commands found in the menu bar, organized by category.

    Panels

    Displays commands associated with panels and menus.

Tools

Displays a list of tool icons.

3. In the Command column, view the command for which you want to create or change a shortcut. If necessary, click the triangle next to the name of a category to reveal the commands it includes.
4. Click in the item's shortcut field to select it.
5. Type the shortcut you want to use for the item. The Keyboard Customization dialog box displays an alert if the shortcut you choose is already in use.
6. Do one of the following:
   - To erase a shortcut and return it to the command that originally had it, click Undo.
   - To jump to the command that previously had the shortcut, click Go To.
   - To simply delete the shortcut you typed, click Clear.
   - To reenter the shortcut you typed previously, click Redo.
7. Repeat the procedure to enter as many shortcuts as you want. When you're finished, click Save As, type a name for your Key Set, and click Save.

Note:

The operating system reserves some commands. You cannot reassign those commands to Premiere Pro. Also, you cannot assign the plus (+) and minus (-) keys on the numeric keypad because they are necessary for entering relative timecode values. You can assign the minus (–) key on the main keyboard, however.

Copy keyboard shortcuts from one computer to another.

Sync keyboard shortcuts using Creative Cloud

Premiere Pro CC lets you quickly and easily sync keyboard shortcuts between computers using the Sync Settings feature. Using Sync Settings, you can upload the customized keyboard shortcuts from your computer to Creative Cloud. Then, you can sync the keyboard shortcuts from Creative Cloud to any other computer.

Note:

Keyboard shortcuts are synchronized for the same platform only, and not between Windows and Mac OS platforms. That is, keyboard shortcuts created for Windows only sync with a Windows computer. Mac OS keyboard shortcuts only sync with a Mac OS computer.

Manually copy keyboard shortcuts

You can copy your customized keyboard shortcuts from one computer to another computer, or to another location on your computer.

1. Locate the keyboard shortcuts (.kys) file that you want to copy to another computer.

   The location of the customized keyboard shortcuts file depends on whether you've signed in to Creative Cloud Sync Settings in Premiere Pro CC or not.

Signed into Creative Cloud Sync Settings

- Win: Users\[user name]\Documents\Adobe\Premiere Pro\[version]\Profile-CreativeCloud-\Win\
- Mac: Users/[user name]/Documents/Adobe/Premiere Pro/[version]/Profile-CreativeCloud-/Mac/

Signed out of Creative Cloud Sync Settings

- Win: Users\[user name]\Documents\Adobe\Premiere Pro\[version]\Profile-username\Win\
- Mac: Users/[user name]/Documents/Adobe/Premiere Pro/[version]/Profile-username/Mac/

Note:

[version] can be 7.0 or 8.0

2. Copy the keyboard shortcuts (.kys) file and paste into the required file location.

   To copy the keyboard shortcuts file to a location on a different computer, copy the .kys file to a removable drive, like a USB thumb drive. Then, copy the .kys file from the removable drive to the appropriate location in the new computer.

Assign multiple keyboard shortcuts to a command.

You can assign multiple keyboard shortcuts for a single command.

The Keyboard Shortcuts dialog displays the keyboard shortcut as an editable button, which lets you change, add multiple shortcuts, or delete shortcuts.

Add more shortcuts

To add more shortcuts to a command, click to the right of an existing shortcut. If there is no existing shortcut, click anywhere in the Shortcut column. A new shortcut button is created in which you can type the shortcut.

Edit a shortcut

To edit a shortcut, click the shortcut text in the Shortcuts column. The text is replaced with an editable button. Type the shortcut that you want to use. If the shortcut you type is already in use, an alert appears.

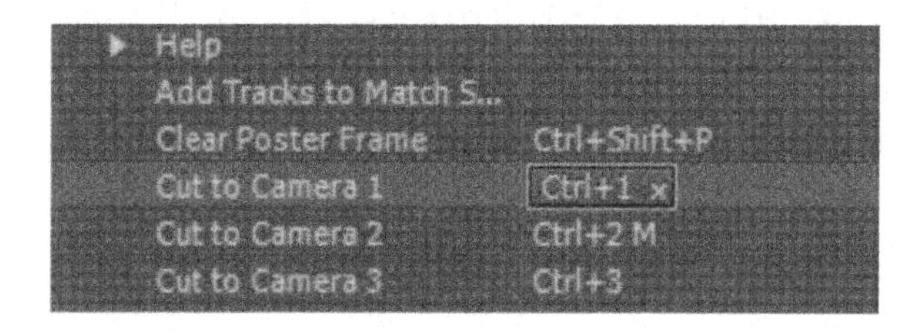

Delete a shortcut

To delete a shortcut, click '**x**' in the editable shortcut button.

Remove Shortcuts

1. Do one of the following:
    - In Windows, choose Edit > Keyboard Shortcuts
    - In Mac OS, choose Premiere Pro > Keyboard Shortcuts
2. Do one of the following:
    - To remove a shortcut, select the shortcut you want to remove, and click Clear.
    - To remove a set of shortcuts, choose the key set from the Set menu and click Delete. When prompted in the warning dialog box, click Delete to confirm your choice.

Applies to: *Adobe Premiere Pro CC.*

CHAPTER 9.

Tips, Tricks, Techniques, and Keyboard Shortcuts for use in Dreamweaver.

About the application: This is a web-design application developed by Adobe Systems Incorporated for creation, publication, and management of websites.

A fresh topic

The Dreamweaver Workspace.

Learn about the Dreamweaver workspace, the different views and workspaces that are available to you, and all the different panels and toolbars in Dreamweaver.

Onboarding Dreamweaver

After installing Dreamweaver, when you first launch the application, a QuickStart menu appears on the screen asking you three questions that help you personalize your Dreamweaver workspace according to your needs.

Based on your responses to these questions, Dreamweaver opens in a Developer workspace (a minimal code-focused layout), or a Standard workspace (a split layout with visual tools and an in-app preview as you code).

After you choose a workspace, you choose a color theme that you are comfortable with. You can then get started.

Note:

You can change these workspace preferences any time later using the Edit > Preferences dialog.

The Start experience

The Start screen in Dreamweaver gives you quick access to your recent files, CC library files, and starter templates.

Depending on your subscription status, the Start workspace may also display content tailored for your requirements.

Dreamweaver displays the Start screen at launch or when no documents are open.

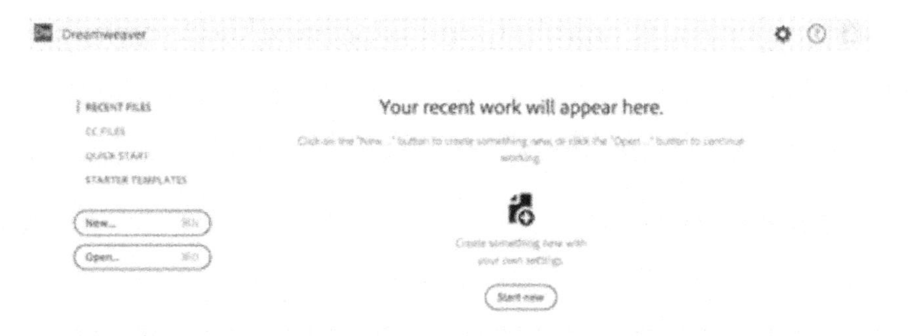

The Start workspace in Dreamweaver

Options in the Dreamweaver Start experience

Recent Files

Open a recently-opened file from a list of recent files.

CC Files

Open recently opened files present in your CC Libraries cloud.

Quick Start

Get started creating documents in Dreamweaver by clicking any of the file types displayed.

Starter Templates

Open one of the starter templates packaged with Dreamweaver.

Note:

This Start screen is enabled, and is opened by default.

If you don't need this Start screen, uncheck Show Start Screen in the Preferences > General dialog box.

Workspace overview

The Dreamweaver workspace lets you view documents and object properties. The workspace also places many of the most common operations in toolbars so that you can quickly make changes to your documents.

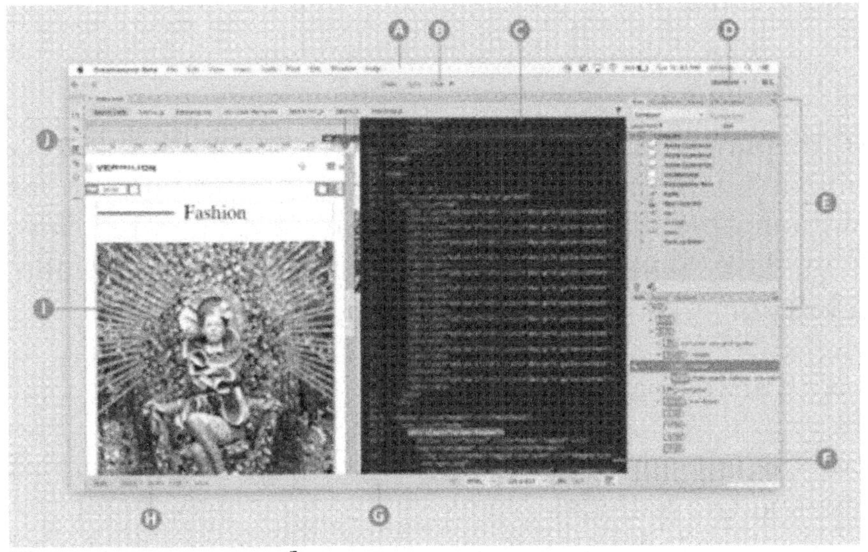

Dreamweaver workspace

A. Application bar **B.** Document toolbar **C.** Document window **D.** Workspace switcher **E.** Panels **F.** Code View **G.** Status bar **H.** Tag selector **I.** Live View **J.** Toolbar

Workspace Elements Overview.

The workspace includes the following elements:

- The Application bar

Is across the top of the application window and contains a workspace switcher, menus (Windows only), and other application controls.

- The Document toolbar

Contains buttons that provide options for different views of the Document window (such as Design view, Live view, and Code view).

- The Standard toolbar

To display the Standard toolbar, select Window > Toolbars > Standard. The toolbar contains buttons for common operations from the File and Edit menus: New, Open, Save, Save All, Print Code, Cut, Copy, Paste, Undo, and Redo.

- The toolbar

Is on the left side of the application window and contains view-specific buttons.

- The Document window

Displays the current document as you create and edit it.

- The Property inspector

Lets you view and change a variety of properties for the selected object or text. Each object has different properties.

- The Tag selector

Located in the Status bar at the bottom of the Document window. Shows the hierarchy of tags surrounding the current selection. Click any tag in the hierarchy to select that tag and all its contents.

- Panels

Help you monitor and modify your work. Examples include the Insert panel, the CSS Designer panel, and the Files panel. To expand a panel, double-click its tab.

The Extract panel

Lets you upload and view your PSD files on Creative Cloud. Using this panel, you can extract CSS, text, images, fonts, colors, gradients, and measurements from your PSD comps into your document.

The Insert panel

Contains buttons for inserting various types of objects, such as images, tables, and media elements, into a document. Each object is a piece of HTML code that lets you set various attributes as you insert it. For example, you can insert a table by clicking the Table button in the Insert panel. If you prefer, you can insert objects using the Insert menu instead of the Insert panel.

The Files panel

Lets you manage your files and folders, whether they are part of a Dreamweaver site or on a remote server. The Files panel also lets you access all the files on your local disk.

The Snippets panel

Lets you save and reuse your code snippets across different web pages, different sites, and different installations of Dreamweaver (using sync settings).

The CSS Designer panel

is a CSS Property Inspector that lets you "visually"create CSS styles, files, and set properties, along with media queries.

Note:

Dreamweaver provides many other panels, inspectors, and windows. To open the panels, inspectors, and windows, use the Window menu.

Document Window Overview.

The Document window shows the current document. To switch views of the document, use the view options on the Document toolbar.

You can also switch views, using the View options in the View menu.

Live view:

displays a realistic representation of what your document will look like in a browser, and lets you interact with the document exactly as you would in a browser. You can edit HTML elements directly in Live View and instantly preview your changes in the same view as well. For more information on editing in Live View, see Edit HTML elments in Live View.

Design view:

is a design environment for visual page layout, visual editing, and rapid application development. In this view, Dreamweaver displays a fully editable, visual representation of the document, similar to what you would see when viewing the page in a browser.

Code view:

is a hand-coding environment for writing and editing HTML, JavaScript, and any other kind of code.

Code – Code:

is a split version of Code view that lets you scroll to work on different sections of the document at the same time.

Code – Live:

Lets you see both Code view and Live view for the same document in a single window.

Code – Design:

Lets you see both Code view and Design view for the same document in a single window.

Live Code:

Displays the actual code that a browser uses to execute the page, and can dynamically change as you interact with the page in Live view.

When a Document window is maximized (the default), tabs appear at the top of the Document window showing the filenames of all open documents. Dreamweaver displays an asterisk after the filename if you have made changes that you haven't saved yet.

Dreamweaver also displays the Related Files toolbar below the document's tab (or below the document's title bar if you are viewing documents in separate windows). Related documents are documents associated with the current file, such as CSS files or JavaScript files. To open one of these related files in the Document window, click its filename in the Related Files toolbar.

Switch between views

Use the Document toolbar to toggle between different views quickly.

You can also switch between views using the following options in the View menu:

- Code view only: Select Code
- Split view: Select Split and select any of the split options
- View mode: Toggle between Live and Design views
- Switch Views: To switch views from one view to another.

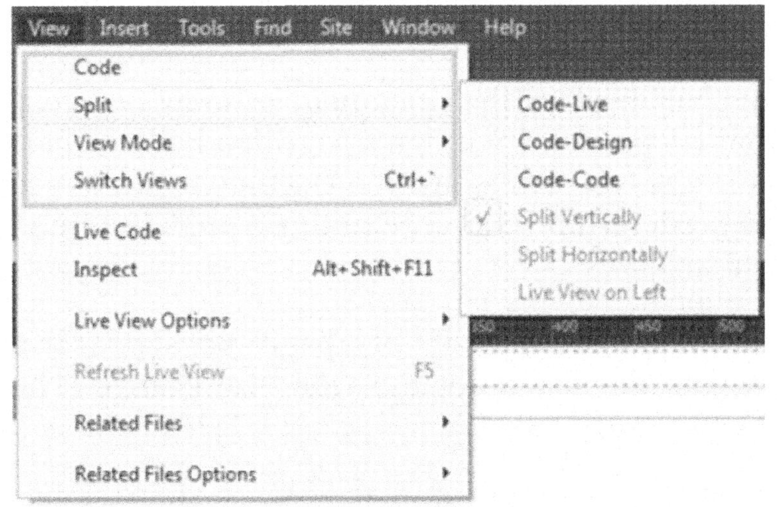

Switching views using the View menu options

Cascade, tile, or rearrange document windows

If you have many documents open at once, you can cascade or tile them.

To cascade document windows: select Window > Arrange > Cascade.

To tile document windows:

- (Windows) Select Window > Arrange > Tile Horizontally or Tile Vertically.
- (Macintosh) Select Window > Arrange >Tile.

When you open more than one file, the Document windows are tabbed. To rearrange the order of tabbed Document windows, drag a window's tab to a new location in the group.

Resize document window

The Status bar displays the Document window's current dimensions (in pixels). To design a page that looks its best at a specific size, you can adjust the Document window to any of the predetermined sizes, edit those predetermined sizes, or create sizes.

When you change the view size of a page in design or live view only the dimensions of the view size change. The document size is unaltered.

In addition to predetermined and custom sizes, Dreamweaver also lists sizes specified in a media query. When you select a size corresponding to a media query, Dreamweaver uses the media query to display the page. You can also change the page orientation to preview the page for mobile devices where the page layout changes based on how the device is held.

To resize the document window, select one of the sizes from the Window Size pop-up menu at the bottom of the Document window.

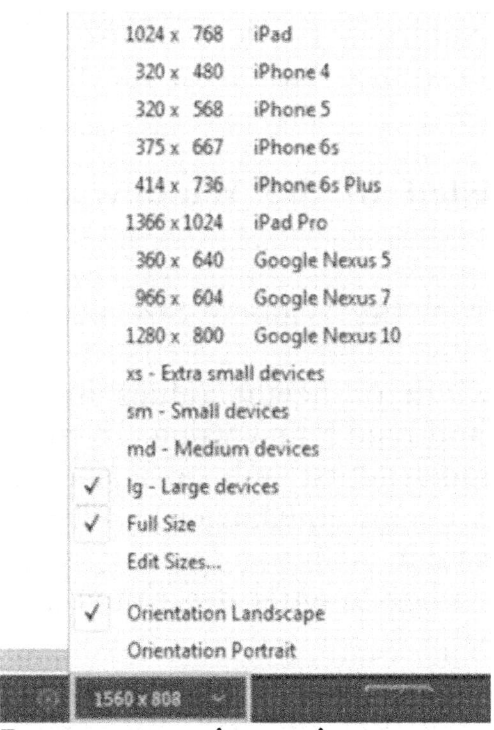

Document resize options

The window size shown reflects the inside dimensions of the browser window, without borders; the monitor size or mobile device is listed to the right.

Note:

For less precise resizing, use your operating system's standard methods of resizing windows, such as dragging the lower-right corner of a window.

Note:

(Windows only) Documents within the Document window are maximized by default, and you can't resize a document when it's maximized. To de-maximize the document, click the de-maximize button in the upper right corner of the document.

Change the values listed in the Window Size pop-up menu

1. Select Edit Sizes from the Window Size pop-up menu.
2. Click any of the width or height values in the Window Sizes list, and type a new value. To make the Document window adjust only to a specific width (leaving the height unchanged), select a height value and delete it.
3. Click the Description box to enter descriptive text about a specific size.

Add a new size to the Window Size pop-up menu

1. Select Edit Sizes from the Window Size pop-up menu.

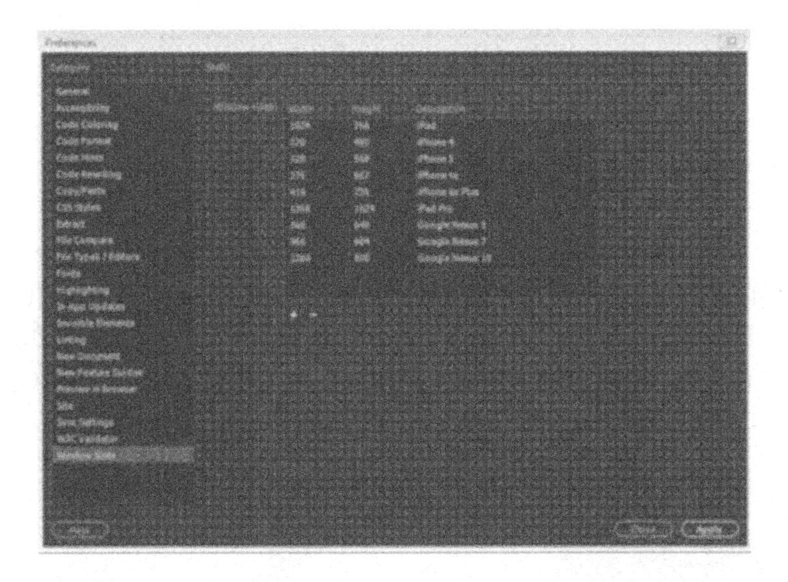

Adding window sizes to the Window size pop-up menu

2. Click the blank space below the last value in the Width column.
3. Enter values for Width and Height.

   To set the Width or Height only, simply leave one field empty.

4. Click the Description field to enter descriptive text about the size you added.

   For example, you might type SVGA or average PC next to the entry for an 800 x 600 pixel monitor, and 17-in. Macnext to the entry for an 832 x 624 pixel monitor. Most monitors can be adjusted to a variety of pixel dimensions.

5. Click Apply and close the dialog box.

Your new window size is now available to use in the Window Size pop-up menu.

Document Toolbar Overview.

The Document toolbar contains buttons that let you toggle between different views of your document quickly. The toolbar also contains some common commands and options related to viewing the document and transferring it between the local and remote sites.

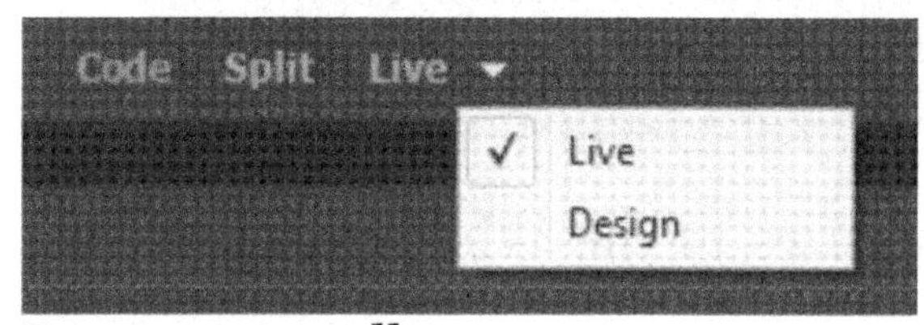

Document toolbar

The following options appear in the Document toolbar:

Code View

Displays only the Code view in the Document window.

Split View

Splits the Document window between the Code and the Live/Design views. Design view option is not available for fluid grid documents.

Live View

Is an interactive preview that accurately renders HTML5 projects and updates in real time to show your changes as you make them. You can also edit HTML elements in Live View. The drop-down list adjacent to the Live options lets you switch between Live and Design views. This drop-down list is not available in fluid grid documents.

Design View

Displays a representation of the document showing how the user views it in a web browser.

Standard Toolbar Overview.

The Standard toolbar

To display the Standard toolbar, select Window > Toolbars > Standard. The toolbar contains buttons for common operations from the File and Edit menus: New, Open, Save, Save All, Print Code, Cut, Copy, Paste, Undo, and Redo.

Browser Navigation Toolbar Overview.

The Browser Navigation toolbar becomes active in Live view, and shows you the address of the page you're looking at in the Document window. Live view acts like a regular browser, so even if you browse to a site outside of your local site (for example, http://www.adobe.com), Dreamweaver will load the page in the Document window.

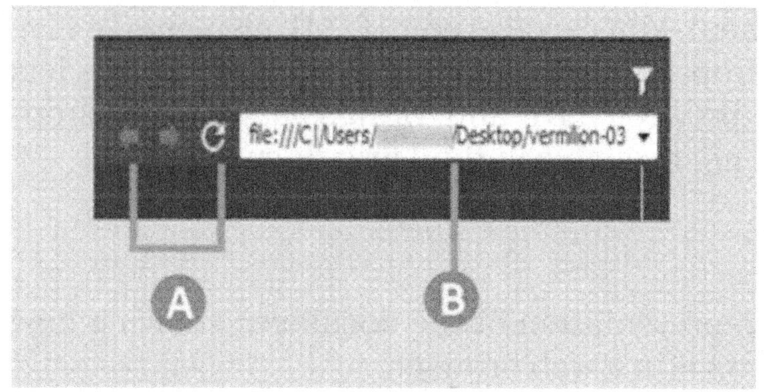

Browser navigation toolbar

A. Browser controls **B.** Address box

By default, links are not active in Live view. Having links non-active lets you select or click link text in the Document window without being taken to another page. To test links in Live view, you can enable one-time clicking or continuous clicking by selecting View > Live View Options > Follow Links (Ctrl+Click Link) or Follow Links Continuously.

Toolbar Overview.

The toolbar appears vertically on the left side of the Document window, and is visible in all views - Code, Live, and Design. The buttons on the toolbar are view-specific and appear only if they are applicable to the view you are working in. For example, if you are working in Live view, then Code view-specific options such as Format Source Code are not visible.

Customize toolbar

You can choose to customize this toolbar according to your needs by adding menu options, or removing unwanted menu options from the toolbar.

To customize the toolbar, do the following:

1. Click in the Toolbar, to open the Customize Toolbar dialog box.

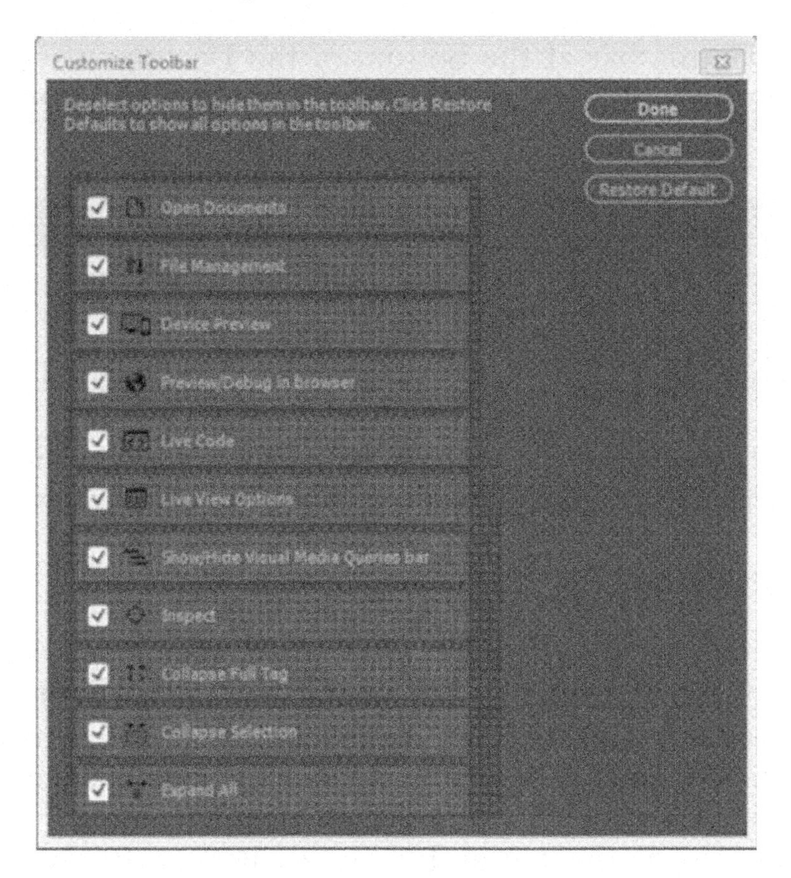

Customize toolbars

2. Select or deselect the menu options that you want available in the toolbar and click Done to save your toolbar.

To restore the default toolbar buttons, click Restore Default in the Customize Toolbar dialog box.

Status bar overview

The Status bar at the bottom of the Document window provides additional information about the document you are creating.

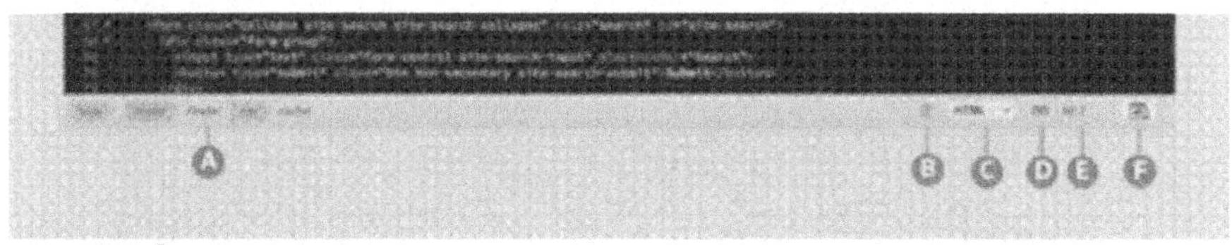

Status bar

A. Tag selector **B.** Output panel **C.** Code coloring **D.** Insert and Overwrite toggle **E.** Line and column number

Tag selector

Shows the hierarchy of tags surrounding the current selection. Click any tag in the hierarchy to select that tag and all its contents. Click <body> to select the entire body of the document. To set the class or ID attributes for a tag in the tag selector, right-click (Windows) or Control-click (Macintosh) the tag and select a class or ID from the context menu.

Output panel

Click this icon to display the Output panel that shows coding errors in your document.

Code coloring

(Only available in Code view)

Select any of the coding languages from this pop-up menu to change the coloring of the code to display according to the programming language.

Insert and Overwrite toggle

(Only available in Code view)

Allows you to toggle between Insert and Overwrite modes while working in Code view.

Line and column number

(Only available in Code view.)

Displays the line number and column number where the cursor is located.

Property Inspector Overview.

The Property Inspector (Window > Properties) lets you examine and edit the most common properties for the currently selected page element, such as text or an inserted object.

The contents of the Property Inspector vary depending on the element selected. For example, if you select an image on your page, the Property Inspector changes to show properties for the image (such as the file path to the image, the width and height of the image, the border around the image, if any, and so on).

Property Inspector

The Property Inspector is at the lower edge of the workspace by default, but you can undock it and make it a floating panel in the workspace.

Note:

Use the Tag inspector to view and edit every attribute associated with a given tag's properties.

To access help for a particular Property inspector, click the help button in the upper right corner of the Property inspector, or select Help from a Property inspector's Options menu.

View and change properties of a page element

1. Select the page element in the Document window.

   You may have to expand the Property inspector to view all the properties of the selected element.

2. Change any of the properties in the Property inspector.

   Note:

   For information on specific properties, select an element in the Document window, and then click the Help icon in the upper-right corner of the Property inspector.

3. If your changes are not immediately applied in the Document window, apply the changes in one of these ways:
    - Click outside the property-editing text fields.
    - Press Enter (Windows) or Return (Macintosh).
    - Press Tab to switch to another property.

Context Menus

Context menus provide convenient access to the most useful commands and properties related to the object or window you're working with. Context menus list only those commands that are applicable to the current selection.

To open a context menu, right-click (Windows) or Ctrl+Click (Mac) a section of code in Code view, or an object in Live or Design Views.

Rearranging Panels in Dreamweaver.

You can customize the placement and appearance of all the Dreamweaver panels according to your requirements.

Dock and undock panels

- To dock a panel, drag it by its tab into the dock, at the top, bottom, or in between other panels.
- To dock a panel group, drag it by its title bar (the solid empty bar above the tabs) into the dock.

- To remove a panel or panel group, drag it out of the dock by its tab or title bar. You can drag it into another dock or make it free-floating.

Move panels

As you move panels, you see blue highlighted drop zones, areas where you can move the panel. For example, you can move a panel up or down in a dock by dragging it to the narrow blue drop zone above or below another panel. If you drag to an area that is not a drop zone, the panel floats freely in the workspace.

- To move a panel, drag it by its tab.
- To move a panel group, drag the title bar.

Note:

Press Ctrl (Windows) or Command (Mac OS) while moving a panel to prevent it from docking. Press Esc while moving the panel to cancel the operation.

Add and remove panels

If you remove all panels from a dock, the dock disappears. You can create a dock by moving panels to the right edge of the workspace until a drop zone appears.

- To remove a panel, right-click (Windows) or Control-click (Mac) its tab and then select Close, or deselect it from the Window menu.
- To add a panel, select it from the Window menu and dock it wherever you want.

Manipulate panel groups

- To move a panel into a group, drag the panel's tab to the highlighted drop zone in the group.
- To rearrange panels in a group, drag a panel's tab to a new location in the group.
- To remove a panel from a group so that it floats freely, drag the panel by its tab outside the group.
- To move a group, drag the title bar (the area above the tabs).

Stack floating panels

When you drag a panel out of its dock but not into a drop zone, the panel floats freely. The floating panel allows you to position it anywhere in the workspace. You can stack floating panels or panel groups so that they move as a unit when you drag the topmost title bar.

- To stack floating panels, drag a panel by its tab to the drop zone at the bottom of another panel.
- To change the stacking order, drag a panel up or down by its tab.
- To remove a panel or panel group from the stack, so that it floats by itself, drag it out by its tab or title bar.

Resize panels

- To minimize or maximize a panel, panel group, or stack of panels, double-click a tab. You can also double-click the tab area (the empty space next to the tabs).
- To resize a panel, drag any side of the panel.

Collapse and expand panel icons

You can collapse panels to icons to reduce clutter on the workspace. In some cases, panels are collapsed to icons in the default workspace.

- To collapse or expand all panel icons in a column, click the double arrow at the top of the dock.
- To expand a single panel icon, click it.
- To resize panel icons so that you see only the icons (and not the labels), adjust the width of the dock until the text disappears. To display the icon text again, make the dock wider.
- To collapse an expanded panel back to its icon, click its tab, its icon, or the double arrow in the panel's title bar.

Create Custom Workspaces.

You can customize your workspace by adding or removing panels according to your requirements. You can then save these changes to your workspace by saving it to access later from the Workspace Switcher in the Document toolbar.

By saving the current size and position of panels as a named workspace, you can restore that workspace even if you move or close a panel.

To save a custom workspace:

1. Choose Window > Workspace Layout > New Workspace.
2. Type a name for the workspace.

The workspace is saved and is visible in the Workspace switcher in the Document toolbar.

To delete a custom workspace:

Select Manage Workspaces from the workspace switcher in the Application bar to open the Manage Workspaces dialog box. Select the workspace, and then click Delete.

Display or switch workspaces

Select a workspace from the workspace switcher in the Document toolbar.

Customizing Dreamweaver in multi-user systems.

You can customize Dreamweaver to suit your needs even in a multiuser operating system such as Windows XP or Mac OS X.

Dreamweaver prevents any user's customized configuration from affecting any other user's customized configuration. To accomplish this goal, the first time you run Dreamweaver in one of the multiuser operating systems that it recognizes, the application creates copies of a variety of configuration files. These user configuration files are stored in a folder that belongs to you.

If you reinstall or upgrade Dreamweaver, Dreamweaver automatically makes backup copies of existing user configuration files, so if you customized those files by hand, you still have access to the changes you made.

Display Tabbed Documents (On Mac only).

You can view multiple documents in a single Document window by using tabs to identify each document. You can also display them as part of a floating workspace, in which each document appears in its own window.

Open a tabbed document in a separate window

Control-click the tab and select Move To New Window from the context menu.

Change the default tabbed document setting

1. Select Dreamweaver > Preferences, and then select the General category.
2. Select or deselect Open Documents in Tabs, and click OK.

Dreamweaver does not alter the display of documents that are currently open when you change preferences. Documents opened after you select a new preference, however, display according to the preference you selected.

The Welcome screen appears when you start Dreamweaver and anytime that you do not have any documents open. You can choose to hide the Welcome screen, and then later display it again. When the Welcome screen is hidden and no documents are open, the Document window is blank.

Common Dreamweaver panels

You work with a number of panels in Dreamweaver. Some of the commonly used panels are described here.

Insert panel overview

The Insert panel (Window > Insert) contains buttons for creating and inserting objects such as tables, images, and links. The buttons are organized into several categories, which you can switch by selecting the desired category from the drop-down list at the top.

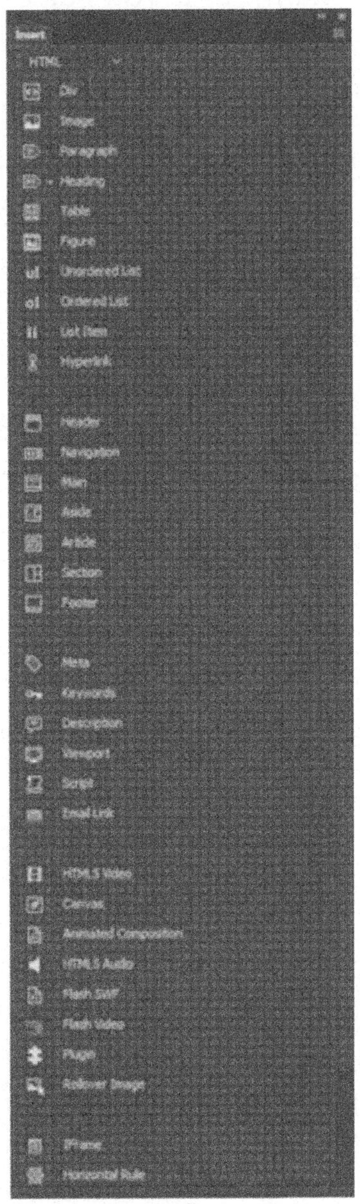

Insert panel

Some categories have buttons with pop-up menus. When you select an option from a pop-up menu, it becomes the default action for the button. For example, if you select **Line Break** from the Character button's pop-up menu, the next time you click the Character button, Dreamweaver inserts a line break. Anytime you select a new option from the pop-up menu, the default action for the button changes.

The Insert panel is organized in the following categories:

HTML

Lets you create and insert the most commonly used HTML elements such as div tags and objects, such as images, and tables.

Form

Contains buttons for creating forms and inserting form elements, such as search, month, and password.

Templates

Lets you save the document as a template and mark specific regions as editable, optional, repeating, or editable optional regions.

Bootstrap components

Contains Bootstrap components to provide navigation, containers, dropdowns, and more that you can use in responsive projects.

jQuery Mobile

Contains buttons for building sites that use jQuery Mobile.

jQuery UI

Lets you insert jQuery UI elements such as accordion, sliders, and buttons.

Favorites

Lets you group and organize the Insert panel buttons you use the most in one common place.

Note:

If you are working with certain types of files, such as XML, JavaScript, Java, and CSS, the Insert panel and the Design view option are dimmed because you cannot insert items into these code files.

Insert object

To insert an object using the Insert panel:

1. Select the appropriate category from the Category pop-up menu of the Insert panel.
2. Do one of the following:
    - Click an object button or drag the button's icon into the Document window (into Design, Live, or Code View).
    - Click the arrow on a button, then select an option from the menu.

      Depending on the object, a corresponding object-insertion dialog box may appear, prompting you to browse to a file or specify parameters for an object. Or, Dreamweaver may insert code into the document, or open a tag editor or a panel for you to specify information before the code is inserted.

For some objects, no dialog box appears if you insert the object in Design view, but a tag editor appears if you insert the object in Code view. For a few objects, inserting the object in Design view causes Dreamweaver to switch to Code view before inserting the object.

Edit Insert panel preferences

1. Select Edit > Preferences (Windows) or Dreamweaver > Preferences (Macintosh).
2. In the General category of the Preferences dialog box, deselect Show Dialog When Inserting Objects to suppress dialog boxes when you insert objects such as images, tables, scripts, and head elements or by holding down the Control key (Windows) or the Option key (Macintosh) while creating the object.

Note:

When you insert an object with this option off, the object is given default attribute values. Use the Property inspector to change object properties after inserting the object.

Add, delete, or manage items in the Favorites category of the Insert panel

1. Select any category in the Insert panel.

2. Right-click (Windows) or Control-click (Macintosh) in the area where the buttons appear, and then select Customize Favorites.
3. In the Cutomize Favorite Objects dialog box, make changes as necessary, and click OK.

   To add an object, select an object in the Available Objects pane on the left, and then click the arrow between the two panes or double-click the object in the Available Objects pane.

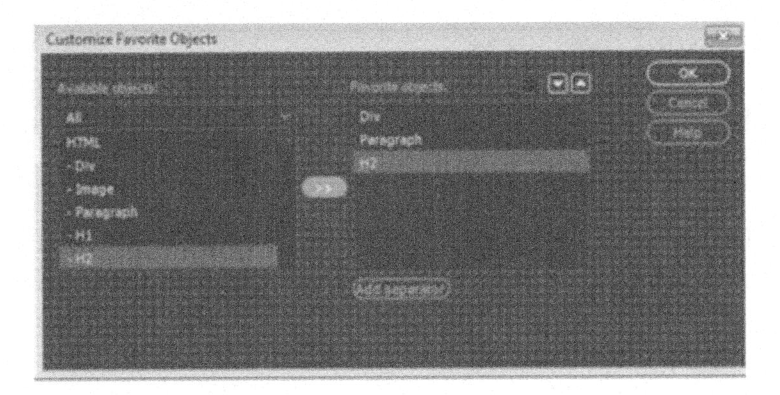

Customize favorites in the Insert panel

Note:

You can add one object at a time. You cannot select a category name, such as Common, to add an entire category to your favorites list.

- To delete an object or separator, select an object in the Favorite Objects pane on the right, and then click the Remove Selected Object in Favorite Objects List button above the pane.

- To move an object, select an object in the Favorite Objects pane on the right, and then click the Up or Down arrow button above the pane.
- To add a separator below an object, select an object in the Favorite Objects pane on the right, and then click the Add Separator button below the pane.

4. If you're not in the Favorites category of the Insert panel, select that category to see your changes.

Files panel overview

Use the Files panel to view and manage the files on your Dreamweaver site.

You can use the Files panel to view files and folders, check whether they are associated with a Dreamweaver site or not, and perform standard file maintenance operations, such as opening and moving files.

The Files panel also helps you manage and transfer files to and from a remote server.

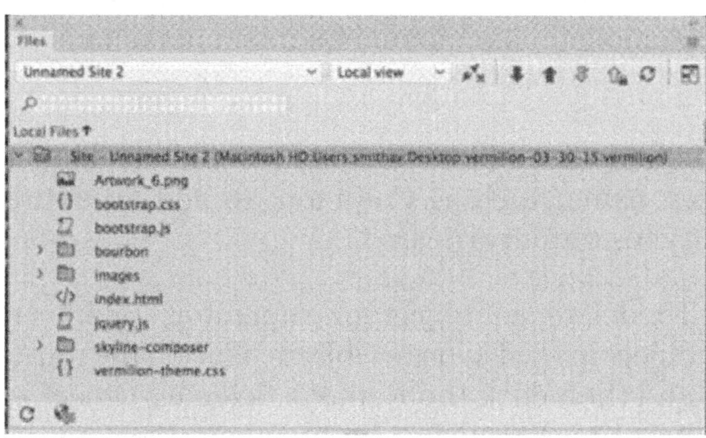

The Files panel

CSS Designer.

CSS Designer panel (Windows > CSS Designer) is a CSS Property Inspector that lets you 'visually' create CSS styles, files, and set properties, along with media queries.

You can use Ctrl/Cmd+ Z to undo or Ctrl/Cmd + Y to redo all actions you perform in CSS Designer. The changes are automatically reflected in Live View and the relevant CSS file is also refreshed. To let you know that the related file has changed, the affected file's tab is highlighted for a while (around 8 seconds).

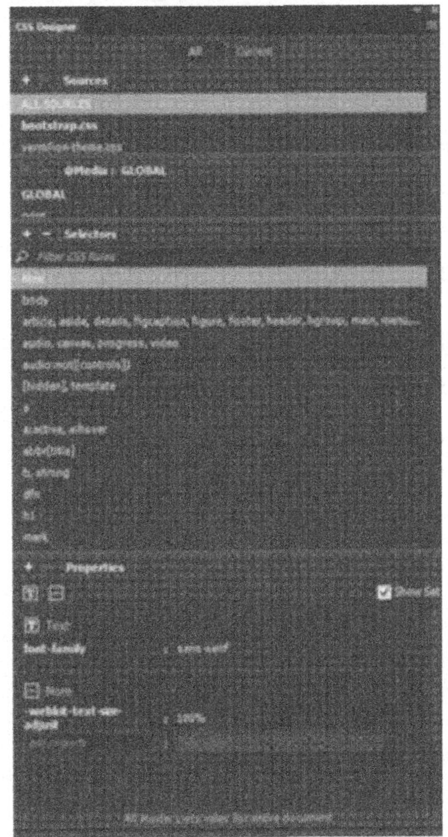

CSS Designer panel

The CSS Designer panel consists of the following panes and options:

All Lists all the CSS, media queries, and selectors associated with the current document. You can filter for the required CSS rules and modify the properties. You can also use this mode to begin creating selectors or media queries.

This mode is not sensitive to the selection. This means, when you select an element on the page, the associated selector, media query, or CSS are not highlighted in CSS Designer.

Current Lists all the computed styles for any selected element in Design or Live view of the current document. When you use this mode for a CSS file in Code view, all the properties for the selector in focus are displayed.

This mode is context-sensitive. Use this option to edit the properties of selectors associated with selected elements in the document.

Sources Lists all the CSS style sheets associated with the document. Using this pane, you can create and attach a CSS to the document, or define styles within the document.

@Media Lists all the media queries in the source selected in the Sources pane. If you do not select a specific CSS, this pane displays all the media queries associated with the document.

Selectors Lists all the selectors in the source selected in the Sources pane. If you also select a media query, this pane narrows down the list of selectors for that media query. If no CSS or media queries are selected, this pane displays all the selectors in the document.

When you select Global in the @Media pane, all the selectors that are not included in a media query of the selected source are displayed.

Properties Displays properties that you can set for the specified selector.

If you collapse or expand the panes in CSS Designer, the sizes of the panes are remembered within a session. Sources and Media panes stick to the customized sizes until you change their sizes again.

Note: When you select a page element, the most specific Selector is selected in the Selectors pane. To view the properties of a specific Selector, click the name of that Selector in the pane.

To view all the selectors, you can choose All Sources in the Sources pane. To view selectors that do not belong to any media query in the selected source, click Global in the @Media pane.

Visual Guides Overview

Dreamweaver provides several kinds of visual guides to help you design documents and predict approximately how they appear in browsers. You can do any of the following:

- Instantly snap the Document window to a desired window size to see how the elements fit on the page.
- Use a tracing image as the page background to help you duplicate a design created in an illustration or image-editing application such as Adobe® Photoshop® or Adobe® Fireworks®.
- Use rulers and guides to provide a visual cue for precise positioning and resizing of page elements.
- Use the grid for precise positioning and resizing of absolutely positioned elements (AP elements).

  Grid marks on the page help you align AP elements, and when snapping is enabled, AP elements automatically snap to the closest grid point when moved or resized. (Other objects, such as images and paragraphs, do not snap to the grid.) Snapping works regardless of whether the grid is visible.

Zoom in and out of a page.

Dreamweaver lets you increase the magnification (zoom in) in the Document window so that you can check the pixel accuracy of graphics, select small items more easily, design pages with small text, design large pages, and so on.

To zoom in or out of a page, select View > Design View Options > Magnification, and choose any of the magnification options available.

You can choose from a variety of magnification options. You can also choose to:

- Fit Selection - Select an object or text, and choose this option to fill the Document window with the selection.
- Fit All - Fill the Document window with an entire page
- Fit Width - Fill the Document window with the entire width of a page

Note:

You can also zoom in without using the Zoom tool by pressing Control+= (Windows) or Command+= (Macintosh). You can also zoom out without using the Zoom tool by pressing Control+- (Windows) or Command+- (Macintosh).

Set General preferences for Dreamweaver

1. Select Edit > Preferences (Windows) or Dreamweaver > Preferences (Macintosh).
2. Set any of the following options:

   Open Documents In Tabs Opens all documents in a single window with tabs that let you switch between documents (Mac only).

   Show Start Screen Displays the Dreamweaver Welcome screen when you start Dreamweaver or when you don't have any documents open.

   Reopen Documents on Startup Opens any documents that were open when you closed Dreamweaver. If this option is not selected,

Dreamweaver displays the Welcome screen or a blank screen when you start (depending on your Show Welcome Screen setting).

Warn When Opening Read-Only Files Alerts you when you open a read-only (locked) file. Choose to unlock/check out the file, view the file, or cancel.

Enable Related Files Lets you see which files are connected to the current document (for example, CSS or JavaScript files). Dreamweaver displays a button for each related file at the top of the document, and opens the file if you click the button.

Discover Dynamically-Related Files Lets you select whether Dynamically-Related Files appear in the Related Files toolbar automatically, or after manual interaction. You can also choose to disable the discovery of Dynamically-Related Files.

Update Links When Moving Files Determines what happens when you move, rename, or delete a document within your site. Set this preference to always update links automatically, never update links, or prompt you to perform an update.

Show Dialog When Inserting Objects Determines whether Dreamweaver prompts you to enter additional information when inserting images, tables, Shockwave movies, and certain other objects by using the Insert panel or the Insert menu. If this option is off, the dialog box does not appear and you must use the Property inspector to specify the source file for images, the number of rows in a table, and so on. For roll over images and Fireworks HTML, a dialog box always appears when you insert the object, regardless of this option setting. (To temporarily override this setting, Control-click (Windows) or Command-click (Macintosh) when creating and inserting objects.)

Enable Double-Byte Inline Input Lets you enter double-byte text directly into the Document window if you are using a development environment or language kit that facilitates double-byte text (such as Japanese characters). When this option is deselected, a text input window appears for entering and converting double-byte text; the text appears in the Document window after it is accepted.

Switch To Plain Paragraph After Heading Specifies that pressing Enter (Windows) or Return (Macintosh) at the end of a heading paragraph in Design or Live view creates a new paragraph tagged with a p tag. (A heading paragraph is one that's tagged with a heading tag such as h1 or h2.) When the option is disabled, pressing Enter or Return at the end of a heading paragraph creates a new paragraph tagged with the same heading tag (allowing you to type multiple headings in a row and then go back and fill in details).

Allow Multiple Consecutive Spaces Specifies that typing two or more spaces in Design or Live view creates nonbreaking spaces that appear in a browser as multiple spaces. (For example, you can type two spaces between sentences, as you would on a typewriter.) This option is designed mostly for people who are used to typing in word processors. When the option is disabled, multiple spaces are treated as a single space (because browsers treat multiple spaces as single spaces).

Use <strong> and <em> in Place of <b> and <i> Specifies that Dreamweaver applies the strong tag whenever you perform an action that would normally apply the b tag, and applies the em tag whenever you perform an action that would normally apply the i tag. Such actions include clicking the Bold or Italic buttons in the text Property inspector in HTML mode and choosing Format > Style > Bold or Format > Style > Italic. To use the b and i tags in your documents, deselect this option.

Note: The World Wide Web Consortium discourages use of the b and i tags; the strong and em tags provide more semantic information than the b and i tags do.

Warn when placing editable regions within <p> or <h1> - <h6> tags Specifies whether a warning message is displayed whenever you save a Dreamweaver template that has an editable region within a paragraph or heading tag. The message tells you that users will not be able to create more paragraphs in the region. It is enabled by default.

Limit undo actions to the active document Limits the maximum number of undo operations.

Maximum Number of History Steps Determines the number of steps that the History panel retains and shows. (The default value should be sufficient for most users.) If you exceed the given number of steps in the History panel, the oldest steps are discarded.

Spelling Dictionary Lists the available spelling dictionaries. If a dictionary contains multiple dialects or spelling conventions (such as American English and British English), the dialects are listed separately in the Dictionary pop-up menu.

Set Fonts preferences for documents in Dreamweaver.

A document's encoding determines how the document appears in a browser. Dreamweaver font preferences let you view a given encoding in the font and size you prefer. The fonts you select in the Fonts Preferences dialog, however, only affect the way fonts appear in Dreamweaver; they do not affect the way the document appears in a visitor's browser. To change the way fonts appear in a browser, you need to change the text by using the Property inspector or by applying a CSS rule.

1. Select Edit > Preferences (Windows) or Dreamweaver > Preferences (Mac).
2. Select Fonts from the Category list on the left.

3. Select an encoding type (such as Western European or Japanese) from the Font Settings list.

   Note:

   To display an Asian language, you must be using an operating system that supports double-byte fonts.

4. Select a font and size to use for each category of the selected encoding.

   Note:

   To appear in the font pop-up menus, a font must be installed on your computer. For example, to see Japanese text you must have a Japanese font installed.

   Proportional Font

   The font that Dreamweaver uses to display normal text (for example, text in paragraphs, headings, and tables). The default depends on your system's installed fonts. For most U.S. systems, the default is Times New Roman 12 pt. (Medium) on Windows and Times 12 pt. on Mac OS.

   Fixed Font

   The font Dreamweaver uses to display text within pre, code, and tt tags. The default depends on your system's installed fonts. For most U.S. systems, the default is Courier New 10 pt. (Small) on Windows and Monaco 12 pt. on Mac OS.

Code View

The font used for all text that appears in the Code view and Code inspector. The default depends on your system's installed fonts.

Customize Dreamweaver Highlighting Colors.

Use the Highlighting preferences to customize the colors that identify template regions, library items, third-party tags, layout elements, and code in Dreamweaver.

1. Select Edit > Preferences and select the Highlighting category.
2. Beside the object you want to change the highlighting color for, click the color box, and then use the color picker to select a new color, or enter a hexadecimal value.
3. To activate or deactivate highlighting for a particular option, select or deselect the Show option.

-by Adobe Systems Inc. experts.

End of Topic.

A fresh topic

What to know about Dreamweaver Keyboard Shortcuts.

Note:

The user interface has been simplified in Dreamweaver CC and later. As a result, you may not find some of the options described in this article in Dreamweaver CC and later.

Customize Keyboard Shortcuts.

Use the Keyboard Shortcut Editor to create your own shortcut keys, including keyboard shortcuts for code snippets. You can also remove shortcuts, edit existing shortcuts, and select a predetermined set of shortcuts in the Keyboard Shortcut Editor.

Create a keyboard shortcut.

Create your own shortcut keys, edit existing shortcuts, or select a predetermined set of shortcuts.

1. Select Edit > Keyboard Shortcuts (Windows) or Dreamweaver > Keyboard Shortcuts (Macintosh).
2. Set any of the following options and click OK:

   Current Set

   Allows you to choose a set of predetermined shortcuts included with Dreamweaver, or any custom set you've defined. The predetermined sets are listed at the top of the menu. For example, if you are familiar with the shortcuts found in HomeSite or BBEdit, you can use those shortcuts by choosing the corresponding predetermined set.

Commands

Allows you to select a category of commands to edit. For example, you can edit menu commands, such as the Open command, or code editing commands, such as Balance Braces.

Note:

To add or edit a keyboard shortcut for a code snippet, select Snippet from the Commands pop-up menu.

The command list

Displays the commands associated with the category you selected from the Commands pop-up menu, along with the assigned shortcuts. The Menu Commands category displays this list as a tree view that replicates the structure of the menus. The other categories list the commands by name (such as Quit Application), in a flat list.

Shortcuts

Displays all shortcuts assigned to the selected command.

Add Item (+)

Adds a new shortcut to the current command. Click this button to add a new blank line to the Shortcuts. Enter a new key combination and click Change to add a new keyboard shortcut for this command. You can assign two different keyboard shortcuts for each command; if there are already two shortcuts assigned to a command, the Add Item button does nothing.

Remove Item (-)

Removes the selected shortcut from the list of shortcuts.

Press Key

Displays the key combination you enter when you're adding or changing a shortcut.

Change

Adds the key combination shown in the Press Key to the list of shortcuts, or changes the selected shortcut to the specified key combination.

Duplicate Set

Duplicates the current set. Give the new set a name; the default name is the current set's name with the word *copy* appended.

Rename Set

Renames the current set.

Export as HTML File

Saves the current set in an HTML table format for easy viewing and printing. You can open the HTML file in your browser and print the shortcuts for easy reference.

Delete Set

Deletes a set. (You cannot delete the active set.)

Remove a shortcut from a command

1. Select Edit > Keyboard Shortcuts (Windows) or Dreamweaver > Keyboard Shortcuts (Macintosh).
2. From the Commands pop-up menu, select a command category.
3. In the Commands list, select a command and then select a shortcut.
4. Click the Remove Item (-) button.

Add a shortcut to a command

1. Select Edit > Keyboard Shortcuts (Windows) or Dreamweaver > Keyboard Shortcuts (Macintosh).
2. From the Commands pop-up menu, select a command category.
3. In the Commands list, select a command.

   Note:

   To add a keyboard shortcut for a code snippet, select Snippet from the Commands pop-up menu.

   The shortcuts assigned to the command appear in the Shortcuts.

4. Prepare to add a shortcut by doing one of the following:
   - If there are fewer than two shortcuts already assigned to the command, click the Add Item (+) button. A new blank line appears in the

Shortcuts and the insertion point moves to the Press Key.
    - If there are already two shortcuts assigned to the command, select one of them (that one will be replaced by the new shortcut). Then click in the Press Key.
5. Press a key combination. The key combination appears in the Press Key.

   Note:

   If there is a problem with the key combination (for example, if the key combination is already assigned to another command), an explanatory message appears just below the Shortcuts and you may be unable to add or edit the shortcut.

6. Click Change. The new key combination is assigned to the command.

Edit an existing shortcut

1. Select Edit > Keyboard Shortcuts (Windows) or Dreamweaver > Keyboard Shortcuts (Macintosh).
2. From the Commands pop-up menu, select a command category.
3. In the Commands list, select a command and then select a shortcut to change.
4. Click in the Press Key and enter a new key combination.
5. Click the Change button to change the shortcut.

   Note:

If there is a problem with the key combination (for example, if the key combination is already assigned to another command), an explanatory message appears just below the Shortcuts field and you may be unable to add or edit the shortcut.

About keyboard shortcuts and non-U.S. keyboards

The default Dreamweaver keyboard shortcuts work primarily on U.S.-standardized keyboards. Keyboards from other countries (including those produced in the United Kingdom), may not provide the functionality necessary for utilizing these shortcuts. If your keyboard does not support certain Dreamweaver-enabled shortcuts, Dreamweaver disables their functionality.

To customize keyboard shortcuts that work with non-U.S.-standardized keyboards, see "Changing keyboard shortcut mappings" in *Extending Dreamweaver*.

End of Topic.

A fresh topic

Adobe Dreamweaver CC Keyboard Shortcuts.

Keyboard shortcuts make it easier and faster to use common functions in Dreamweaver. Use the quick reference guide below to become more familiar with the Dreamweaver workspace.

Use the following list of keyboard shortcuts to enhance your productivity in Adobe Dreamweaver.

Shortcuts for Document Editing.

Function	Mac OS Shortcut	Windows OS Shortcut
Preview in Primary Browser	Opt + F12	Alt + F12
Preview in Secondary Browser	Cmd + F12, Shift + F12	Ctrl + F12, Shift + F12
Preview in Secondary Browser	Shift + F12	Shift + F12
Extract	Cmd + K	Ctrl + K
Element Quick View	Cmd + /	Ctrl + /
Switch Views	Ctrl + '	Ctrl + '
Toggle Live View	Opt + F11	Alt + F11
Inspect	Opt + Shift + F11	Alt + Shift + F11
Zoom In	Cmd + =	Ctrl + =
Zoom Out	Cmd + -	Ctrl + -
Go to Source Code	Cmd + Opt + '	Ctrl + Alt + '

Shortcuts for Code Options.

Function	Mac OS Shortcut	Windows OS Shortcut
Check page - Links	Shift + F8	Shift + F8
Paste Special	Cmd + Shift + V	Ctrl + Shift + V
Select Parent Tag	Cmd + [	Ctrl + [
Select Child	Cmd +]	Ctrl +]
Go to Line	Cmd + G	Ctrl + G
Show code hints	Ctrl + space	Ctrl + space
Refresh code hints	Ctrl + .	Ctrl + .
Balance braces	Cmd + '	Ctrl + '
Indent Code	Cmd + Shift + >	Ctrl + Shift + >
Outdent Code	Cmd + Shift + <	Ctrl + Shift + <
Refresh Design View	F5	F5
Insert - Image	Cmd + Opt + I	Ctrl + Alt + I
Insert - Table	Cmd + Opt + T	Ctrl + Alt + T
Insert - Named Anchor	Cmd + Opt + A	Ctrl + Alt + A
Insert - Line Break	Shift + Return	Shift + Return
Insert - Non-breaking Space	Cmd + Shift + Space	Ctrl + Shift + Space

Shortcuts for Text Options.

Function	Mac OS Shortcut	Windows OS Shortcut
Format - Bold	Cmd + B	Ctrl + B
Format - Italic	Cmd + I	Ctrl + I

Format - Paragraph	Cmd + Shift + P	Ctrl + Shift + P
Format - Heading 1	Cmd + 1	Ctrl + 1
Format - Heading 2	Cmd + 2	Ctrl + 2
Format - Heading 3	Cmd + 3	Ctrl + 3
Align - Left	Cmd + Shift + Opt + L	Ctrl + Shift + Alt + L
Align - Center	Cmd + Shift + Opt + C	Ctrl + Shift + Alt + C
Align - Right	Cmd + Shift + Opt + R	Ctrl + Shift + Alt + R
Align - Justify	Cmd + Shift + Opt + J	Ctrl + Shift + Alt + J
Check Spelling	Shift + F7	Shift + F7

Shortcuts for CSS Designer.

Function	Mac OS Shortcut	Windows OS Shortcut
Add selector (if control is in the selector section)	Ctrl + Alt + [Shift =]	Ctrl + Alt + [Shift =]
Add selector (if control is anywhere in the app)	Ctrl + Alt + S	Ctrl + Alt + S
Add property (if control is	Ctrl + Alt + [Shift =]	Ctrl + Alt + [Shift =]

anywhere in the app)		
Add property (if control is in the property section)	Ctrl + Alt + P	Ctrl + Alt + P
Delete Selector	Select + Delete	Select + Delete
Jump between sections (in properties panel)	Ctrl + Alt + (PgUp/PgDn)	Ctrl + Alt + (PgUp/PgDn)

Shortcuts for Live View Property Inspector

Function	Mac OS Shortcut	Windows OS Shortcut
"Hide Live View Displays" toggle option	Ctrl + Cmd + H	Ctrl + Alt + H
Display HUD	Cmd + E	Ctrl + E
Commit the current text editing session	Cmd + Return	Ctrl + Enter
Enter text editing session on a selected text element	Return	Enter

Applies to: *Dreamweaver CC.*

CHAPTER 10.

Keyboard Shortcuts for use in InDesign.

About the application: It is a desktop publishing application developed by Adobe Systems. It helps in the production of flyers, brochures, posters, magazines, newspapers, and books.

A fresh topic ↳

Default keyboard shortcuts in Adobe InDesign.

Adobe InDesign provides shortcuts to help you quickly work in documents without using the mouse. Many keyboard shortcuts appear next to the command names in menus. You can use the default InDesign shortcut set, the QuarkXPress 4.0 or Adobe PageMaker 7.0 shortcut set, or a shortcut set that you create. You can share shortcut sets with others using InDesign on the same platform.

InDesign provides shortcuts to help you quickly work in documents without using the mouse. Many keyboard shortcuts appear next to the command names in menus.

You can use the default InDesign shortcut set or a shortcut set that you create. You can share shortcut sets with others using InDesign on the same platform.

Keys for Tools .

Note:

This table isn't a complete list of keyboard shortcuts. It lists only those shortcuts that aren't displayed in menu commands or tool tips.

Note:

Choose Window > Utilities > Tool Hints, and then select a tool to view its shortcuts and modifier keys.

Use the following list of keyboard shortcuts to enhance your productivity in Adobe InDesign.

Tool	Windows Shortcut	Mac OS Shortcut
Selection tool	V, Esc	V, Esc
Direct Selection tool	A	A
Toggle Selection and Direct Selection tool	Ctrl+Tab	Command+Control+Tab
Page tool	Shift+P	Shift+P
Gap tool	U	U

Pen tool	P	P
Add Anchor Point tool	=	=
Add Anchor Point tool	=	= (on the numeric pad)
Delete Anchor Point tool	-	-
Delete Anchor Point tool		-
Convert Direction Point tool	Shift+C	Shift+C
Type tool	T	T
Type On A Path tool	Shift+T	Shift+T
Pencil tool (Note tool)	N	N
Line tool	\	\
Rectangle Frame tool	F	F
Rectangle tool	M	M
Ellipse tool	L	L
Rotate tool	R	R
Scale tool	S	S
Shear tool	O	O
Free Transform tool	E	E
Eyedropper tool	I	I

Measure tool	K	K
Gradient tool	G	G
Scissors tool	C	C
Hand tool	H	H
Temporarily selects Hand tool	Spacebar (Layout mode), Alt (Text mode), or Alt+Spacebar (both)	Spacebar (Layout mode), Option (Text mode), or Option+Spacebar (both)
Zoom tool	Z	Z
Temporarily selects Zoom In tool	Ctrl+Spacebar	Command+Spacebar
Toggle Fill and Stroke	X	X
Swap Fill and Stroke	Shift+X	Shift+X
Toggle between Formatting Affects Container and Formatting Affects Text	J	J
Apply Color	, [comma]	, [comma]
Apply Gradient	. [period]	. [period]

Apply No Color	/	/
Switch between Normal View and Preview Mode	W	W
Frame Grid tool (horizontal)	Y	Y
Frame Grid tool (vertical)	Q	Q
Gradient Feather tool	Shift+G	Shift+G

Keys for Selecting and Moving Objects.

This table lists only keyboard shortcuts that aren't displayed in menu commands or tool tips.

Result	Windows Shortcut	Mac OS Shortcut
Temporarily select Selection or Direct Selection tool (last used)	Any tool (except selection tools)+Ctrl	Any tool (except selection tools)+ Command

Temporarily select Group Selection tool	Direct Selection tool+Alt; or Pen, Add Anchor Point, or Delete Anchor Point tool+Alt+Ctrl	Direct Selection tool+Option; or Pen, Add Anchor Point, or Delete Anchor Point tool+Option+Command
Select container of selected content	Esc or double-click	Esc or double-click
Select content of selected container	Shift+Esc or double-click	Shift+Esc or double-click
Add to or subtract from a selection of multiple objects	Selection, Direct Selection, or Group Selection tool+Shift–click (to deselect, click center point)	Selection, Direct Selection, or Group Selection tool+Shift–click (to deselect, click center point)
Duplicate selection	Selection, Direct Selection, or Group Selection tool+Alt–drag*	Selection, Direct Selection, or Group Selection tool+ Option–drag*
Duplicate and offset selection	Alt+Left Arrow, Right Arrow, Up Arrow, or	Option+Left Arrow, Right Arrow, Up Arrow, or Down Arrow key

	Down Arrow key	
Duplicate and offset selection by 10 times**	Alt+Shift+Left Arrow, Right Arrow, Up Arrow, Down Arrow key	Option+Shift+Left Arrow, Right Arrow, Up Arrow, Down Arrow key
Move selection**	Left Arrow, Right Arrow, Up Arrow, Down Arrow key	Left Arrow, Right Arrow, Up Arrow, Down Arrow key
Move selection by 10th**	Ctrl+Shift+Left Arrow, Right Arrow, Up Arrow, Down arrow key	Command+Shift+Left Arrow, Right Arrow, Up Arrow, Down arrow key
Move selection by 10 times**	Shift+Left Arrow, Right Arrow, Up Arrow, Down Arrow key	Shift+Left Arrow, Right Arrow, Up Arrow, Down Arrow key
Select master page item from document page	Selection or Direct Selection tool+Ctrl+Shift –click	Selection or Direct Selection tool+ Command+Shift–click
Select next object behind or in front	Selection tool+Ctrl–click, or Selection tool+Alt+Ctrl–click	Selection tool+Command–click or Selection tool+Option+ Command–click

Select next or previous frame in story	Alt+Ctrl+Page Down/ Alt+Ctrl+Page Up	Option+Command+Page Down/ Option+Command+Page Up
Select first or last frame in story	Shift+Alt+Ctrl +Page Down/ Shift+Alt+Ctrl +Page Up	Shift+Option+Command+Page Down/ Shift+Option+Command+Page Up
*Press Shift to constrain movement to 45° angles. **Amount is set in Edit > Preferences > Units & Increments (Windows) or InDesign > Preferences > Units & Increments (Mac OS).		

Keys for Transforming Objects.

This table lists only keyboard shortcuts that aren't displayed in menu commands or tool tips.

Result	**Windows Shortcut**	**Mac OS Shortcut**
Duplicate and transform selection	Transformation tool+Alt–drag*	Transformation tool+Option–drag*
Display Transform tool dialog box	Select object+double-click Scale tool, Rotate tool, or Shear tool in Toolbox	Select object+double-click Scale tool, Rotate tool, or Shear tool in Toolbox

Decrease scale by 1%	Ctrl+,	Command+,
Decrease scale by 5%	Ctrl+Alt+,	Command+Option+,
Increase scale by 1%	Ctrl+.	Command+.
Increase scale by 5%	Ctrl+Alt+.	Command+Option+.
Resize frame and content	Selection tool+Ctrl–drag	Selection tool+Command–drag
Resize frame and content proportionately	Selection tool+Shift+Ctrl–drag	Selection tool+Shift+Command–drag
Constrain proportion	Ellipse tool, Polygon tool, or Rectangle tool+Shift–drag	Ellipse tool, Polygon tool, or Rectangle tool+Shift–drag
Switch image from High Quality Display to Fast Display	Ctrl+Alt+Shift+Z	Command+Option+Shift+Z
*After you select a transformation tool, hold down the mouse button, and then hold down Alt (Windows) or Option (Mac OS) and drag. Press Shift to constrain movement to 45° angles.		

Keys for Editing Paths and Frames.

This table lists only keyboard shortcuts that aren't displayed in menu commands or tool tips.

Result	Windows Shortcut	Mac OS Shortcut
Temporarily select Convert Direction Point tool	Direct Selection tool+Alt+Ctrl, or Pen tool+Alt	Direct Selection tool+Option+ Command, or Pen tool+Option
Temporarily switch between Add Anchor Point and Delete Anchor Point tool	Alt	Option
Temporarily select Add Anchor Point tool	Scissors tool+Alt	Scissors tool+Option
Keep Pen tool selected when pointer is over path or anchor point	Pen tool+Shift	Pen tool+Shift
Move anchor point and handles while drawing	Pen tool+spacebar	Pen tool+spacebar
Display the Stroke panel	F10	Command+F10

Keys for Tables.

This table lists only keyboard shortcuts that aren't displayed in menu commands or tool tips.

Result	Windows Shortcut	Mac OS Shortcut
Insert or delete rows or columns while dragging	Begin dragging row or column border, and then hold down Alt as you drag	Begin dragging row or column border, and then hold down Option as you drag
Resize rows or columns without changing the size of the table	Shift–drag interior row or column border	Shift–drag interior row or column border
Resize rows or columns proportionally	Shift–drag right or bottom table border	Shift–drag right or bottom table border
Move to next/previous cell	Tab/Shift+Tab	Tab/Shift+Tab
Move to first/last cell in column	Alt+Page Up/ Alt+Page Down	Option+Page Up/ Option+Page Down
Move to first/last cell in row	Alt+Home/ Alt+End	Option+Home/ Option+End
Move to first/last row in frame	Page Up/Page Down	Page Up/Page Down
Move up/down one cell	Up Arrow/Down Arrow	Up Arrow/Down Arrow
Move left/right one cell	Left Arrow/Right Arrow	Left Arrow/Right Arrow

Select cell above/below the current cell	Shift+Up Arrow/ Shift+Down Arrow	Shift+Up Arrow/ Shift+Down Arrow
Select cell to the right/left of the current cell	Shift+Right Arrow/ Shift+Left Arrow	Shift+Right Arrow/ Shift+Left Arrow
Start row on next column	Enter (numeric keypad)	Enter (numeric keypad)
Start row on next frame	Shift+Enter (numeric keypad)	Shift+Enter (numeric keypad)
Toggle between text selection and cell selection	Esc	Esc

Keys for Finding and Changing Text.

This table lists only keyboard shortcuts that aren't displayed in menu commands or tool tips.

Result	**Windows Shortcut**	**Mac OS Shortcut**
Insert selected text into Find What box	Ctrl+F1	Command+F1
Insert selected text into Find What box and finds next	Shift+F1	Shift+F1

Find next occurrence of Find What text	Shift+F2 or Alt+Ctrl+F	Shift+F2 or Option+Command+F
Insert selected text into Change To box	Ctrl+F2	Command+F2
Replace selection with Change To text	Ctrl+F3	Command+F3

Keys for Working with Type.

This table lists only keyboard shortcuts that aren't displayed in menu commands or tool tips.

Result	**Windows Shortcut**	**Mac OS Shortcut**
Bold (only for fonts with bold face)	Shift+Ctrl+B	Shift+Command+B
Italic (only for fonts with italic face)	Shift+Ctrl+I	Shift+Command+I
Normal	Shift+Ctrl+Y	Shift+Command+Y
Underline	Shift+Ctrl+U	Shift+Command+U
Strikethrough	Shift+Ctrl+/	Control+Shift+Command+/
All caps (on/off)	Shift+Ctrl+K	Shift+Command+K

Asian language hyphenation	Shift+Ctrl+K	Shift+Command+K
Small caps (on/off)	Shift+Ctrl+H	Shift+Command+H
Tate-chu-yoko setting	Shift+Ctrl+H	Shift+Command+H
Superscript	Shift+Ctrl+(+) [plus sign]	Shift+Command+(+) [plus sign]
Subscript	Shift+Alt+Ctrl+(+) [plus sign]	Shift+Option+Command+(+) [plus sign]
Reset horizontal or vertical scale to 100%	Shift+Ctrl+X or Shift+Alt+Ctrl+X	Shift+Command+X or Shift+Option+Command+X
Basic letter group setting or detail setting	Shift+Ctrl+X or Shift+Alt+Ctrl+X	Shift+Command+X or Shift+Option+Command+X
Align left, right, or center	Shift+Ctrl+L, R, or C	Shift+Command+L, R, or C
Justify all lines	Shift+Ctrl+F (all lines) or J (all but last line)	Shift+Command+F (all lines) or J (all but last line)

Align both ends or equal spacing	Shift+Ctrl+F (align both end) or J (equal spacing)	Shift+Command+F (align both ends) or J (equal spacing)
Increase or decrease point size*	Shift+Ctrl+> or <	Shift+Command+> or <
Increase or decrease point size by five times*	Shift+Ctrl+Alt+ > or <	Shift+Command+ Option+> or <
Increase or decrease leading (horizontal text)*	Alt+Up Arrow/ Alt+Down Arrow	Option+Up Arrow/ Option+Down Arrow
Increase or decrease leading (vertical text)*	Alt+Right Arrow/ Alt+Left Arrow	Option+Right Arrow/ Option+Left Arrow
Increase or decrease leading by five times (horizontal text)*	Alt+Ctrl+Up Arrow/ Alt+Ctrl+Down Arrow	Option+Command+Up Arrow/ Option+Command+Down Arrow

Increase or decrease leading by five times (vertical text)*	Alt+Ctrl+Right Arrow/ Alt+Ctrl+Left Arrow	Option+Command+Right Arrow/ Option+Command+Left Arrow
Auto leading	Shift+Alt+Ctrl+A	Shift+Option+Command+A
Align to grid (on/off)	Shift+Alt+Ctrl+G	Shift+Option+Command+G
Auto-hyphenate (on/off)	Shift+Alt+Ctrl+H	Shift+Option+Command+H
Increase or decrease kerning and tracking (horizontal text)	Alt+Left Arrow/Alt+Right Arrow	Option+Left Arrow/ Option+Right Arrow
Increase or decrease kerning and tracking (vertical text)	Alt+Up Arrow/ Alt+Down Arrow	Option+Up Arrow/ Option+Down Arrow
Increase or	Alt+Ctrl+Left Arrow/	Option+Command+Left Arrow/

decrease kerning and tracking by five times (horizontal text)	Alt+Ctrl+Right Arrow	Option+Command+Right Arrow
Increase or decrease kerning and tracking by five times (vertical text)	Alt+Ctrl+Up Arrow/ Alt+Ctrl+Down Arrow	Option+Command+Up Arrow/ Option+Command+Down Arrow
Increase kerning between words*	Alt+Ctrl+\	Option+Command+\
Decrease kerning between words*	Alt+Ctrl+Backspace	Option+Command+Delete
Clear all manual kerning and reset tracking to 0	Alt+Ctrl+Q	Option+Command+Q

Increase or decrease baseline shift** (horizontal text)	Shift+Alt+Up Arrow/ Shift+Alt+Down Arrow	Shift+Option+Up Arrow/ hift+Option+Down Arrow
Increase or decrease baseline shift** (vertical text)	Shift+Alt+Right Arrow/ Shift+Alt+Left Arrow	Shift+Option+Right Arrow/ Shift+Option+Left Arrow
Increase or decrease baseline shift by five times (horizontal text)	Shift+Alt+Ctrl+ Up Arrow/ Shift+Alt+Ctrl+ Down Arrow	Shift+Option+Command+Up Arrow/ Shift+Option+Command+Down Arrow
Increase or decrease baseline shift by five times (vertical text)	Shift+Alt+Ctrl+ Right Arrow/ Shift+Alt+Ctrl+ Left Arrow	Shift+Option+Command+Right Arrow/ hift+Option+Command +Left Arrow
Automatically flow story	Shift–click loaded text icon	Shift–click loaded text icon

Semi-automatically flow story	Alt–click loaded text icon	Option–click loaded text icon
Recompose all stories	Alt+Ctrl+/	Option+Command+/
Insert current page number	Alt+Ctrl+N	Option+Command+N
*Press Shift to increase or decrease kerning between words by five times. **Amount is set in Edit > Preferences > Units & Increments (Windows) or InDesign > Preferences > Units & Increments (Mac OS).		

Keys for Navigating Through and Selecting Text.

This table lists only shortcuts that aren't displayed in menu commands or tool tips.

Result	Windows Shortcut	Mac OS Shortcut
Move to right or left one character	Right Arrow/ Left Arrow	Right Arrow/ Left Arrow

Move up or down one line	Up Arrow/ Down Arrow	Up Arrow/ Down Arrow
Move to right or left one word	Ctrl+Right Arrow/ Ctrl+Left Arrow	Command+Right Arrow/ Command+Left Arrow
Move to start or end of line	Home/End	Home/End
Move to previous or next paragraph	Ctrl+Up Arrow/ Ctrl+Down Arrow	Command+Up Arrow/ Command+Down Arrow
Move to start or end of story	Ctrl+Home/ Ctrl+End	Command+Home/ Command+End
Select one word	Double-click word	Double-click word
Select one character right or left	Shift+Right Arrow/ Shift+Left Arrow	Shift+Right Arrow/ Shift+Left Arrow
Select one line above or below	Shift+Up Arrow/ Shift+Down Arrow	Shift+Up Arrow/ Shift+Down Arrow
Select start or end of line	Shift+Home/ Shift+End	Shift+Home/ Shift+End
Select one paragraph	Triple-click or quadruple-click paragraph, depending on Text Preferences setting	Triple-click or quadruple-click paragraph, depending on Text Preferences setting

Select one paragraph before or after	Shift+Ctrl+Up Arrow/ Shift+Ctrl+Down Arrow	Shift+Command+Up Arrow/ Shift+Command+Down Arrow
Select current line	Shift+Ctrl+\	Shift+Command+\
Select characters from insertion point	Shift–click	Shift–click
Select start or end of story	Shift+Ctrl+Home/ Shift+Ctrl+End	Shift+Command+Home/ Shift+Command+End
Select all in story	Ctrl+A	Command+A
Select first/last frame	Shift+Alt+Ctrl+ Page Up/ Shift+Alt+Ctrl+ Page Down	Shift+Option+ Command+Page Up/ Shift+Option+ Command+Page Down
Select previous/next frame	Alt+Ctrl+Page Up/ Alt+Ctrl+Page Down	Option+Command+Page Up/ Option+Command+Page Down
Delete word in front of insertion point (Story Editor)	Ctrl+Backspace or Delete	Command+Delete or Del (numeric keypad)

Update missing font list	Ctrl+Alt+Shift+/	Command+Option+Shift+/

Keys for viewing documents and document workspaces.

This table lists only shortcuts that aren't displayed in menu commands or tool tips.

Result	Windows Shortcut	Mac OS Shortcut
Temporarily select Hand tool	Spacebar (with no text insertion point), Alt-drag (with text insertion point), or Alt+spacebar (in both text and non-text modes)	Spacebar (with no text insertion point), Option–drag (with text insertion point), or Option+spacebar (in both text and nontext modes)
Temporarily select Zoom In tool	Ctrl+spacebar	Command+spacebar
Temporarily select Zoom Out tool	Alt+Ctrl+spacebar or Alt+Zoom In tool	Option+Command+spacebar or Option+Zoom In tool

Zoom to 50%, 200%, or 400%	Ctrl+5, 2, or 4	Command+5, 2, or 4
Redraw screen	Shift+F5	Shift+F5
Open new default document	Ctrl+Alt+N	Command+Option+N
Switch between current and previous zoom levels	Alt+Ctrl+2	Option+Command+2
Switch to next/previous document window	Ctrl+~ [tilde]/ Shift+Ctrl+F6 or Ctrl+Shift+~ [tilde]	Command+F6 or Command+~ [tilde]/ Command+Shift+~ [tilde]
Scroll up/down one screen	Page Up/Page Down	Page Up/Page Down
Go back/forward to last-viewed page	Ctrl+Page Up/ Ctrl+Page Down	Command+Page Up/ Command+Page Down
Go to previous/next spread	Alt+Page Up/ Alt+Page Down	Option+Page Up/ Option+Page Down
Fit spread in window	Double-click Hand tool	Double-click Hand tool

Activate the Go To command	Ctrl+J	Command+J
Fit selection in window	Ctrl+Alt+(+) [plus sign]	Command+Option+(+) [plus sign]
Display the entire object	Ctrl+Alt+(+) [plus sign]	Command+Option+(+) [plus sign]
Go to master page while \ panel is closed	Ctrl+J, type prefix of master, press Enter	Command+J, type prefix of master, press Return
Cycle through units of measurement	Shift+Alt+Ctrl+U	Shift+Option+Command+U
Snap guide to ruler increments	Shift–drag guide	Shift–drag guide
Switch between page and spread guides (creation only)	Ctrl–drag guide	Command–drag guide
Temporarily turn on/off snap to		Control-drag object

Create vertical and horizontal ruler guides for the spread	Ctrl–drag from zero point	Command–drag from zero point
Select all guides	Alt+Ctrl+G	Option+Command+G
Lock or unlock zero point	Right-click zero point and choose an option	Control–click zero point and choose an option
Use current magnificati on for view threshold of new guide	Alt–drag guide	Option–drag guide
Select buttons in alert dialog boxes	Press first letter of button name, if underlined	Press first letter of button name
Show information on installed plug-ins and InDesign component s	Ctrl+Help > About Design	Command+InDesign menu > About InDesign

Keys for Working with XML.

This table lists only shortcuts that aren't displayed in menu commands or tool tips.

Result	Windows Shortcut	Mac OS Shortcut
Expand/Collapse element	Right Arrow/Left Arrow	Right Arrow/Left Arrow
Expand/Collapse element and child elements	Alt+Right Arrow/ Alt+Left Arrow	Option+Right Arrow/ Option+Left Arrow
Extend XML selection up/down	Shift+Up Arrow/ Shift+Down Arrow	Shift+Up Arrow/ Shift+Down Arrow
Move XML selection up/down	Up Arrow/ Down Arrow	Up Arrow/ Down Arrow
Scroll structure pane up/down one screen	Page Up/ Page Down	Page Up/ Page Down
Select first/last XML node	Home/ End	Home/ End
Extend selection to first/last XML node	Shift+Home/ Shift+End	Shift+Home/ Shift+End
Go to previous/nex	Ctrl+Left Arrow/	Command+Left Arrow/

t validation error	Ctrl+Right Arrow	Command+Right Arrow
Automatically tag text frames and tables	Ctrl+Alt+Shift+F7	Command+Option+Shift+F7

Keys for Indexing.

This table lists only shortcuts that aren't displayed in menu commands or tool tips.

Result	**Windows Shortcut**	**Mac OS Shortcut**
Create index entry without dialog box (alphanumeric only)	Shift+Ctrl+Alt+[	Shift+Command+Option+[
Open index entry dialog box	Ctrl+7	Command+7
Create proper name index entry (last name, first name)	Shift+Ctrl+Alt+]	Shift+Command+Option+]

Keys for Panels.

This table lists only shortcuts that aren't displayed in menu commands or tool tips.

Result	Windows Shortcut	Mac OS Shortcut
Delete without confirmation	Alt-click Delete icon	Option-click Delete icon
Create item and set options	Alt-click New button	Option-click New button
Apply value and keep focus on option	Shift+Enter	Shift+Enter
Activate last-used option in last-used panel	Ctrl+Alt+~ [tilde]	Command+Option+~ [tilde]
Select range of styles, layers, links, swatches, or library objects in a panel	Shift-click	Shift-click
Select nonadjacent styles, layers, links, swatches, or library objects in a panel	Ctrl-click	Command-click

Apply value and select next value	Tab	Tab
Move focus to selected object, text, or window	Esc	Esc
Show/Hide all panels, Toolbox, and Control panel (with no insertion point)	Tab	Tab
Show/Hide all panels except the Toolbox and Control panel (docked or not)	Shift+Tab	Shift+Tab
Open or close all stashed panels	Ctrl+Alt+Tab	Command+Option+Tab
Stash a panel group	Alt+drag any panel tab (in the group) to edge of screen	Option+drag any panel tab (in the group) to edge of window
Select item by name	Alt+Ctrl-click in list, and then use	Option+Command-click in list and then use

	keyboard to select item by name	keyboard to select item by name
Open the Drop Shadow panel	Alt+Ctrl+M	Command+Option+M

Keys for the Control Panel.

This table lists only shortcuts that aren't displayed in menu commands or tool tips.

Result	**Windows Shortcut**	**Mac OS Shortcut**
Toggle focus to/from Control panel	Ctrl+6	Command+6
Toggle Character/Paragraph text attributes mode	Ctrl+Alt+7	Command+Option +7
Change reference point when proxy has focus	Any key on the numeric keypad or keyboard numbers	Any key on the numeric keypad or keyboard numbers
Display the pop-up menu that has focus	Alt+Down Arrow	

Open Units & Increments Preferences	Alt-click Kerning icon	Option-click Kerning icon
Open the Text Frame Options dialog box	Alt-click Number Of Columns icon	Option-click Number of Columns icon
Open the Move dialog box	Alt-click X or Y icon	Option-click X or Y icon
Open the Rotate dialog box	Alt-click Angle icon	Option-click Angle icon
Open the Scale dialog box	Alt-click X or Y Scale icon	Option-click X or Y Scale icon
Open the Shear dialog box	Alt-click Shear icon	Option-click Shear icon
Open Text Preferences	Alt-click Superscript, Subscript, or Small Caps button	Option-click Superscript, Subscript, or Small Caps button
Open the Underline Options dialog box	Alt-click Underline button	Option-click Underline button
Open the Strikethrough Options dialog box	Alt-click Strikethrough button	Option-click Strikethrough button
Open the Grids Preferences	Alt-click Align To Baseline Grid, or Do Not Align To	Option-click Align To Baseline Grid, or Do Not Align To Baseline Grid button

	Baseline Grid button	
Open the Drop Caps & Nested Styles dialog box	Alt-click Drop Cap Number Of Lines, or Drop Cap One Or More Characters icon	Option-click Drop Cap Number Of Lines, or Drop Cap One Or More Characters icon
Open the Justification dialog box	Alt-click Leading icon	Option-click Leading icon
Open Named Grid dialog box	Double-click Named Grid icon	Double-click Named Grid icon
Open New Named Grid Options dialog box	Alt-click Named Grid icon	Option-click Named Grid icon
Open Frame Grid Options dialog box	Alt-click Number of characters Horizontal, Number of Characters Vertical, Character Aki, Line Aki, Vertical Scale, Horizontal Scale, Grid	Option-click Number of characters Horizontal, Number of Characters Vertical, Character Aki, Line Aki, Vertical Scale, Horizontal Scale, Grid View, Font Size, Number of Columns, or

	View, Font Size, Number of Columns, or Column Gutter icon	Column Gutter icon

Keys for Type Panels and Dialog Boxes.

This table isn't a complete list of keyboard shortcuts. It lists only those shortcuts that aren't displayed in menu commands or tool tips.

Result	**Windows Shortcut**	**Mac OS Shortcut**
Open Justification dialog box	Alt+Ctrl+Shift+J	Option+Command+Shift+J
Open Paragraph Rules dialog box	Alt+Ctrl+J	Option+Command+J
Open Keep Options dialog box	Alt+Ctrl+K	Option+Command+K
Activate Character panel	Ctrl+T	Command+T
Activate Paragraph panel	Ctrl+Alt+T	Command+Option+T

Keys for the Character and Paragraph Styles.

This table lists only shortcuts that aren't displayed in menu commands or tool tips.

Result	Windows Shortcut	Mac OS Shortcut
Make character style definition match text	Select text and press Shift+Alt+Ctrl +C	Select text and press Shift+Option+Command +C
Make paragraph style definition match text	Select text and press Shift+Alt+Ctrl +R	Select text and press Shift+Option+Command +R
Change options without applying style	Shift+Alt+Ctrl-double-click style	Shift+Option+Command -double-click style
Remove style and local formattin g	Alt-click paragraph style name	Option-click paragraph style name
Clear overrides from paragraph style	Alt+Shift-click paragraph style name	Option+Shift-click paragraph style name

Show/hide Paragraph and Character Styles panels, respectively	F11, Shift+F11	Command+F11, Command+Shift+F11

Keys for the Tabs Panel.

This table lists only shortcuts that aren't displayed in menu commands or tool tips.

Result	**Windows Shortcut**	**Mac OS Shortcut**
Activate Tabs panel	Shift+Ctrl+T	Shift+Command+T
Switch between alignment options	Alt-click tab	Option-click tab

Keys for the Layers Panel.

This table lists only shortcuts that aren't displayed in menu commands or tool tips.

Result	**Windows Shortcut**	**Mac OS Shortcut**

Select all objects on layer	Alt-click layer	Option-click layer
Copy selection to new layer	Alt-drag small square to new layer	Option-drag small square to new layer
Add new layer below selected layer	Ctrl-click Create New Layer	Command-click Create New Layer
Add new layer to the top of the layer list	Shift+Ctrl-click Create New Layer	Shift+Command-click Create New Layer
Add new layer to the top of the layer list and open New Layer dialog box	Shift+Alt+Ctrl-click Create New Layer	Cmd+Option+Shift-click Create New Layer
Add new layer and open New Layer dialog box	Alt-click Create New Layer	Option-click Create New Layer

Keys for the Pages Panel.

This table lists only shortcuts that aren't displayed in menu commands or tool tips.

Result	Windows Shortcut	Mac OS Shortcut
Apply master to selected page	Alt-click master	Option-click master
Base another master page on selected master	Alt-click the master you want to base the selected master on	Option-click the master you want to base the selected master on
Create master page	Ctrl-click Create New Page button	Command-click Create New Page button
Display Insert Pages dialog box	Alt-click New Page button	Option-click New Page button
Add new page after last page	Shift+Ctrl+P	Shift+Command+P

Keys for the Color Panel.

This table lists only shortcuts that aren't displayed in menu commands or tool tips.

Result	Windows Shortcut	Mac OS Shortcut
Move color sliders in tandem	Shift-drag slider	Shift-drag slider

Select a color for the nonactive fill or stroke	Alt-click color bar	Option-click color bar
Switch between color modes (CMYK, RGB, LAB)	Shift-click color bar	Shift-click color bar

Keys for using the Separations Preview Panel.

This table lists only shortcuts that aren't displayed in menu commands or tool tips.

Result	**Windows Shortcut**	**Mac OS Shortcut**
Turn on Overprint preview	Ctrl+Alt+Shift+Y	Command+Option+Shift+Y
Show all plates	Ctrl+Alt+Shift+~ [tilde]	Command+Option+Shift+~ [tilde]
Show Cyan plate	Ctrl+Alt+Shift+1	Command+Option+Shift+1
Show Magenta plate	Ctrl+Alt+Shift+2	Command+Option+Shift+2
Show Yellow plate	Ctrl+Alt+Shift+3	Command+Option+Shift+3
Show Black plate	Ctrl+Alt+Shift+4	Command+Option+Shift+4

Show 1st Spot plate	Ctrl+Alt+Shift+5	Command+Option+Shift+5
Show 2nd Spot plate	Ctrl+Alt+Shift+6	Command+Option+Shift+6
Show 3rd Spot plate	Ctrl+Alt+Shift+7	Command+Option+Shift+7

Keys for the Swatches Panel.

This table lists only shortcuts that aren't displayed in menu commands or tool tips.

Result	**Windows Shortcut**	**Mac OS Shortcut**
Create new swatch based on the current swatch	Alt-click New Swatch button	Option-click New Swatch button
Create spot color swatch based on the current swatch	Alt+Ctrl-click New Swatch button	Option+Command-click New Swatch button

Change options without applying swatch	Shift+Alt+Ctrl-double-click swatch	Shift+Option+Command-double-click swatch

Keys for the Transform Panel.

This table lists only shortcuts that aren't displayed in menu commands or tool tips.

Result	**Windows Shortcut**	**Mac OS Shortcut**
Apply value and copy object	Alt+Enter	Option+Enter
Apply width, height, or scale value proportionally	Ctrl+Enter	Command+Enter

Keys for Resolving Conflicts between Mac OS 10.3x and 10.4

This table lists only shortcuts that aren't displayed in menu commands or tool tips.

Result	**Mac OS Shortcut**
Open Preferences dialog box	Command+K
Open Paragraph Styles panel	Command+F11
Open Character Styles panel	Command+Shift+F11
Open Swatches panel	F5

Open Pages panel	Command+F12
Minimize active application window	Command+M
Hide application	Command+H

Applies to: *Adobe InDesign.*

CHAPTER 11.

Tips, Techniques, and Keyboard Shortcuts for use in Adobe Bridge.

About the application: It is a great media manager for visual people, developed and sold by adobe Systems Incorporated.

A fresh topic

Adobe Bridge Workspace.

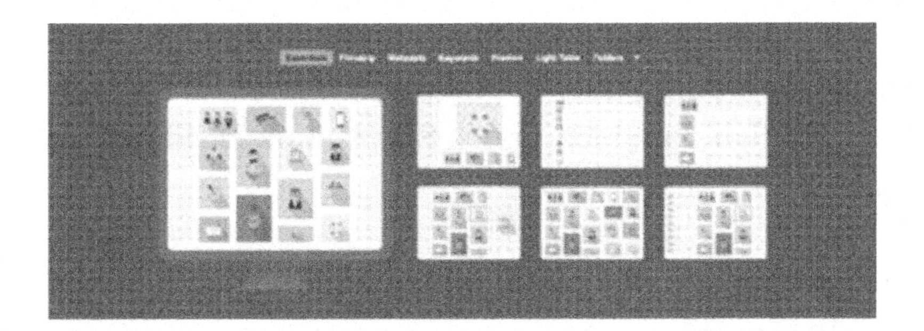

Workspace Overview.

The Adobe Bridge workspace consists of three columns, or panes, that contain various panels. You can adjust the

Adobe Bridge workspace by moving or resizing panels. You can create custom workspaces or select from several preconfigured Adobe Bridge workspaces.

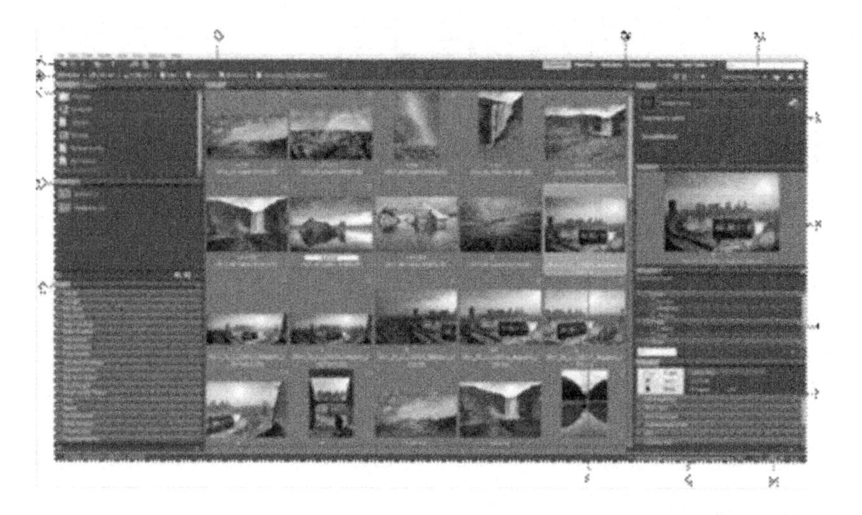

Adobe Bridge workspace

A. Application bar **B.** Path bar **C.** Favorites panel & Folders panel (tabbed) **D.** Collections panel **E.** Filter panel **F.** Selected item **G.** Thumbnail slider **H.** View options **I.** Metadata panel **J.** Keywords panel **K.** Preview panel **L.** Publish panel **M.** Quick Search box **N.** Standard workspaces **O.** Content panel

The following are the main components of the Adobe Bridge workspace:

Application bar

Provides buttons for essential tasks, such as navigating the folder hierarchy, switching workspaces, and searching for files.

Path bar

Shows the path for the folder you're viewing and allows you to navigate the directory.

Favorites panel

Gives you quick access to frequently browsed folders.

Folders panel

Shows the folder hierarchy. Use it to navigate folders.

Filter panel

Lets you sort and filter files that appear in the Content panel.

Collections panel

Lets you create, locate, and open collections and smart collections.

Content panel

Displays files specified by the navigational menu buttons, Path bar, Favorites panel, Folders panel, or Collections panel.

Publish panel

Lets you upload photos to Adobe Stock from within the Bridge app. See Publish images to Adobe Stock for details. To view this panel in any workspace, choose Window > Publish Panel.

Preview panel

Displays a preview of the selected file or files. Previews are separate from, and typically larger than, the thumbnail image displayed in the Content panel. You can reduce or enlarge the preview by resizing the panel.

Metadata panel

Contains metadata information for the selected file. If multiple files are selected, shared data (such as keywords, date created, and exposure setting) is listed.

Keywords panel

Helps you organize your images by attaching keywords to them.

Search Adobe Stock.

Introduced in Bridge CC 2017

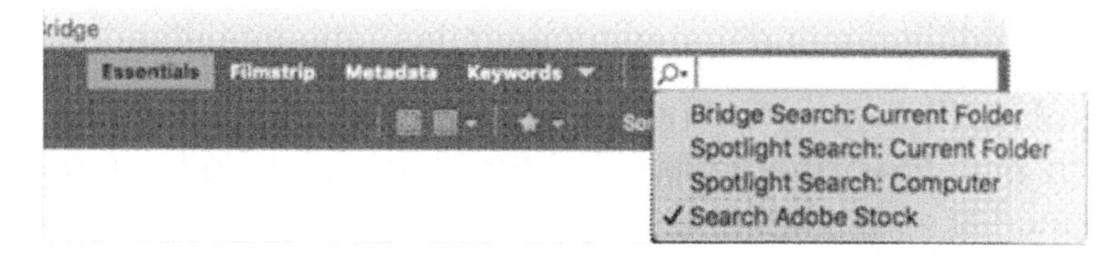

In addition to searching for assets in Bridge or on your computer, you can also use the Quick Search box (on the right side of the Application bar) to search for high-quality Adobe Stock illustrations, vectors, and photos. When you search, the results appear on the Adobe Stock website in your default web browser.

To switch your search between Adobe Stock search and Windows (Win)/Spotlight (Mac) search options, use the drop-down list in the Quick Search box.

Adjust Panels.

You can adjust the Adobe Bridge window by moving and resizing its panels. However, you can't move panels outside the Adobe Bridge window.

- Do any of the following:
    - Drag a panel by its tab into another panel.
    - Drag the horizontal divider bar between panels to make them larger or smaller.
    - Drag the vertical divider bar between the panels and the Content panel to resize the panels or Content panel.
    - To show or hide all panels except the center panel, Press Tab (the center panel varies depending on the workspace you've chosen).
    - Choose Window, followed by the name of the panel you want to display or hide.
    - Right-click (Windows) or Control-click (Mac OS) a panel tab and choose the name of the panel you want to display.

Work with Favorites.

- To specify Favorites preferences, choose Edit > Preferences (Windows) or Adobe Bridge CC > Preferences (Mac OS). Click General, and select desired options in the Favorite Items area of the Preferences dialog box.
- To add items to Favorites, do one of the following:
    - Drag a file or folder to the Favorites panel from Windows Explorer (Windows), the Finder (Mac OS), or the Content or Folders panel of Adobe Bridge.
    - Select a file, folder, or collection in Adobe Bridge and choose File > Add To Favorites.

Note:

To remove an item from the Favorites panel, select it and choose File > Remove From Favorite. Or right-click (Windows) or Control-click (Mac OS) the item and choose Remove From Favorites from the context menu.

Select and Manage Workspaces.

An Adobe Bridge workspace is a certain configuration or layout of panels. You can select either a preconfigured workspace or a custom workspace that you have previously saved.

By saving various Adobe Bridge workspaces, you can work in (and quickly switch between) different layouts. For example, use one workspace to sort new photos and another to work with footage files from an After Effects composition.

Adobe Bridge provides the following preconfigured workspaces:

Metadata

Displays the Content panel in List view, along with the Favorites, Metadata, Filter, and Export panels.

Essentials

Displays the Favorites, Folders, Filter, Collections, Export, Content, Preview, Metadata, and Keywords panels.

Filmstrip

Displays thumbnails in a scrolling horizontal row (in the Content panel) along with a preview of the currently selected item (in the Preview panel). Also displays the Favorites, Folders, Filter, Collections, and Export panels.

Keywords

Displays the Content panel in Details view, along with the Favorites, Keywords, Filter, and Export panels.

Note:

In Mac OS, pressing Command+F5 to load the Keywords workspace starts Mac OS voice-over by default. To load the Preview workspace by using the keyboard shortcut, first disable the voice-over shortcut in Mac OS Keyboard Shortcuts preferences. For instructions, see Mac OS Help.

Preview

Displays a large Preview panel; a narrow, vertical Content panel in Thumbnails view; and the Favorites, Folders, Filter, Collections, and Export panels.

Light Table

Displays only the Content panel. Files are displayed in Thumbnails view.

Folders

Displays the Content panel in Thumbnails view, along with the Favorites, Folders, and Export panels.

- To select a workspace, choose Window > Workspace, and then choose the desired workspace. Or, click one of the workspace buttons in the Adobe Bridge application bar.

Note:

Drag the vertical bar to the left of the workspace buttons to show more or fewer buttons. Drag the buttons to rearrange their order.

- To save the current layout as a workspace, choose Window > Workspace > New Workspace. In the New Workspace dialog box, enter a name for the workspace, specify options, and then click Save.
- To delete or restore a custom workspace, choose Window > Workspace, and then choose one of the following commands:

Delete Workspace

Deletes the saved workspace. Choose the workspace from the Workspace menu in the Delete Workspace dialog box, and click Delete.

Reset Workspace

Restores the currently selected saved workspace to its default settings.

Reset Standard Workspace

Restores the default settings for the Adobe pre-defined workspaces (Essentials, Output, and so on)

Adjust Brightness and Colors.

Brighten or darken the Adobe Bridge background and specify accent colors in General preferences. To open preferences, choose Edit > Preferences (Windows) or Adobe Bridge > Preferences (Mac OS).

- To brighten or darken the background, go to the General panel of the Preferences dialog box and do the following:
  - Drag the User Interface Brightness slider to make the Adobe Bridge background darker or lighter.
  - Drag the Image Backdrop slider to make the background of slideshows and of the Content and Preview panels darker or lighter.
- To specify accent colors, go to the General panel of the Preferences dialog box and choose a color from the Accent Color menu.

Manage Color.

In Adobe Bridge, the thumbnail quality determines whether color profile settings are used. High-quality thumbnails use color-profile settings, while quick thumbnails do not. In CS5 only, use the Advanced Preferences and the Options For Thumbnail Quality and Preview Generation button in the application bar to determine thumbnail quality.

If you are a Creative Cloud member or own Adobe Creative Suite, you can use Adobe Bridge to synchronize color settings across all color-managed apps and components. When you specify color settings using the Edit > Color Settings (Bridge CC) or Edit > Creative Suite Color Settings (Bridge CS) command, color settings are automatically synchronized. Synchronizing color settings ensures that colors look the same in all color-managed Adobe products.

Change Language Settings.

Adobe Bridge can display menus, options, and tool tips in multiple languages. You can also specify that Adobe Bridge use a specific language for keyboard shortcuts.

1. Choose Edit > Preferences (Windows) or Adobe Bridge > Preferences (Mac OS), and click Advanced.
2. Do either or both of the following:
    - Choose a language from the Language menu to display menus, options, and tool tips in that language.

    - Choose a language from the Keyboard menu to use that language keyboard configuration for keyboard shortcuts.
3. Click OK, and restart Adobe Bridge.

   The new language takes effect the next time you start Adobe Bridge.

Enable Startup Scripts.

You can enable or disable startup scripts in Adobe Bridge preferences. Scripts listed vary depending on the Creative Suite® components you've installed. Disable startup scripts to improve performance or to resolve incompatibilities between scripts.

1. Choose Edit > Preferences (Windows) or Adobe Bridge > Preferences (Mac OS), and click Startup Scripts.
2. Do any of the following:
    - Select or deselect the desired scripts.
    - To enable or disable all scripts, click Enable All or Disable All.
    - Click Reveal My Startup Scripts to go to Adobe Bridge Startup Scripts folder on your hard drive.

HiDPI and Retina Display Support.

HiDPI monitors and Apple's Retina displays allow more pixels to be displayed on your screen. To take advantage of advancements in high-resolution display technologies, Adobe Bridge CC includes native support for high-resolution monitor displays running on Windows and

Mac OS X (for example, the MacBook Pro with Retina display).

Bridge CC is aware of different monitor dots per inch (DPI) settings. When you are working on a HiDPI monitor set at a DPI of 150% or higher, Bridge's user interface automatically scales to 200% so that you continue to see sharp and clear UI elements, readable font size, and crisp icons across a wide variety of DPI display settings.

Note:

Bridge supports a minimum screen resolution of 2560 x 1600. Working on HiDPI monitors with screen resolution set below 2560 x 1600 truncates the Bridge user interface and some of the items may not fit on the screen.

User interface scaling preferences (Windows only)

With High DPI support enabled on Windows, the Bridge user interface scales to 200% on HiDPI monitors. However, Bridge also allows you to manually set the scaling preference:

1. Choose Edit > Preferences > Interface.
2. In the Preferences dialog, click Interface.

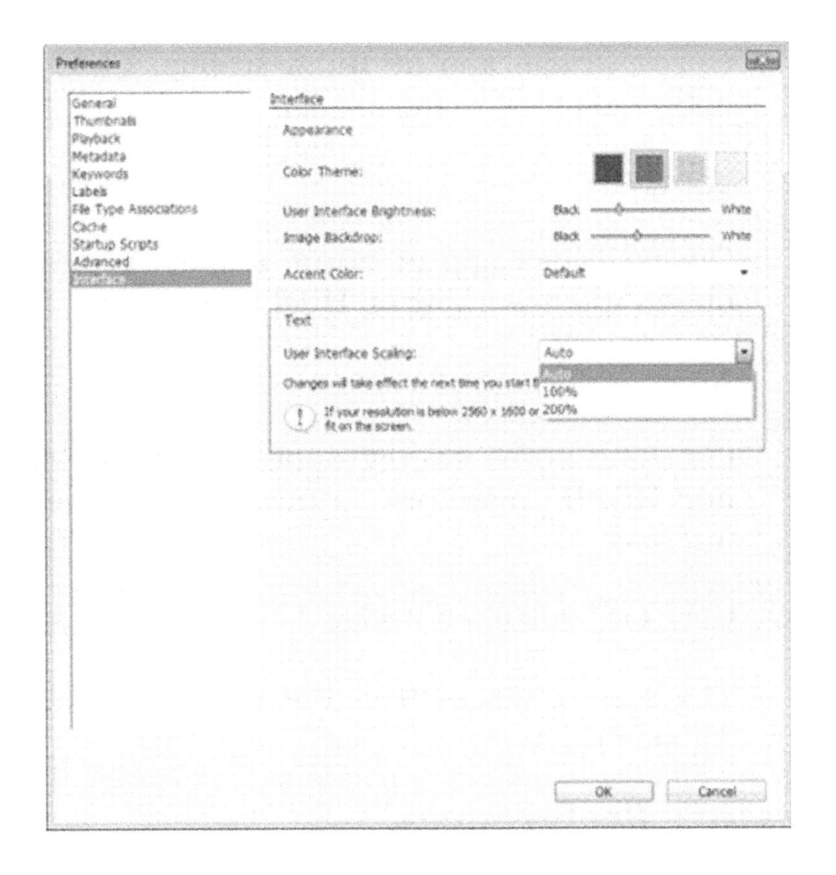

3. Select a User Interface Scaling option. You can choose any of the following:

   Auto

   (Default) Automatically scales the Bridge user interface to the following percentages based on the DPI setting of the display monitor:

   - 200% at DPI >= 150%
   - 100% at DPI < 150%

   100%

Opens Bridge app at 100% scaling. Choose this option to revert to the pre-HiDPI look.

200%

Opens Bridge app at 200% scaling. Choose this option when working on HiDPI monitors.

Note:

Choosing 200% scaling option when working on non-HiDPI monitors truncates/cuts the user interface.

4. Click OK. Relaunch Bridge.

   The scaling takes effect the next time you start Adobe Bridge.

Restore Preferences.

Numerous program settings are stored in the Adobe Bridge preferences file, including display, Adobe Photo Downloader, performance, and file-handling options.

Restoring preferences returns settings to their defaults and can often correct unusual application behavior.

1. Press and hold the Ctrl key (Windows) or the Option key (Mac OS) while starting Adobe Bridge.
2. In the Reset Settings dialog box, select one or more of the following options:

Reset Preferences

Returns preferences to their factory defaults. Some labels and ratings may be lost. Adobe Bridge creates a preferences file when it starts.

Purge Entire Thumbnail Cache

Purging the thumbnail cache can help if Adobe Bridge is not displaying thumbnails properly. Adobe Bridge re-creates the thumbnail cache when it starts.

Reset Standard Workspaces

Returns Adobe predefined workspaces to their factory default configurations.

3. Click OK, or click Cancel to open Adobe Bridge without resetting preferences.

A fresh topic

Keyboard Shortcuts in Adobe Bridge.

Keyboard shortcuts let you quickly select tools and execute commands without using a menu. When available, the keyboard shortcut appears to the right of the command name in the menu.

Note:

In addition to using keyboard shortcuts, you can access many commands using context-sensitive menus. Context-sensitive menus display commands that are relevant to the active tool, selection, or panel. To display a context-sensitive menu, right-click (Windows) or Ctrl-click (Mac OS) an area.

This is not a complete list of keyboard shortcuts. This table primarily lists only those shortcuts that aren't displayed in menu commands or tool tips.

Use the following list of keyboard shortcuts to enhance your productivity in Adobe Bridge.

Result	**Windows Shortcut**	**Mac OS Shortcut**
Go to next view	Ctrl+\	Command+\
Go to previous view	Ctrl+Shift+\	Command+Shift+\
Show/hide panels	Tab	Tab
Switch between 0- and 1-star rating	Ctrl+'	Command+'

Increase thumbnail size	Ctrl+plus sign (+)	Command+plus sign (+)
Decrease thumbnail size	Ctrl+minus sign (-)	Command+minus sign (-)
Step thumbnail size up	Ctrl+Shift+plus sign (+)	Command+Shift+plus sign (+)
Step thumbnail size down	Ctrl+Shift+minus sign (-)	Command+Shift+minus sign (-)
Move up a folder (in Folders panel or a row)	Up Arrow	Up Arrow
Move down a folder (in Folders panel or a row)	Down Arrow	Down Arrow
Move up a level (in Folders panel)	Ctrl+Up Arrow	Command+Up Arrow
Move left one item	Left Arrow	Left Arrow
Move right one item	Right Arrow	Right Arrow
Move to the first item	Home	Home

Move to the last item	End	End
Add to selection (discontiguous)	Ctrl-click	Command-click
Refresh Contents panels	F5	F5
Add an item to the selection	Shift + Right Arrow, Left Arrow, Up Arrow, or Down Arrow	Shift + Right Arrow, Left Arrow, Up Arrow, or Down Arrow
Display Help	F1	Command+/
Rename next (with filename selected in Content panel)	Tab	Tab
Rename previous (with filename selected in Content panel)	Shift+Tab	Shift+Tab
Show items with star rating of 1-5 or higher in Filter panel	Ctrl+Alt+1 through 5	Command+Option+1 through 5

Show items with selected star rating in Filter panel	Ctrl+Alt+Shift +1 through 5	Command+Option+Sh ift+1 through 5
Show items with labels 1-4 in Filter panel	Ctrl+Alt+6 through 9	Command+Option+6 through 9
Show all items with selected rating or higher in Filter panel	Shift-click	Shift-click
Clear filters	Ctrl+Alt+A	Command+Option+A
Select inverse in Filter panel	Alt-click	Option-click
Display Loupe tool in Preview panel or Review mode	Click	Click
Move Loupe tool	Click or drag	Click or drag
Display additional Loupes in Preview panel (multiple selection)	Click	Click

Move multiple Loupe tools simultaneously	Ctrl-click or Ctrl-drag	Command-click or Command-drag
Zoom in with Loupe tool	+	+
Zoom out with Loupe tool	-	-
Zoom in with Loupe tool (multiple selection)	Ctrl+plus sign (+)	Command+plus sign (+)
Zoom out with Loupe tool (multiple selection)	Ctrl+minus sign (-)	Command+minus sign (-)
Select all items in a stack	Alt-click	Option-click
Apply or remove current keyword and all parent keywords in Keywords panel	Shift-click	Shift-click
Forcibly remove current	Alt-click	Option-click

keyword in Keywords panel		
Open disclosure triangle in Keywords panel	Ctrl+Right Arrow	Command+Right Arrow
Close disclosure triangle in Keywords panel	Ctrl+Left Arrow	Command+Left Arrow

Applies to: *Adobe Bridge.*

CHAPTER 12.

Keyboard Shortcuts for use in Adobe Reader.

About the application: This is an application developed by Adobe that is used by readers to create, view, manipulate, print, and manage Portable Document Format (PDF) files.

A fresh topic

Keyboard Shortcuts in Adobe Reader.

Note:

This topic provides instructions for Acrobat DC. If you're using Acrobat Reader DC, see What can I do with Adobe Reader. If you're using Acrobat XI, see Acrobat XI Help.

Keys for Selecting Tools.

To enable single-key shortcuts, open the Preferences dialog box, and under General, select the Use Single-Key Accelerators To Access Tools option.

Use the following list of keyboard shortcuts to enhance your productivity in Adobe Acrobat Reader.

Tool	Windows/UNIX Shortcut	Mac OS Shortcut
Hand tool	H	H
Temporarily select Hand tool	Spacebar	Spacebar
Select tool	V	V
Marquee Zoom tool	Z	Z
Cycle through zoom tools: Marquee Zoom,Dynamic Zoom, Loupe	Shift+Z	Shift+Z
Temporarily select Dynamic Zoom tool (when Marquee Zoom tool is selected)	Shift	Shift
Temporarily zoom out (when Marquee Zoom tool is selected)	Ctrl	Option

Temporarily select Zoom In tool	Ctrl+spacebar	Spacebar+Command
Select Object tool	R	R
Edit Object tool	O	O
Enter/Exit Forms editing	A	A
Crop tool	C	C
Link tool	L	L
Text Field tool	F	F
Cycle through tools in forms authoring mode: Text Field, Check Box, Radio Button, List Box, Dropdown Box, Button, Digital Signature, Barcode	Shift+F	Shift+F
3D tool	M	M
Cycle through Multimedia tools: 3D object, SWF, Sound, Video	Shift+M	Shift+M

Edit Document Text tool	T	T
Redaction	Shift+Y	Shift+Y
Cycle through Touch Up tools: Touch Up Text, Touch Up Reading Order, Touch Up Object	Shift+T	Shift+T
JavaScript Debugger	Ctrl+J	Command+J
Insert Blank Pages tool	Shift+Ctrl+T	Shift+Command+T
Insert Files	Ctrl+Shift+I	Shift+Command+I
Delete pages	Ctrl+Shift+D	Shift+Command+D
Open Output Preview	~	~
Touch Up Reading Order tool (or if already selected, return focus to dialog box)	Shift+Ctrl+U	Shift+Command+U

Keys for Working with Comments.

To enable single-key shortcuts, select the Use Single-Key Accelerators To Access Tools option in General preferences.

Result	Windows/UNIX Shortcut	Mac OS Shortcut
Sticky Note tool	S	S
Text Edits tool	E	E
Stamp tool	K	K
Current highlighting tool	U	U
Cycle through highlighting tools: Highlighter,Underline Text, Cross Out Text	Shift+U (Windows only)	Shift+U
Current drawing markup tool	D	D
Cycle through drawing markup tools: Cloud, Arrow, Line, Rectangle, Oval, Polygon Line, Polygon, Pencil Tool, Eraser Tool	Shift+D (Windows only)	Shift+D
Cloud tool	Q (Windows only)	Q
Text Box tool	X	X
Current Stamp or Attach tool	J	J
Cycle through Stamp, Attach File, Record Audio Comment	Shift+J	Shift+J

Move focus to next comment or form field	Tab	Tab
Move focus to previous comment or form field	Shift+Tab	Shift+Tab
Open pop-up note (or text field in Comments List) for comment that has focus	Enter	Return
Closes pop-up (or text field in Comments List) for comment that has focus	Esc	Esc

Keys for Navigating a PDF.

Result	**Windows/UNIX Shortcut**	**Mac OS Shortcut**
Previous screen	Page Up or Shift+Enter	Page Up or Shift+Return
Next screen	Page Down or Enter	Page Down or Return
First page	Home or Shift+Ctrl+Page Up or Shift+Ctrl+Up Arrow	Home or Shift+Command+Up Arrow
Last page	End or Shift+Ctrl+Page Down or Shift+Ctrl+Down Arrow	End or Shift+Command+Down Arrow

Previous page	Left Arrow or Ctrl+Page Up	Left Arrow or Command+Page Up
Next page	Right Arrow or Ctrl+Page Down	Right Arrow or Command+Page Down
Previous open document	Ctrl+F6 (UNIX)	Command+F6
Next open document	Shift+Ctrl+F6 (UNIX)	Shift+Command+F6
Scroll up	Up Arrow	Up Arrow
Scroll down	Down Arrow	Down Arrow
Scroll (when Hand tool is selected)	Spacebar	Spacebar
Zoom in	Ctrl+equal sign	Command+equal sign
Zoom out	Ctrl+hyphen	Command+hyphen

Keys for Working with Forms.

Result	Windows/UNIX Shortcut	Mac OS Shortcut
Toggle between editing and previewing your form	P	P

Toggle Guides On / Off	G	G
Align selected fields left	L	L
Align selected fields right	R	R
Align selected fields top	T	T
Align selected fields bottom	B	B
Align selected fields horizontal	H	H
Align selected fields vertical	V	V
Center fields horizontally	Shift+H	Shift+H
Center fields vertically	Shift+V	Shift+V
Highlight fields	Shift+L	Shift+L
Show Tab Order	Shift+N	Shift+N
Document JavaScripts	Shift+D	Shift+D

Keys for Working with PDF Portfolios.

These keys are available in the files list of the Details pane.

Result	**Windows Shortcut**	**Mac OS Shortcut**
Move focus to the next or previous row	Up Arrow or Down Arrow	Up Arrow or Down Arrow

when in the body of the file list on the left		
If pressed in the body of the file list, navigate one level up from within a folder	Backspace	Delete
Press the Go Back button in a folder if focus is on the button.	Enter or Spacebar	Enter or Spacebar
If pressed when focus is on a row in the file list representing a subfolder, navigate to a subfolder, or open an attachment in Preview mode.	Enter	Enter
If in the body of the file list, move to the first or last row	Home or End	Home or End
If in the body of the file list, move to the next or last set	Page Down or Page Up	Page Down or Page Up

of rows to fit the screen		
Select or deselect all files	Ctrl+A or Shift+Ctrl+A	Command+A or Shift+Command+A
If in the body of the file list, extend the selection by adding the next row above or below the selected row	Shift+Up Arrow or Shift+Down Arrow	Shift+Up Arrow or Shift+Down Arrow
Change whether the row with focus is in the selection	Ctrl+Spacebar	Command+Spacebar
Move focus up or down one row without changing the selection	Ctrl+Up Arrow or Ctrl+Down Arrow	Command+Up Arrow or Command+Down Arrow

Keys for Navigating Task Panes.

Result	Windows Shortcut	Mac OS Shortcut
Move focus to the next item among Document pane, Task panes, Message	F6	F6

bar, and Navigation bar		
Move focus to the previous item among Document pane, Task panes, message bar, and Navigation bar	Shift+F6	Shift+F6
Move focus to the next panel in the Task pane	Ctrl+Tab	Option +Tab
Move focus to the previous panel in the Task pane	Ctrl+Shift+Tab	Command+ Shift+Tab
Navigate to the next panel and panel control within an open Task pane	Tab	Tab
Navigate to the previous panel and panel control within an open Task pane	Shift+Tab	Shift+Tab
Navigate to the next command button within a panel	Down Arrow	Down Arrow
Navigate to the previous command button within a panel	Up Arrow	Up Arrow
Expand or collapse panel in focus (press F6 to move focus to	Spacebar or Enter	Spacebar or Enter

Tools pane, then tab to desired panel)		
Open or close the Task pane	Shift+F4	Shift+F4
Close the pane that lists the tasks of an Action	Ctrl+Shift+F4	Ctrl+Shift+F4
Open the menu and move the focus to the first menu option when focus is on a command with a submenu or submenu element with a flyout	Spacebar or Enter	Spacebar or Enter
Move the focus back to the parent command button with a submenu or submenu element with a flyout	Esc	Esc
Run the command in focus	Spacebar or Enter	Spacebar or Enter
Navigate to the next item in the active panel in the Create New Action, Edit Action, Create Custom Tool, or the Edit Custom Tool dialog boxes	Tab	Tab
Navigate to the previous item in the	Shift+Tab	Shift+Tab

active panel in the Create New Action, Edit Action, Create Custom Tool, or the Edit Custom Tool dialog boxes		

Keys for General Navigating.

Result	Windows/UNIX Shortcut	Mac OS Shortcut
Move focus to menus (Windows, UNIX); expand first menu item (UNIX)	F10	Control+F2
Move focus to toolbar in browser and application (In application, sets focus to the first button in the top bar - Home)	Shift+F8	Shift+F8

Navigate through the other controls in the top bar - Home, Tools, Document	Right/Left Arrow or Tab/Shift Tab	Right/Left Arrow or Tab/Shift Tab
Select a highlighted control in the top bar	Enter or Spacebar	Return or Spacebar
Move to next open document tab (when multiple documents are open in same window)	Ctrl+Tab	Control+Tab
Move to previous open document tab (when multiple documents are open in same window)	Ctrl+Shift+Tab	Control+Shift+Tab

Move to next open document window (when focus is on document pane)	Ctrl+F6	Command+F6
Move to previous open document window (when focus is on document pane)	Ctrl+Shift+F6	Command+Shift+F6
Close current document	Ctrl+F4	Command+F4
Close all open documents	Not available	Command+Option+W
Move focus to next comment, link, or form field in the document pane	Tab	Tab
Move focus to	F5	F5

document pane		
Move focus to previous comment, link, or form field in the document pane	Shift+Tab	Shift+Tab
Activate selected tool, item (such as a movie clip or bookmark), or command	Spacebar or Enter	Spacebar or Return
Open context menu	Shift+F10	Control+click
Close context menu	F10	Esc
Return to Hand tool or Select tool	Esc	Esc
Move focus to next tab in a tabbed dialog box	Ctrl+Tab	Not available

Move to previous search result and highlight it in the document	Shift + F3 or Ctrl + Shift + G	Shift + Command + G
Move to next search result and highlight it in the document	F3 or Ctrl + G	Command + G
Search previous document (with Search results displaying multiple files)	Alt+Shift+Left Arrow (Windows only)	Command+Shift+Left Arrow
Search next document (with Search results displaying multiple files)	Alt+Shift+Right Arrow (Windows only)	Command+Shift+Right Arrow

Select text (with Select tool selected)	Shift+arrow keys	Shift+arrow keys
Select next word or deselect previous word (with Select tool selected)	Shift+Ctrl+Right Arrow or Left Arrow	Not available

Keys for Working with Navigation Panels.

Result	**Windows/UNIX Shortcut**	**Mac OS Shortcut**
Open and move focus to navigation pane	Ctrl+Shift+F5	Command+Shift+F5
Move focus among the document, message bar, and navigation panels	F6	F6
Move focus to previous pane or panel	Shift+F6	Shift+F6

Move among the elements of the active navigation panel	Tab	Tab
Move to previous or next navigation panel and make it active (when focus is on the panel button)	Up Arrow or Down Arrow	Up Arrow or Down Arrow
Move to next navigation panel and make it active (when focus is anywhere in the navigation pane)	Ctrl+Tab	Not available
Expand the current bookmark (focus on Bookmarks panel)	Right Arrow or Shift+plus sign	Right Arrow or Shift+plus sign

Collapse the current bookmark (focus on Bookmarks panel)	Left Arrow or minus sign	Left Arrow or minus sign
Expand all bookmarks	Shift+*	Shift+*
Collapse current selected bookmark	Forward Slash (/)	Forward Slash (/)
Move focus to next item in a navigation panel	Down Arrow	Down Arrow
Move focus to previous item in a navigation panel	Up Arrow	Up Arrow

Keys for Navigating the Help Window.

Result	**Windows/UNIX Shortcut**	**Mac OS Shortcut**
Open Help window	F1	F1 or Command+?
Close Help window	Ctrl+W (Windows only) or Alt+F4	Command+W

Move back to previously opened topic	Alt+Left Arrow	Command+Left Arrow
Move forward to next topic	Alt+Right Arrow	Command+Right Arrow
Move to next pane	Ctrl+Tab	See Help for your default browser
Move to previous pane	Shift+Ctrl+Tab	See Help for your default browser
Move focus to the next link within a pane	Tab	Not available
Move focus to the previous link within a pane	Shift+Tab	Not available
Activate highlighted link	Enter	Not available
Print Help topic	Ctrl+P	Command+P

Keys for Accessibility.

Result	Windows Shortcut	Mac OS Shortcut
Change reading settings for the	Shift+Ctrl+5	Shift+Command+5

current document		
Reflow a tagged PDF, and return to unreflowed view	Ctrl+4	Command+4
Activate and deactivate Read Out Loud	Shift+Ctrl+Y	Shift+Command+Y
Read only the current page out loud	Shift+Ctrl+V	Shift+Command+V
Read out loud from the current page to the end of the document	Shift+Ctrl+B	Shift+Command+B
Pause reading out loud	Shift+Ctrl+C	Shift+Command+C
Stop reading out loud	Shift+Ctrl+E	Shift+Command+E

Applies to: *Adobe Acrobat DC.*

CHAPTER 13.

Tips, Tricks, Techniques, and Keyboard Shortcuts for use in Audition.

About the application: This, formerly known as Cool Edit Pro, is an application used for recording and mixing audio for video, podcasting, and sound effect design; developed, maintained and marketed by Adobe Systems Incorporated.

A fresh topic ↳

Noise Reduction Techniques and Restoration Effects for Audition.

Techniques for Restoring Audio.

You can fix a wide array of audio problems by combining two powerful features. First, use Spectral Display to visually identify and select ranges of noise or individual artifacts. Then, use either Diagnostic or Noise Reduction effects to fix problems like the following:

- Crackle from wireless microphones or old vinyl records. (See Automatic Click Remover effect.)

- Background noise like wind rumble, tape hiss, or power-line hum. (See Adaptive Noise Reduction effect and DeHummer effect.)
- Phase cancelation from poorly placed stereo microphones or misaligned tape machines. (See Automatic Phase Correction effect.)

Note:

The real-time restoration effects above, which are available in both the Waveform and Multitrack editors, quickly address common audio problems. For unusually noisy audio, however, consider using offline, process effects unique to the Waveform Editor, such as Hiss Reduction and Noise Reduction.

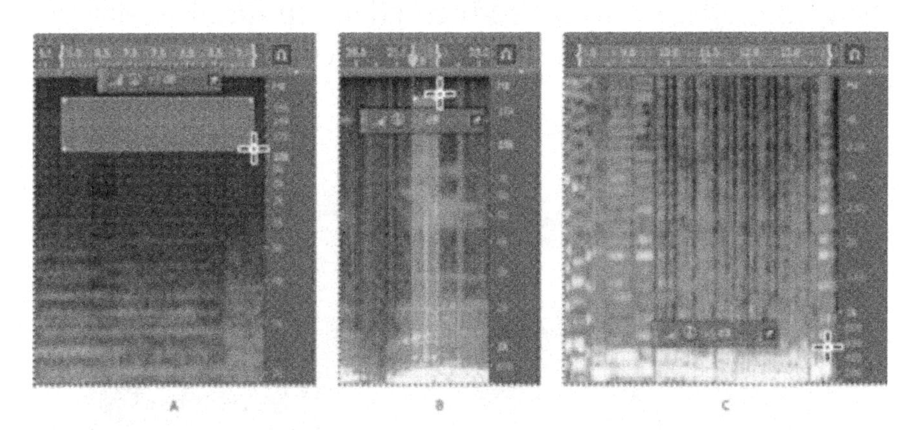

Selecting various types of noise in Spectral Display

A. Hiss **B.** Crackle **C.** Rumble

Noise Reduction Effect (Waveform Editor only).

The Noise Reduction/Restoration > Noise Reduction effect dramatically reduces background and broadband noise with a minimal reduction in signal quality. This effect can remove a combination of noise, including tape hiss, microphone background noise, power-line hum, or any noise that is constant throughout a waveform.

The proper amount of noise reduction depends upon the type of background noise and the acceptable loss in quality for the remaining signal. In general, you can increase the signal-to-noise ratio by 5 to 20 dB and retain high audio quality.

To achieve the best results with the Noise Reduction effect, apply it to audio with no DC offset. With a DC offset, this effect may introduce clicks in quiet passages. (To remove a DC offset, choose Favorites > Repair DC Offset.)

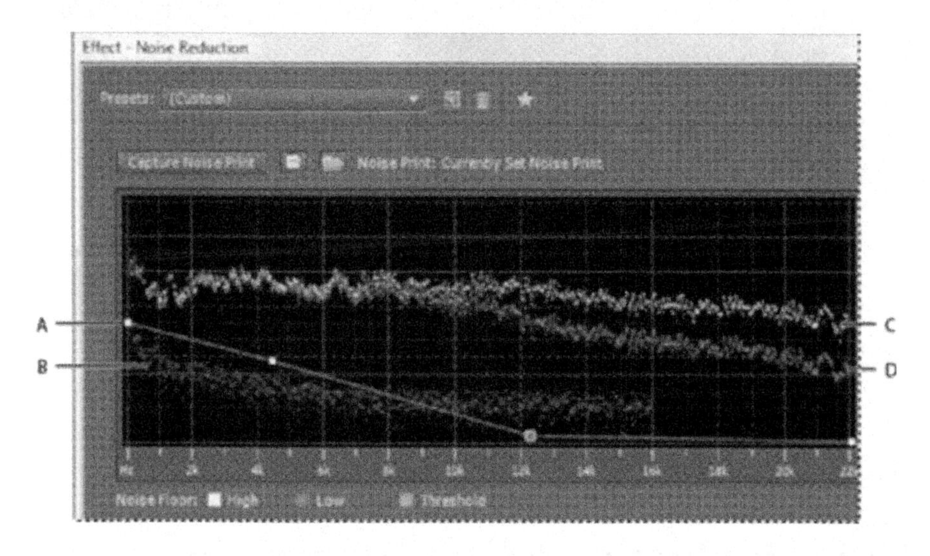

Evaluating and adjusting noise with the Noise Reduction graph:

A. Drag control points to vary reduction in different frequency ranges **B.** Low amplitude noise. **C.** High amplitude noise **D.** Threshold below which noise reduction occurs.

Apply the Noise Reduction effect

1. In the Waveform Editor, select a range that contains only noise and is at least half a second long.

   Note:

   To select noise in a specific frequency range, use the Marquee Selection tool.

2. Choose Effects > Noise Reduction/Restoration > Capture Noise Print.
3. In the Editor panel, select the range from which you want to remove noise.
4. Choose Effects > Noise Reduction/Restoration > Noise Reduction.
5. Set the desired options.

Note:

When recording in noisy environments, record a few seconds of representative background noise that can be used as a noise print later on.

NOISE Reduction options

Capture Noise Print

Extracts a noise profile from a selected range, indicating only background noise. Adobe Audition gathers statistical information about the background noise so it can remove it from the remainder of the waveform.

***Tip**: If the selected range is too short, Capture Noise Print is disabled. Reduce the FFT Size or select a longer range of noise. If you can't find a longer range, copy and paste the currently selected range to create one. (You can later remove the pasted noise by using the Edit > Delete command.)*

Save the Current Noise Print

Saves the noise print as an .fft file, which contains information about sample type, FFT (Fast Fourier Transform) size, and three sets of FFT coefficients: one for the lowest amount of noise found, one for the highest amount, and one for the power average.

Load a Noise Print from Disk

Opens any noise print previously saved from Adobe Audition in FFT format. However, you can apply noise prints only to identical sample types. (For example, you can't apply a 22 kHz mono profile to 44kHz stereo samples.)

***Note**: Because noise prints are so specific, a print for one type of noise won't produce good results with other* *types. If you regularly remove similar noise, however, a saved profile can greatly increase efficiency.*

Graph

Depicts frequency along the *x*-axis (horizontal) and the amount of noise reduction along the *y*-axis (vertical).

The blue control curve sets the amount of noise reduction in different frequency ranges. For example, if you need noise reduction only in the higher frequencies, adjust the control curve downward to the right of the graph.

If you click the Reset button to flatten the control curve, the amount of noise reduction is based entirely on the noise print.

***Tip**: To better focus on the noise floor, click the menu button to the upper right of the graph, and deselect Show Control Curve and Show Tooltip Over Graph.*

Noise Floor

High shows the highest amplitude of detected noise at each frequency; Low shows the lowest amplitude. Threshold shows the amplitude below which noise reduction occurs.

***Tip**: The three elements of the noise floor can overlap in the graph. To better distinguish them, click the menu button , and select options from the Show Noise Floor menu.*

Scale

Determines how frequencies are arranged along the horizontal *x*-axis:

- For finer control over low frequencies, select Logarithmic. A logarithmic scale more closely resembles how people hear sound.
- For detailed, high-frequency work with evenly spaced intervals in frequency, select Linear.

Channel

Displays the selected channel in the graph. The amount of noise reduction is always the same for all channels.

Select Entire File

Lets you apply a captured noise print to the entire file.

Noise Reduction

Controls the percentage of noise reduction in the output signal. Fine-tune this setting while previewing audio to achieve maximum noise reduction with minimum artifacts. (Excessively high noise reduction levels can sometimes cause audio to sound flanged or out-of-phase.)

Reduce By

Determines the amplitude reduction of detected noise. Values between 6 and 30 dB work well. To reduce bubbly artifacts, enter lower values.

Output Noise Only

Previews only noise so you determine if the effect is removing any desirable audio.

Advanced settings

Click the triangle to display the following options:

Spectral Decay Rate

Specifies the percentage of frequencies processed when audio falls below the noise floor. Fine-tuning this percentage allows greater noise reduction with fewer artifacts. Values of 40% to 75% work best. Below those values, bubbly-sounding artifacts are often heard; above those values, excessive noise typically remains.

Smoothing

Takes into account the variance of the noise signal in each frequency band. Bands that vary greatly when analyzed (such as white noise) will be smoothed differently than constant bands (like 60-Hz hum). In general, increasing the smoothing amount (up to 2 or so) reduces burbly background artifacts at the expense of raising the overall background broadband noise level.

Precision Factor

Controls changes in amplitude. Values of 5-10 work best, and odd numbers are ideal for symmetrical processing. With values of 3 or less, the Fast Fourier transform is performed in giant blocks, and between them drops or spikes in volume can occur. Values beyond 10 cause no noticeable change in quality, but they increase processing time.

Transition Width

Determines the amplitude range between noise and desirable audio. For example, a width of zero applies a sharp, noise gate to each frequency band. Audio just above the threshold remains; audio just below is truncated to silence. Alternatively, you can specify a range over which the audio fades to silence based upon the input level. For example, if the transition width is 10 dB, and the noise level for the band is -60 dB, audio at -60 dB stays the same, audio at -62 dB is reduced slightly, and audio at -70 dB is removed entirely.

FFT Size

Determines how many individual frequency bands are analyzed. This option causes the most drastic changes in quality. The noise in each frequency band is treated separately, so with more bands, noise is removed with finer frequency detail. Good settings range from 4096 to 8192.

Fast Fourier Transform size determines the tradeoff between frequency- and time-accuracy. Higher FFT sizes might cause swooshing or reverberant artifacts, but they very accurately remove noise frequencies. Lower FFT sizes result in better time response (less swooshing before cymbal hits, for example), but they can produce poorer frequency resolution, creating hollow or flanged sounds.

Noise Print Snapshots

Determines how many snapshots of noise to include in the captured profile. A value of 4000 is optimal for producing accurate data.

Very small values greatly affect the quality of the various noise reduction levels. With more snapshots, a noise reduction level of 100 will likely cut out more noise, but also cut out more original signal. However, a low noise reduction level with more snapshots will also cut out more noise, but likely retain the intended signal.

Sound Remover Effect.

The Sound Remover effect (**Effects > Noise Reduction/Restoration**) removes unwanted audio sources from a recording. This effect analyzes a selected portion of the recording, and builds a sound model, which is used to find and remove the sound.

The generated model can also be modified using parameters that indicate its complexity. A high complexity sound model requires more refinement passes to process the recording, but provides more accurate results. You can also save the sound model for later use. Several common presets are also included to remove some common noise sounds, such as sirens and ringing mobile phones.

Learn Sound Model

Uses the selected waveform to learn the sound model. Select an area on the waveform that only contains the sound to remove, and then press Learn Sound Model. You can also save and load sound models on disc.

Sound Model Complexity

Indicates the complexity of the Sound Model. The more complex or mixed the sound is, the better results you'll get with a higher complexity setting, though the longer it will take to calculate. Settings range from 1 to 100.

Sound Refinement Passes

Defines the number of refinement passes to make to remove the sound patterns indicated in the sound model. Higher number of passes require longer processing time, but offer more accurate results.

Content Complexity

Indicates the complexity of the signal. The more complex or mixed the sound is, the better results you'll get with a higher complexity setting, though the longer it will take to calculate. Settings range from 5 to 100.

Content Refinement Passes

Specifies the number of passes to make on the content to remove the sounds that match the sound model. A higher number of passes require more processing time, but generally provide more accurate results.

Enhanced Supression

This increases the aggressiveness of the sound removal algorithm, and can be modified on the Strength value. A higher value will remove more of the sound model from mixed signals, which can result in greater loss of desired signal, while a lower value will leave more of the overlapping signal and therefore, more of the noise may be audible (though less than the original recording.)

Enhance for Speech

Specifies that the audio includes speech and is careful in removing audio patterns that closely resemble speech. The end result makes sure that speech is not removed, while removing noise.

FFT Size

Determines how many individual frequency bands are analyzed. This option causes the most drastic changes in quality. The noise in each frequency band is treated separately, so with more bands, noise is removed with finer frequency detail. Good settings range from 4096 to 8192.
Fast Fourier Transform size determines the tradeoff between frequency- and time-accuracy. Higher FFT sizes might cause swooshing or reverberant artifacts, but they very accurately remove noise frequencies. Lower FFT sizes result in better time response (less swooshing before cymbal hits, for example), but they can produce poorer frequency resolution, creating hollow or flanged sounds.

Adaptive Noise Reduction Effect.

The Noise Reduction/Restoration > Adaptive Noise Reduction effect quickly removes variable broadband noise such as background sounds, rumble, and wind. Because this effect operates in real time, you can combine it with other effects in the Effects Rack and apply it in the

Multitrack Editor. By contrast, the standard Noise Reduction effect is available only as an offline process in the Waveform Editor. That effect, however, is sometimes more effective at removing constant noise, such as hiss or hum.

For best results, apply Adaptive Noise Reduction to selections that begin with noise followed by desirable audio. The effect identifies noise based on the first few seconds of audio.

Note:

This effect requires significant processing. If your system performs slowly, lower FFT Size and turn off High Quality Mode.

Reduce Noise By

Determines the level of noise reduction. Values between 6 and 30 dB work well. To reduce bubbly background effects, enter lower values.

Noisiness

Indicates the percentage of original audio that contains noise.

Fine Tune Noise Floor

Manually adjusts the noise floor above or below the automatically calculated floor.

Signal Threshold

Manually adjusts the threshold of desirable audio above or below the automatically calculated threshold.

Spectral Decay Rate

Determines how quickly noise processing drops by 60 decibels. Fine-tuning this setting allows greater noise reduction with fewer artifacts. Values that are too short create bubbly sounds; values that are too long create a reverb effect.

Broadband Preservation

Retains desirable audio in specified frequency bands between found artifacts. A setting of 100 Hz, for example, ensures that no audio is removed 100 Hz above or below found artifacts. Lower settings remove more noise but may introduce audible processing.

FFT Size

Determines how many individual frequency bands are analyzed. Choose a high setting to increase frequency resolution; choose a low setting to increase time resolution. High settings work well for artifacts of long duration (like squeaks or power-line hum), while low settings better address transient artifacts (like clicks and pops).

Automatic Click Remover Effect.

To quickly remove crackle and static from vinyl recordings, use the Noise Reduction/Restoration >

Automatic Click Remover effect. You can correct a large area of audio or a single click or pop.

This effect provides the same options as the DeClicker effect, which lets you choose which detected clicks to address (see DeClicker options). However, because the Automatic Click Remover operates in real time, you can combine it with other effects in the Effects Rack and apply it in the Multitrack Editor. The Automatic Click Remover effect also applies multiple scan and repair passes automatically; to achieve the same level of click reduction with the DeClicker, you must manually apply it multiple times.

Threshold

Determines sensitivity to noise. Lower settings detect more clicks and pops but may include audio you wish to retain. Settings range from 1 to 100; the default is 30.

Complexity

Indicates the complexity of noise. Higher settings apply more processing but can degrade audio quality. Settings range from 1 to 100; the default is 16.

Automatic Phase Correction Effect.

The Noise Reduction/Restoration > Automatic Phase Correction effect addresses azimuth errors from misaligned tape heads, stereo smearing from incorrect microphone placement, and many other phase-related problems.

Global Time Shift

Activates the Left and Right Channel Shift sliders, which let you apply a uniform phase shift to all selected audio.

Auto Align Channels and Auto Center Panning

Align phase and panning for a series of discrete time intervals, which you specify using the following options:

Time Resolution

Specifies the number of milliseconds in each processed interval. Smaller values increase accuracy; larger ones increase performance.

Responsiveness

Determines overall processing speed. Slow settings increase accuracy; fast settings increase performance.

Channel

Specifies the channels phase correction will be applied to.

Analysis Size

Specifies the number of samples in each analyzed unit of audio.

Note:

For the most precise, effective phase correction, use the Auto Align Channels option. Enable the Global Time Shift sliders only if you are confident that a uniform adjustment is necessary, or if you want to manually animate phase correction in the Multitrack Editor.

Click/Pop Eliminator Effect.

Use the **Click/Pop Eliminator** effect (**Effects > Noise Reduction/Restoration**) to remove microphone pops, clicks, light hiss, and crackles. Such noise is common on recordings such as old vinyl records and on-location recordings. The effect dialog box stays open, and you can adjust the selection, and fix multiple clicks without reopening the effect several times.

Detection and correction settings are used to find clicks and pops. The detection and rejection ranges are displayed graphically.

Detection graph

Shows the exact threshold levels to be used at each amplitude, with amplitude along the horizontal ruler (x-axis) and threshold level along the vertical ruler (y-axis). Adobe Audition uses values on the curve to the right (above -20 dB or so) when processing louder audio and values on the left when processing softer audio. Curves are color-coded to indicate detection and rejection.

Scan for All Levels

Scans the highlighted area for clicks based on the values for Sensitivity and Discrimination, and determines values for Threshold, Detect, and Reject. Five areas of audio are selected, starting at the quietest and moving to the loudest.

Sensitivity

Determines the level of clicks to detect. Use a lower value, such as 10, to detect lots of subtle clicks, or a value of 20 to detect a few louder clicks. (Detected levels with Scan for All Levels are always higher than with this option.)

Discrimination

Determines how many clicks to fix. Enter high values to fix very few clicks and leave most of the original audio intact. Enter lower values, such as 20 or 40, if the audio contains a moderate number of clicks. Enter extremely low values, such as 2 or 4, to fix constant clicks.

Scan for Threshold Levels

Automatically sets the Maximum, Average, and Minimum Threshold levels.

Maximum, Average, Minimum

Determine the unique detection and rejection thresholds for the maximum, average, and minimum amplitudes of the audio. For example, if audio has a maximum RMS amplitude of -10 dB, you should set Maximum Threshold to -10 dB. If the minimum RMS amplitude is -55 dB, then set Minimum Threshold to -55.

Set the threshold levels before you adjust the corresponding Detect and Reject values. (Set the Maximum and Minimum Threshold levels first, because once they're in place, you shouldn't need to adjust them much.) Set the Average Threshold level to about three quarters of the way between the Maximum and Minimum Threshold levels. For example, if Maximum Threshold is set to 30 and Minimum Threshold is set to 10, set Average Threshold to 25.

After you audition a small piece of repaired audio, you can adjust the settings as needed. For example, if a quiet part still has a lot of clicks, lower the Minimum Threshold level a bit. If a loud piece still has clicks, lower the Average or Maximum Threshold level. In general, less correction is required for louder audio, as the audio itself masks many clicks, so repairing them isn't necessary. Clicks are very noticeable in very quiet audio, so quiet audio tends to require lower detection and rejection thresholds.

Second Level Verification (Reject Clicks)

Rejects some of the potential clicks found by the click detection algorithm. In some types of audio, such as trumpets, saxophones, female vocals, and snare drum hits, normal peaks are sometimes detected as clicks. If these peaks are corrected, the resulting audio will sound muffled. Second Level Verification rejects these audio peaks and corrects only true clicks.

Detect

Determines sensitivity to clicks and pops. Possible values range from 1 to 150, but recommended values range from 6 to 60. Lower values detect more clicks.

Start with a threshold of 35 for high-amplitude audio (above -15 dB), 25 for average amplitudes, and 10 for low-amplitude audio (below-50 dB). These settings allow for the most clicks to be found, and usually all of the louder ones. If a constant crackle is in the background of the source audio, try lowering the Min Threshold level or increasing the dB level to which the threshold is assigned. The level can be as low as 6, but a lower setting can cause the filter to remove sound other than clicks.

If more clicks are detected, more repair occurs, increasing the possibility of distortion. With too much distortion of this type, audio begins to sound flat and lifeless. If this occurs, set the detection threshold rather low, and select Second Level Verification to reanalyze the detected clicks and disregard percussive transients that aren't clicks.

Reject

Determines how many potential clicks (found using the Detection Threshold) are rejected if Second Level Verification box is selected. Values range from 1 to 100; a setting of 30 is a good starting point. Lower settings allow for more clicks to be repaired. Higher settings can prevent clicks from being repaired, as they might not be actual clicks.

You want to reject as many detected clicks as possible but still remove all audible clicks. If a trumpet-like sound has clicks in it, and the clicks aren't removed, try lowering the value to reject fewer potential clicks. If a particular sound becomes distorted, then increase the setting to keep repairs at a minimum. (The fewer repairs that are needed to get good results, the better.)

FFT Size

Determines the FFT size used to repair clicks, pops, and crackle. In general, select Auto to let Adobe Audition determine the FFT size. For some types of audio, however, you might want to enter a specific FFT size (from 8 to 512). A good starting value is 32, but if clicks are still quite audible, increase the value to 48, and then 64, and so on. The higher the value, the slower the correction will be, but the better the potential results. If the value is too high, rumbly, low frequency distortion can occur.

Fill Single Click

Corrects a single click in a selected audio range. If Auto is selected next to FFT Size, then an appropriate FFT size is used for the restoration based on the size of the area being restored. Otherwise, settings of 128 to 256 work very well for filling in single clicks. Once a single click is filled, press the F3 key to repeat the action. You can also create a quick key in the Favorites menu for filling in single clicks.

Pop Oversamples Width

Includes surrounding samples in detected clicks. When a potential click is found, its beginning and end points are marked as closely as possible. The Pop Oversamples value (which can range from 0 to 300) expands that range, so more samples to the left and right of the click are considered part of the click.
If corrected clicks become quieter but are still evident, increase the Pop oversamples value. Start with a value of 8, and increase it slowly to as much as 30 or 40. Audio that doesn't contain a click shouldn't change very much if it's corrected, so this buffer area should remain mostly untouched by the replacement algorithm.

Increasing the Pop Oversamples value also forces larger FFT sizes to be used if Auto is selected. A larger setting may remove clicks more cleanly, but if it's too high, audio will start to distort where the clicks are removed.

Run Size

Specifies the number of samples between separate clicks. Possible values range from 0 to 1000. To independently correct extremely close clicks, enter a low value; clicks that occur within the Run Size range are corrected together.

A good starting point is around 25 (or half the FFT size if Auto next to FFT Size isn't selected). If the Run Size value is too large (over 100 or so), then the corrections may become more noticeable, as very large blocks of data are repaired at once. If you set the Run Size too small, then clicks that are very close together may not be repaired completely on the first pass.

Pulse Train Verification

Prevents normal waveform peaks from being detected as clicks. It may also reduce detection of valid clicks, requiring more aggressive threshold settings. Select this option only if you've already tried to clean up the audio but stubborn clicks remain.

Link Channels

Processes all channels equally, preserving the stereo or surround balance. For example, if a click is found in one channel, a click will most likely be detected in the other.

Detect Big Pops

Removes large unwanted events (such as those more than a few hundred samples wide) that might not be detected as clicks. Values can range from 30 to 200.

Note that a sharp sound like a loud snare drum hit can have the same characteristic as a very large pop, so select this option only if you know the audio has very large pops (like a vinyl record with a very big scratch in it). If this option causes drum hits to sound softer, slightly increase the threshold to fix only loud, obvious pops.

If loud, obvious pops aren't fixed, select Detect Big Pops, and use settings from about 30 (to find quiet pops) to 70 (to find loud pops).

Ignore Light Crackle

Smooths out one-sample errors when detected, often removing more background crackle. If the resulting audio sounds thinner, flatter, or tinnier, deselect this option.

Passes

Performs up to 32 passes automatically to catch clicks that might be too close together to be repaired effectively. Fewer passes occur if no more clicks are found and all detected clicks are repaired. In general, about half as many clicks are repaired on each successive pass. A higher detection threshold might lead to fewer repairs and increase the quality while still removing all clicks.

DeHummer effect

The Noise Reduction/Restoration > DeHummer effect removes narrow frequency bands and their harmonics. The most common application addresses power line hum from lighting and electronics. But the DeHummer can also apply a notch filter that removes an overly resonant frequency from source audio.

Note:

To quickly address typical audio problems, choose an option from the Presets menu.

Frequency

Sets the root frequency of the hum. If you're unsure of the precise frequency, drag this setting back and forth while previewing audio.

Note:

To visually adjust root frequency and gain, drag directly in the graph.

Q

Sets the width of the root frequency and harmonics above. Higher values affect a narrower range of frequencies, and lower values affect a wider range.

Gain

Determines the amount of hum attenuation.

Number of Harmonics

Specifies how many harmonic frequencies to affect.

Harmonic Slope

Changes the attenuation ratio for harmonic frequencies.

Output Hum Only

Lets you preview removed hum to determine if it contains any desirable audio.

Hiss Reduction effect (Waveform Editor only).

The Noise Reduction/Restoration > Hiss Reduction effect reduces hiss from sources such as audio cassettes, vinyl records, or microphone preamps. This effect greatly lowers the amplitude of a frequency range if it falls below an amplitude threshold called the *noise floor*. Audio in frequency ranges that are louder than the threshold remain untouched. If audio has a consistent level of background hiss, that hiss can be removed completely.

Note:

To reduce other types of noise that have a wide frequency range, try the Noise Reduction effect.

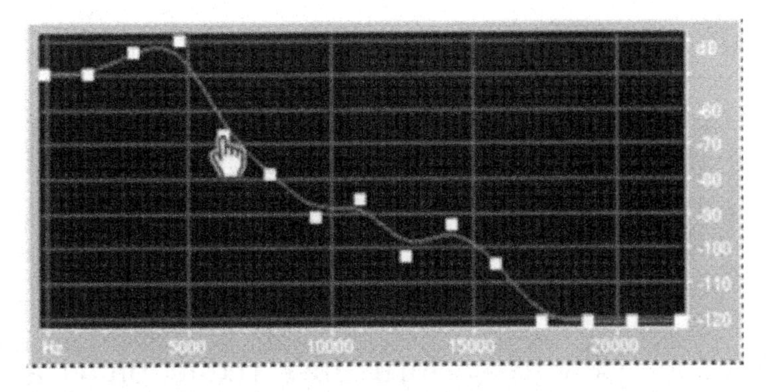

Using the Hiss Reduction graph to adjust the noise floor.

Capture Noise Floor

Graphs an estimate of the noise floor. The estimate is used by the Hiss Reduction effect to more effectively remove only hiss while leaving regular audio untouched. This option is the most powerful feature of Hiss Reduction.

To create a graph that most accurately reflects the noise floor, click Get Noise Floor with a selection of audio that contains only hiss. Or, select an area that has the least amount of desirable audio, in addition to the least amount of high frequency information. (In the spectral display, look for an area without any activity in the top 75% of the display.)

After you capture the noise floor, you might need to lower the control points on the left (representing the lower frequencies) to make the graph as flat as possible. If music is present at any frequency, the control points around that frequency will be higher than they should be.

Graph

Represents the estimated noise floor for each frequency in the source audio, with frequency along the horizontal ruler (*x*-axis) and the amplitude of the noise floor along the vertical ruler (*y*-axis). This information helps you distinguish hiss from desirable audio data.

The actual value used to perform hiss reduction is a combination of the graph and the Noise Floor slider, which shifts the estimated noise floor reading up or down for fine-tuning.

Note:

To disable tooltips for frequency and amplitude, click the menu button to the upper right of the graph, and deselect Show Tooltip Over Graph.

Scale

Determines how frequencies are arranged along the horizontal *x*-axis:

- For finer control over low frequencies, select Logarithmic. A logarithmic scale more closely resembles how people hear sound.
- For detailed, high-frequency work with evenly spaced intervals in frequency, select Linear.

Channel

Displays the selected audio channel in the graph.

Reset

Resets the estimated noise floor. To reset the floor higher or lower, click the menu button to the upper right of the graph, and choose an option from the Reset Control Curve menu.

Note:

For quick, general-purpose hiss reduction, a complete noise floor graph isn't always necessary. In many cases, you can simply reset the graph to an even level and manipulate the Noise Floor slider.

Noise Floor

Fine-tunes the noise floor until the appropriate level of hiss reduction and quality is achieved.

Reduce By

Sets the level of hiss reduction for audio below the noise floor. With higher values (especially above 20 dB) dramatic hiss reduction can be achieved, but the remaining audio might become distorted. With lower values, not as much noise is removed, and the original audio signal stays relatively undisturbed.

Output Hiss Only

Lets you preview only hiss to determine if the effect is removing any desirable audio.

Advanced settings

Click the triangle to display these options:

Spectral Decay Rate

When audio is encountered above the estimated noise floor, determines how much audio in surrounding frequencies is assumed to follow. With low values, less audio is assumed to follow, and hiss reduction will cut more closely to the frequencies being kept.

Values of 40% to 75% work best. If the value is too high (above 90%), unnaturally long tails and reverbs might be heard. If the value is too low, background bubbly effects might be heard, and music might sound artificial.

Precision Factor

Determines the time-accuracy of hiss reduction. Typical values range from 7 to 14. Lower values might result in a few milliseconds of hiss before and after louder parts of audio. Larger values generally produce better results and slower processing speeds. Values over 20 don't ordinarily improve quality any further.

Transition Width

Produces a slow transition in hiss reduction instead of an abrupt change. Values from 5 to 10 usually achieve good results. If the value is too high, some hiss may remain after processing. If the value is too low, background artifacts might be heard.

FFT Size

Specifies a Fast Fourier Transform size, which determines the tradeoff between frequency- and time-accuracy. In general, sizes from 2048 to 8192 work best.

Lower FFT sizes (2048 and below) result in better time response (less swooshing before cymbal hits, for example), but they can produce poorer frequency resolution, creating hollow or flanged sounds.

Higher FFT sizes (8192 and above) might cause swooshing, reverb, and drawn out background tones, but they produce very accurate frequency resolution.

Control Points

Specifies the number of points added to the graph when you click Capture Noise Floor.

End of Topic.

A fresh topic

Default Keyboard Shortcuts in Audition.

These partial lists include the shortcuts that Adobe Audition experts find most useful.

Use the following list of keyboard shortcuts to enhance your productivity in Adobe Audition.

Keys for Playing and Zooming Audio.

Result	Windows Shortcut	Mac OS Shortcut
Toggle between Waveform and Multitrack Editor	8	8
Start and stop playback	Spacebar	Spacebar
Move current-time indicator to beginning of timeline	Home	Home
Move current-time indicator to end of timeline	End	End
Move current-time	Ctrl+left arrow	Command+left arrow

indicator to previous marker, clip, or selection edge		
Move current-time indicator to next marker, clip, or selection edge	Ctrl+right arrow	Command+right arrow
Toggle preference for Return CTI To Start Position On Stop	Shift+X	Shift+X
Zoom in horizontally	=	=
Zoom in vertically	Alt+=	Option+=
Zoom out horizontally	-	-
Zoom out vertically	Alt+minus sign	Option+minus sign

Add marker	M or * (asterisk)	M or * (asterisk)
Move to previous marker	Crtl+Alt+left arrow	Cmd+Option+left arrow
Move to next marker	Crtl+Alt+righ t arrow	Cmd+Option+right arro w

Keys for Editing Audio Files.

The following keyboard shortcuts apply only in the Waveform Editor.

Result	**Windows Shortcut**	**Mac OS Shortcut**
Repeat previous command (opening its dialog box and clicking OK)	Shift+R	Shift+R
Repeat previous command (opening its dialog box but not clicking OK)	Ctrl+R	Command+R
Open Convert	Shift+T	Shift+T

Sample Type dialog box		
Capture a noise reduction profile for the Noise Reduction effect	Shift+P	Shift+P
Activate left channel of a stereo file for editing	Up arrow	Up arrow
Activate right channel of a stereo file for editing	Down arrow	Down arrow
Make spectral display more logarithmic or linear	Ctrl+Alt+up or down arrow	Option+Command+up or down arrow
Make spectral display fully logarithmic or linear	Ctrl+Alt+Page Up or Down	Option+Command+Page Up or Down
Increase or decrease	Shift+Ctrl+up or down arrow	Shift+Command-up or down arrow

spectral resolution		

Keys for Mixing Multitrack Sessions.

The following keyboard shortcuts apply only in the Multitrack Editor.

Result	Windows Shortcut	Mac OS Shortcut
Select the same input or output for all audio tracks	Ctrl+Shift-select	Command+Shift-select
Activate or deactivate Mute, Solo, Arm For Record, or Monitor Input in all tracks	Ctrl+Shift-click	Command+Shift-click
Adjust knobs in large increments	Shift-drag	Shift-drag
Adjust knobs in small increments	Ctrl-drag	Command-drag
Nudge selected clip to the left	Alt+comma	Option+comma
Nudge selected clip to the right	Alt+period	Alt+period
Maintain keyframe time position or parameter value	Shift-drag	Shift-drag
Reposition envelope segment without creating keyframe	Ctrl-drag	Command-drag

Applies to: *Adobe Audition.*

Customer's Page.

This page is for customers who enjoyed Top 11 Adobe Keyboard Shortcuts.

Our beloved and respectable reader, we thank you very much for your patronage. Please we will appreciate it more if you rate and review this book; that is if it was helpful to you. We also advise you to get the ebook version of this book in order to access the numerous useful links included in it. Thank you.

Download Our EBooks Today For Free.

In order to appreciate our customers, we have made some of our titles available at 0.00. They are totally free. Feel free to get a copy of the free titles.

Here are books we give to our customers free of charge:

(A) For Keyboard Shortcuts in Windows check:

Windows 7 Keyboard Shortcuts.

(B) For Keyboard Shortcuts in Office 2016 for Windows check:

Word 2016 Keyboard Shortcuts For Windows.

(C) For Keyboard Shortcuts in Office 2016 for Mac check:

OneNote 2016 Keyboard Shortcuts For Macintosh.

Follow this link to download any of the titles listed above for free.

Note: Feel free to download them from our website or your favorite bookstore today. Thank you.

Other Books By This Publisher.

S/N	Title	Series
Series A: Limits Breaking Quotes.		
1	Discover Your Key Christian Quotes	Limits Breaking Quotes
Series B: Shortcut Matters.		
1	Windows 7 Shortcuts	Shortcut Matters
2	Windows 7 Shortcuts & Tips	Shortcut Matters
3	Windows 8.1 Shortcuts	Shortcut Matters
4	Windows 10 Shortcut Keys	Shortcut Matters
5	Microsoft Office 2007 Keyboard Shortcuts For Windows.	Shortcut Matters
6	Microsoft Office 2010 Shortcuts For Windows.	Shortcut Matters
7	Microsoft Office 2013 Shortcuts For Windows.	Shortcut Matters
8	Microsoft Office 2016 Shortcuts For Windows.	Shortcut Matters
9	Microsoft Office 2016 Keyboard Shortcuts For Macintosh.	Shortcut Matters
10	Top 11 Adobe Programs Keyboard Shortcuts	Shortcut Matters
11	Top 10 Email Clients Keyboard Shortcuts	Shortcut Matters
12	Hot Corel Programs Keyboard Shortcuts	Shortcut Matters

13	Top 10 Browsers Keyboard Shortcuts	Shortcut Matters
Series C: Teach Yourself.		
1	Teach Yourself Computer Fundamentals	Teach Yourself
Series D: For Painless Publishing		
1	Self-Publish it with CreateSpace.	For Painless Publishing
2	Where is my money? Now solved for Kindle and CreateSpace	For Painless Publishing
3	Describe it on Amazon	For Painless Publishing
4	How To Market That Book.	For Painless Publishing

Made in United States
North Haven, CT
15 October 2021

10354735R00282